FRIENDS—THE POWER AND POTENTIAL OF THE COMPANY YOU KEEP

Also by Jerry Gillies:

MY NEEDS, YOUR NEEDS, OUR NEEDS

FRIENDS

The Power and Potential of the Company You Keep

JERRY GILLIES

COWARD, McCANN & GEOGHEGAN, INC.

NEW YORK

 Published on the same day in Canada by Longman Canada Limited, Toronto.

SBN: 698-10758-6

Library of Congress Cataloging in Publication Data

Gillies, Jerry, 1940–
Friends: the power and potential of the company you keep.

Bibliography: p.
1. Friendship. 2. Humanistic psychology. I. Title.
BF575.F66G54 1976 158'.25 76-17587

PRINTED IN THE UNITED STATES OF AMERICA

CONTENTS

ACKNOWLEDGMENTS

The comments, suggestions, and conceptual views generously shared by many psychologists, psychiatrists, educators, poets, and social scientists are deeply incorporated into the very heart of this exploration. In a very real sense, these friends and colleagues are my collaborators. Warm thanks to Leo Buscaglia, PhD; Emily Coleman; Edna Foa, PhD; Jack Gibb, PhD; Jerry Greenwald, PhD; Harold Greenwald, PhD; Ken Keyes, Jr.; Bart Knapp, PhD; Terry Levy, PhD; Daniel Malamud, PhD; Ric Masten; Louis Mobley; Claude Nolte, PhD; Dorothy Nolte, PhD; Judith Osgood, PhD; Patricia Peabody; Robert Resnick, PhD; Susan Scholz, PhD; Gerald Walker Smith, PhD; Mary Ann Somervill, PhD; Marjorie Toomim, PhD; Marta Vago, MSW; Eileen Walkenstein, MD; Leonard Zunin, MD.

Particular appreciation to Nena O'Neill and Dr. George O'Neill for the many meaningful and insightful concepts in their books *Open Marriage* and *Shifting Gears* and for their stimulating friendship.

Special thanks to my agent, Ellen Levine, for her steadfast belief in this project, and to my editor, Peggy Brooks, for her continuous encouragement. Also, for their early support back when this book was just a wisp of an idea in 1973, Julia Coopersmith, Bonnie Cousins, and Rachel Shane. And to Jessica Calise, a loving hug for being there at just the right moment, and to Elisabeth Fehl, for her proofreading and support throughout the creative process.

Deep appreciation to all my friends for providing that sense of belonging so nourishing to any creative project. And to the thousands of beautiful people who have attended my classes and workshops and lectures at Miami-Dade Community College, Cornucopia, Association for Humanistic Psychology conferences, and around the country, I acknowledge that I couldn't have done it without your valuable feedback and all the personal experiences you so generously shared with me, many of which appear as case histories in the following pages.

To Susannah Lippman

Our friendship has enriched my life

AUTHOR'S NOTE

Unless specifically identified as a quote from a book, article, or public lecture, all comments and quoted statements on the following pages are from interviews and conversations between the author and the subject. Dr. Robert Resnick's comments are primarily excerpted from a talk he gave for the 1973 annual meeting of the Association for Humanistic Psychology entitled *Gestalt Therapy: What It Is and What It Ain't*.

INTRODUCTION

The spark that led to this book appeared simultaneously in two separate places. It is perhaps fitting that the book evolved into two major concepts, one focused on inner awareness, the other on outside stimulus. In 1973 I was responsible for an invitation extended by Miami-Dade Community College to two of my closest friends, Dr. Bart Knapp and Marta Vago. They flew to Miami from Philadelphia, and lectured on Transactional Analysis to a highly enthusiastic college audience. During this lecture, as they discussed the transactions which occurred between friends, I had a flash. I thought to myself that here was a possible whole new thrust for therapeutic effort, that by looking at the friends a patient chose, a therapist might obtain valuable information the patient was either unwilling or unable to contribute about his personality and needs. I discussed this with a number of therapists across the country, and they responded most favorably, some going so far as to say they would devote some time and attention to this aspect of their patients' lives.

At the same time, my personal life underwent some changes which underlined for me the vital importance of loving friendships in providing nourishment and support. I had moved to Miami from New York, and left behind a number of highly rewarding friendships. I still maintained contact with these people to some extent, but no longer had the kind of satisfying intimate interaction I had taken for granted. And I missed it. It took several months to build new friendships in my new city, and this experience gave me a deep appreciation for the value of a loving friend.

Thus, the importance and power of friendship struck me at both a highly intellectual level and at a deeply emotional one. This book is the result of that twin awareness.

As I did the research for this book, I discovered something that fascinated and astounded me, and it also seemed to astound the dozens of psychologists, psychiatrists, and social scientists I interviewed and talked to. That something was the fact that friendship has been almost totally ignored as an important and significant factor in human emotional experience. British psychologist Derek Wright, in an article for the journal *New Society,* says most psychologists have assumed that friendship has no important and distinctive features of its own as compared to other types of relationship bonds. He calls this assumption "facile and misleading" and goes on to say, "Friendship forms the unobtrusive backcloth against which we play out our professional, sexual and familial lives." Considering this, it seemed rather odd to me that so little attention was paid to friendship. There have been books galore on man-woman relationships, and those of parent-child, teacher-student, employer-employee, doctor-patient, even owner-dog, but almost none on friendship, and certainly none indicating the important role friends play in our emotional makeups and growth patterns.

In this book I have attempted not only to illuminate this subject but to provide you, the reader, with many tools with which to explore your own friendship patterns, so as to draw your own conclusions about the significance of friends in your life. I have also designed a number of experiences to help you make the most of your current friends, and decide how you want to expand your friendship horizons. Also included are dozens of techniques focused on enhancing interpersonal contact and communication between you and your friends. This, then, is not a sociological study, but a very personal handbook for you to use to examine your friendship patterns and actualize your friendship potential.

As I have stated, and as you'll note from the extensive acknowledgments, I spent a lot of time with people who know a lot about human behavior. I have done something with those interviews that isn't often done in this type of book: I have quoted them almost word for word. I did this for two reasons. First, after twelve years as a working journalist, I learned how very easy it is to distort comments and concepts by taking them out of context. I remember how we newsmen in a large broadcasting facility's newsroom used to play with tapes made by leading politicians, making them sound like idiots by deftly removing a word or two from their statements. Also, I have often been misquoted and misrepresented in newspaper and magazine articles. I was determined, as much as possible, to avoid this. Secondly, I learned a lot by talking to these human relations experts, and found their comments informative and enjoyable. I thought you might feel the same way, and should at least have the opportunity to judge for yourself. There are times when I might have easily edited someone's comments to make their words more exactly conform with my theories and viewpoint. I resisted this impulse, so you may sometimes find slight contradictions in the various quoted statements. I trust you enough to let you decide for yourself which viewpoint fits your needs and your situation. In psychology, an inexact science to say the least, there are many seeming paradoxes. This is because we are always moving, always changing, always experiencing in different ways, from very different perspectives. Hence the two old clichés "Out of sight, out of mind" and "Absence makes the heart grow fonder" are both true, at different times, in different situations. A lot of so-called self-help books pretend to offer definitive answers, easy cures for your problems. An honest author, an honest psychologist or psychiatrist, will tell you that you can only be aware for yourself, you can only change yourself. You may get guidelines and stimuli from outside sources, but it all comes back to you. The more choices you have, the more likely you are to be able to internalize any experience in useful and productive ways.

This is a book offering a lot of alternative approaches, and inviting you to pick and choose among them. If you do, you will have new understanding of the roles friends play in your life, and new tools with which to make the most of friends as a supportive interpersonal environment.

We invest a lot of time and energy in our friends. Time and energy exist for us in limited quantities, and we really can't afford to waste much of either. This book is aimed at helping you make wise investments of your available time and energy.

Some friends make us feel good just by being around. Some help to bring out the best in us. Some challenge or stimulate us, and we look to them for guidance in certain areas, or for a different viewpoint. Some of our friends make us feel they really like us, really respect and appreciate us. Some friends make us feel more alive and energetic and optimistic. Some especially valuable friends may fulfill our needs in several of these areas.

Other friends we choose may not have such positive effects on our lives. Recognizing this and understanding why we choose or need them can tell us much about ourselves. Awareness must precede positive change. But both awareness and change require tools and methods. This book contains many such tools, many viewpoints, and many ways to explore the phenomenon of friendship. All of these involve direct reader participation. You must explore for yourself how you feel about your friends, and whether they indeed provide you with a supportive interpersonal environment. You must decide where change is indicated, and how to best facilitate that change.

Dr. Judith Osgood, a counseling psychologist, says, "From youth to old age, each person is significantly affected, both psychologically and socially, by the meaningful friendships that he develops or by his lack of ability to develop such friendships." There are many possibilities to explore, and the exploration itself can become a strong positive growth experience.

One of the most articulate and friendly people I interviewed in preparation for this book was psychiatrist and author Dr. Leonard Zunin. At one point he said, "Inanimate objects become our friends also. Cars, homes, drapes, tables." My fondest hope is that in some small way you might come to see this book as your friend, allowing it to stimulate your own internal process, your own awareness, your own emotional power. And allowing it, as only the best of friends can do, to bring you a new appreciation for yourself.

JERRY GILLIES

Miami, Florida
March, 1976

CHAPTER 1

YOU ARE YOUR FRIENDS

You are your friends in many ways. They reflect your moods and your characteristics, your weaknesses and your strengths, and they very realistically indicate your needs, some of which you yourself may not be aware of. Looking at your friends individually and collectively, a pattern emerges, and that pattern can be a highly accurate barometer of your emotional state.

It has been said, "Show me his friends and I the man shall know." We are suggesting that you show yourself your friends so as to know yourself better.

One of the primary reasons you can learn so much about yourself by looking at your friends is the fact that you voluntarily choose friends, as compared to most other relationships. In fact, psychologist Derek Wright defines friendship in an article in *New Society* as "a relationship between two people of equal status that serves no ulterior motives such as economic, political or sexual gain and which is felt by the participants to be a result of free choice."

Of course, "free choice" is a relative term. Our prejudices, early conditioning, and emotional needs have a great deal to do with our choice of friends. Nevertheless, you probably exercise as much or more free choice in the selection of your friends than any other aspect of your life involving decision. So, looking at why and how you make the choices you make can produce much in the way of insight and self-knowledge. Dr. Judith Osgood says, "The outside world mirrors you. Each friend is a mirror, and seeing what aspects of yourself are represented in that person usually gives a lot of information, since most of us don't see people that way." This is not a new idea. Back in the seventeenth century, George Herbert said, "The best mirror is an old friend." Perhaps, then, this "friendship mirror" is merely a tool we've forgotten how to use.

In the chapters that lie ahead, you'll have an opportunity to examine the friends you have gathered throughout your life, and your feelings about them. This will help you gain insights into your needs and your self-image, and your capacity for sustaining healthy relationships. You'll be able to look at what you really get from the friends you now have, and what you are willing to give to them. You'll be exploring the reality of what your friends tell about you. In writing a biography, one of the author's first tasks is to carefully interview the subject's friends. You are going to undertake the same kind of research project, but it should prove to be a much more fascinating effort, since you are going to be delving into the most interesting subject in all the world: YOU!

Once you explore the whys and wherefores of your friendship choices, you can move on to the next task from a position of strength. That task involves deciding whether you like the reflection of yourself projected back from your friends, and deciding whether you want to do anything to modify the situation. Friends not only can guide you toward a more realistic view of yourself, but they can be constructively used to help you enhance the positive and eliminate the negative factors in your life. Friends can thus be our greatest natural resource, but not if we leave many of the possibilities and potentials buried beneath the surface.

One of the underlying premises of this book is that you probably will be more willing to examine your friends carefully than you would be to examine your emotional attitudes and needs. Your friends therefore provide an important set of clues to your emotional makeup that may not be otherwise available. Your friends, in many respects, are a monument and a living trophy of your life. You learn much of what you feel about life itself by looking at the friends with whom you choose to share it.

FRIENDS AS ASSISTANT SCRIPTWRITERS

We all have our own life script, consisting of the way we perceive ourselves and define our roles. Much of our life script material may be invalid, and a lot of it comes from parental programming and other early conditioning. Sometimes we use our friends to reinforce this life script, and, in effect, help ourselves sustain the negative aspects of it.

Psychotherapist Marta Vago, codirector of Laurel Institute, a therapy and counseling center in Philadelphia, says, "I think friendships are basically a way of affirming your life position, how you feel about yourself. I'll give a clinical example of a woman I'm seeing. One of the first things that she complained about as one of the things that was bothering her was the fact that her friends were always taking advantage of her. She was so good to them and yet they asked for too much, and they didn't give anything back to her, and so on. What we got to very quickly was that the only way this woman knew how to be close to other people was by constantly giving things to them. She couldn't relate on any other level, just by mothering them and nurturing them. So she tended to choose people who needed to be mothered and nurtured. Now, of course she had her own needs: being mothered and nurtured and so on; but because her basic life issue was that she needed to be taking care of people, she tended to choose more people who were dependent and needed a lot of stuff from her, rather than people who would be able to give things to her. Until she learns how to feel good about herself without having people lean on her, she will tend to surround herself with people who need a lot of help, and she will feel that she's not getting back as much as she's giving out."

Does this ring any familiar bells for you? It is one of the problems seen most often by therapists, particularly in relation to patients and their friends. Dr. Harold Greenwald, clinical psychologist and author, says, "If you decided a long time ago that the world is a lousy place and that people are no goddamn good and are untrustworthy, you will pick friends to illustrate this thesis. If you think that people are nice and good, you pick those kinds of friends. You tend to pick friends to prove your way of looking at the world."

Psychiatrist Eileen Walkenstein illustrates this point with a personal episode. "I had a friend who used to call me from time to time. She was a woman who was wasting her life. Very intelligent, very creative, but she got stuck in the mold of being a professional man's wife and spent her weekends with other women who were also wasting their lives, mostly drinking, partying. Every Saturday and Sunday she would spend her time at these social things, cocktail parties and whatnot, where the women were drinking their lives away. Then they complained to one another during the week about how rotten life was and how depressed they were. Well, from time to time she would call me. At first I was sucked into it like anyone else would be, and then, gradually, it dawned on me what she was doing: she was dumping on me the same kind of shit she was dumping on them and they were dumping on her. When I realized that, it came as an impact, and I said, 'I don't want you to dump your shit on me. I don't want to hear this shit.' She was stunned, and she said, 'Wow! That's all we do. That's what I do with my friends and that's what they do with me. That's *all* we really do with one another!' Somehow, after that, she broke away. She began withdrawing from those friends. Ultimately she went back to school and on to a higher degree, and got a tremendous interest in finding some creative direction in her life."

This episode in Dr. Walkenstein's life is almost a synthesis of the major premises of this book in the way in which it focuses on some of the remarkable facets of friendship. First of all, this woman reinforced her own poor self-image by the friends she chose and the way she interacted with them. Then she became aware of what she was doing through the affirmative action of another friend, Dr. Walkenstein. In effect, Eileen Walkenstein stimulated positive action by being aware of the behavior she wasn't willing to put up with from a friend, and firmly letting her friend know how she felt. By threatening to withdraw her friendship, Dr. Walkenstein forced her friend to sharply focus on the reality of her life.

The friends we choose are often a reflection of our image of ourselves. The sad part about this is that it quite often becomes a vicious circle. If we have a poor self-image, and choose friends based on that poor self-image, then those friends constantly reinforce that poor self-image. Our ignorance of any or all of the factors involved compounds the problem. We may not know we have a poor self-image. We may not know that we are choosing our friends on the basis of that image. We may not know that the friends we choose are contributing to that poor self-image. Becoming aware of any of these factors can help us get out of the destructive pattern.

A SENSE OF WORTH

It all boils down to this: Do you think you are worthwhile? This is the crucial difference between success and failure in all our activities throughout our lives. If you feel lovable and capable, you will enter into relationships that complement and enhance those feelings. In his delightful book *Love*, Dr. Leo Buscaglia says, "First of all the loving individual has to care about himself. This is number one. I don't mean an ego trip. I'm talking about somebody who really cares about himself, who says, 'Everything is filtered through me, and so the greater I am, the more I have to give. The greater knowledge I have, the more I'm going to have to give. The greater understanding I have, the greater is my ability to teach others and to make myself the most fantastic, the most beautiful, the most wondrous, the most tender human being in the world.' "

Even the Bible presupposes self-love. "Thou shalt love thy neighbour as thyself" assumes you already love yourself.

Love is energy. Self-love is your basic energy source, and the stronger this source, the more love-energy you have to share with others. Noted therapist Virginia Satir describes the person with a healthy sense of worth in her book *Peoplemaking:* "He feels that he matters, that the world is a better place because he is here. He has faith in his own competence. He is able to ask others for help, but he believes he can make his own decisions and is his own best resource. Appreciating his own worth, he is ready to see and respect the worth of others. He radiates trust and hope. He doesn't have rules against anything he feels. He accepts all of himself as human."

Acceptance is an important part of self-love. In *Love*, Dr. Buscaglia says, "If you know, accept and appreciate yourself and your uniqueness, you will permit others to do so. If you value and appreciate the discovery of yourself, you will encourage others to engage in self-discovery. If you recognize your need to be free to discover who you are, you will allow others their freedom to do so, also. When you realize you are the best you, you will accept the fact that others are the best they. But it follows that it all starts with you. To the extent to which you know yourself, and we are all more alike than different, you can know others. When you love yourself, you will love others. And to the depth and extent to which you can love yourself, only to that depth and extent will you be able to love others."

Reading these words is one thing, but feeling worthwhile, lovable, and capable may be quite another. You have to believe it for yourself. Your friendships can help, both in illuminating your current self-image and in providing the supportive environment in which you can increase your sense of worth.

YOU AS A FRIEND

What kind of friend are you? Are you the best friend anyone could have? Do you really believe that it's worth making an effort to win your friendship? Most important of all: Are you the kind of friend you would choose as a friend?

Try to write a paragraph about yourself, entitled "A Wonderful Friend." In this paragraph, say everything good about yourself you really believe is true.

Make a list of ten characteristics you believe qualify you as a good friend.

Read over both the paragraph and the list with this question in mind: Would these attributes be the ones you would seek in a potential friend? On reading over what you have written, you may notice you've left some good stuff about yourself out. Put it in! At the end of this book, you might try doing these two little exercises again, and you just might be surprised at the results!

WHAT IS A FRIEND?

You can start to learn something about yourself and your self-image by simply looking at how you perceive and define the word "friend."

For example, which of the following two statements is closest to your own attitude:

> "Friends are those you turn to when you're in trouble."
>
> or:
>
> "Friends are those you turn to when you're very happy and want to share that feeling with someone."

Or is your definition closer to a combination of the above two statements, and more like this comment by Cicero:

> "Friendship doubles our joy and divides our grief."

It's really a question of whether you choose your friends because you want to be able to depend on them, or because you want to share your independence with them.

THE ISLAND

One way to help yourself decide which definition has more meaning for you is to simulate a situation in your imagination. Imagine that you are visiting an unexplored island with a potential new friend, someone you don't know very well. Do you think you would feel closer to this person at the beginning of your visit, when you are both in unfamiliar territory and perhaps a bit fearful? Or would you feel closer as you discovered all the beauty and good things the island had to offer and wanted to share these with someone. Perhaps both situations would produce a degree of closeness, but which do you think would have the most meaning for you?

DEPENDENCY IN FRIENDSHIP

If you "need" your friends rather than "want" them, you may be experiencing an unhealthy life situation. If you are unhappy in your life and in your friendships, this may be the first place to look.

Willard and Marguerite Beecher, in *Beyond Success and Failure*, state: "Dependency always degrades. It degrades by mutual enslavement both the dependent and the one on whom he leans. *Both are equally guilty* of dependence. The individual who is physically and psychologically self-reliant will not allow anyone to lean on him, as it would result in his enslavement if he permitted it. It becomes evident, then, that the one who leans and the one who allows himself to be leaned on are equally lacking in self-sufficiency. They are in a kind of mutual admiration society, which amounts to a conspiracy to exploit each other. Both are in a condition of second-class citizenship, although one may imagine himself mistakenly as the strong one in the relationship. The fact remains that they degrade, inhibit and enslave each other and that, in such cases, 'two is less than one.' "

A SENSE OF BALANCE

A sense of balance is thus of prime importance in friendship. A sense that one friend is not leaning or depending on the other, a sense that both are gaining from the relationship, a sense that the friendship is of equal importance to both individuals. This balance is easier to attain in friendship than in any other interpersonal relationship. This may be why good feelings persist in friendships over much longer periods of time than in parent-child relationships, man-woman love relationships, etc. Dr. Derek Wright in an article for the journal, *New Society*, calls this balance "status symmetry," and notes: "It is a relationship of mutual respect, as distinct from one of unilateral respect. In relationships of unilateral respect one person advises, controls, persuades and influences to a much greater extent than the other does; there is a considerable discrepancy in the relative 'weights' of the opinions and judgements expressed by each within the relationship. In relationships of mutual respect, discrepancies of this kind are bound to arise in particular situations, but there is an overall balance in the influence of each of the two participants."

FRIENDSHIP CREDO

What kind of feeling is evoked in you by the following statement on friendship?:

> You are my friend. I choose you as a friend because you bring out in me things I like about myself. I feel comfortable and warm in your presence. My life is more interesting because you are there. I don't have to have you in my life to be happy, but I am very happy you are in my life. I know you care and you know I do, even if we are separated by time and space. You touch me in a way that no other human being does, and what flows between us is quite unique. You matter to me, and I take great pride and pleasure in knowing that I matter to you. The essence of we two together has to remain a feeling, never totally captured in words or thoughts. In some indescribable way we communicate that feeling to each other. And that is, most of all, why you are my friend.

Is this a statement you could make about any of your current friends? Do you see it as a statement that comes from someone with a healthy self-image? Do you think a person making this statement would be a happy person? If you can't honestly make this statement now about any of your friendships, do you think you would eventually like to be able to do so?

You are asked to make your own decisions about the friendship credo, just as you will be asked to make your own decisions throughout this book. Friendship is a highly personal and private experience. Only you know the reality of what causes you to choose the friends you choose, and how you really feel about them, and how you really feel about yourself. No one else can define these conditions for you, though guidelines can be offered. Any judgments made will have to be your own. Thus the risk and the responsibility are totally yours, as are all the rewards.

YOUR LIST OF FRIENDS

So let's start looking at your self-image as indicated and measured by your friends. One of the innovative techniques in self-confrontation developed by Dr. Dan Malamud for his classes at New York University is for each individual to make a list of his or her friends, writing down the characteristics of each friend. Dr. Malamud says, "Like a detective, you can make a deduction about your needs or fears, based upon those particular characteristics that seem to run through your descriptions of your friends."

In making your own list, spend as much time as necessary to make it as complete as possible. You'll be using it as a basic foundation for many of the exercises in this book, and might even consider putting it on heavy cardboard. Don't attempt to list your friends in any particular order. Just write down their names as they occur to you, and try to include all of your friends, even those from childhood you may no longer see or hear from. Write down the names of all of the friends you can now think of, and then go over the list and write down the characteristics of each person. One list of friends looked like this:

1. *Tommy Barnett.* Dynamic. A leader. Inconsiderate. Braggart.
2. *Jimmy Dugan.* A lot of fun. Womanizer. Irresponsible.
3. *Marc Logan.* Gentle. Dependable. Bright and creative.
4. *Harry Goldstein.* Warm. Down to earth. Generous.
5. *Sharon Albertson.* Pushy. Selfish. Attractive. Bright.
6. *Steve Feldson.* Very masculine. Confident. Good-natured. Stimulating.
7. *Murray Wilson.* Strong-willed. Stubborn. Selfish. Exciting.
8. *Jeff Stern.* Lonely. Warm. Needy. Dependable.
9. *Adam Carnes.* A loner. Strong and silent. Intellectually aware.
10. *Judy Belven.* Creative. Compassionate. Stimulating. Generous.
11. *Sue Lasser.* Warm and good-natured. Creative. Brilliant. Fun.

If you haven't done so yet, make your own list now. You may want to make more detailed comments on your friends' characteristics than were made on the above list, so take as much time and as much space as you need.

Let's look for a moment at our sample list. Just glancing at it, what does it tell you about the man who wrote it? What kind of people is he attracted to and what kind are attracted to him? It might be hard to tell with any degree of accuracy, until we make a slight modification. You were asked to put down all your friends as you thought of them, in no particular order. But to define who you are *now*, you have to know who your friends are now. We may even learn a lot by seeing which ones we no longer consider as our friends. Do this for your list by putting a C in front of each current friend, and a P in front of each friend from the past with whom you no longer have any contact. In the case of our sample list, friends 1,2,5,7, and 8 are no longer friends. Now you can get a much clearer picture of where this person is in relation to the friends in his life. It's a rather healthy picture. Do you see why?

Now, look at your list and what it can tell you at this point. We'll be adding more material to it as we go along, but look it over in its present form and see if it tells you anything at all about yourself.

TO THE FEELING LEVEL

Up to this point you've been doing some thinking about your friends; now you're going to examine them emotionally. Do this by going down each name on your list and trying to visualize that person's face. Do this with your eyes closed, in a comfortable position, and taking as much time as you need to clearly see that friend's face. When you are sharply tuned in to a friend's face, examine what you are feeling. Does this friend make you feel happy, sad, warm, excited? Try to focus on one strong feeling, and right next to that friend's name on your list, write down that feeling.

When you've finished doing this with your whole list, look over the feelings evoked by the people you consider your friends. Are these the feelings you enjoy the most? In other words, are your friends making you feel the way you would like to feel?

STRONGER-WEAKER

Go over your list once again, and this time decide whether each of these friends is emotionally stronger or weaker than you are. You might consider such factors as whether they seem to be happier and more fulfilled than you, or how they handle their love relationships compared to how you handle yours, or some other hint of emotional well-being. In front of each name, preceding the C or P you've already marked, place either a plus sign (+) to indicate you feel this friend is emotionally stronger than you or a minus sign (−) to indicate that you feel this friend is emotionally weaker. If you feel this friend is your emotional equal, place an equal sign (=) in front of his or her name.

These choices may seem arbitrary, but remember they are merely your current perceptions, not necessarily final judgments.

Look at the results of this exercise. Can you see a clear pattern of strength or weakness in the friends you've chosen? How would you like to see this pattern evolve?

YOUR LIST OF NONFRIENDS

Throughout your life you've come in contact with people you haven't been attracted to and have probably shunned them. Psychologist Dan Malamud also has his groups in self-confrontation make a list of the people they dislike and *their* characteristics. Dr. Malamud sees this as a valuable exploration, especially in the comparing of the two lists. Try it for yourself. List those people you have negative feelings about and the characteristics you've noted in them. Compare your two lists. Are the characteristics really different? Does this new list tell you anything new about yourself?

LIMITING YOURSELF

If all your friends fall into a clear-cut personality grouping, you may be avoiding or eliminating a lot of possible types of friends who could offer you a great deal. Can you see any indication from your list of friends that you might be putting very rigid limitations on the types of people you feel comfortable with?

Dr. Dorothy Nolte, a humanistic psychologist says, "In a sense, sometimes we gain out of what looks like a poor friendship. I've heard people say, 'We started out as enemies; we ended up as friends.' "

Dr. Nolte describes how we can limit our possibilities in choosing friends: "I'm reminded of a woman who found that she had a feeling that people didn't really like her. In terms of friends, this negative determined whom she gravitated toward. She had to test the person against this feeling before she explored a possible friendship. Our inner expectation will thus determine the people that we gravitate toward, or allow to gravitate toward us, whether it be a positive or a negative feeling on our part. These feeling states, or wishes or fantasies, do determine how we move into the sphere of choice. If we have a negative feeling going, this would be a filter that all people must be fed through. You don't have spontaneity anymore, you don't have a reaching and an allowing going on, so that we're afraid to really have choice. Out here, then, is the proving ground: life, the social situation, the intimate situation. If you get all these negative people around you, there's got to be something that matches within you."

Her husband and colleague, Dr. Claude Nolte, agrees: "If we take a person who has a broader spectrum of acceptance, who does not limit himself, this individual will have a broader spectrum of the type of people he will have as friends. I would say that a measure of the growth of a person could be the spectrum of the type of friends that person would have."

THE UNPREDICTABLE FRIEND

If you choose all your friends based on a negative self-image or lack of a positive self-image, then your choices have to be very structured and limited. You'll only be willing to choose a friend whose actions you can safely predict will reinforce that self-image. As Dr. Dan Malamud says, "People tend to develop idealized images of themselves, which they either think they do live up to, or which they strain to live up to. And these idealized images of themselves are ways that people have of reassuring themselves about the basic underlying shithood that they feel they are in. I would expect that people gravitate toward those people who will give support to their idealized image, and stay away from people who will threaten their idealized image."

A sign of growth, therefore, might be the ability to choose a friend not knowing whether he or she will reinforce your self-image. In other words, taking a risk on intimacy with no guarantees. Psychiatrist Dr. Eileen Walkenstein says, "Healthy friendships are those that are provocative and unpredictable. If I know everything you're going to tell me before you tell it to me, there's no point in your saying a word; we might just as well sit in silence." Does this make any sense to you? Could you feel comfortable having a friend who was unpredictable? If you need the absolute security of total predictability in all your relationships, then your self-esteem may need some bolstering.

GIVING AND GETTING

What do you give to your friends? What do you get from them? Go over your list of friends and answer these two questions for each friend you now have. Only when there is some equity in the giving and getting exchange can there really be a full friendship experience.

Relationships are not static things, and yet many friendships haven't moved in years, though they are still regarded as current friendships by the two people involved. These could be called stagnant friendships, and if you have any of these on your list, you probably found it difficult to come up with an answer to the giving and getting question. These stagnant friendships are debilitating, time and energy consuming, and self-defeating. You may have a false sense of loyalty to friends who are producing negative vibrations in your life. When friends no longer nurture, they are no longer really friends. Sentences like "He's a good friend, but I really can't stand being around him for very long" or "I feel drained whenever she comes over" are not really describing friendships. Counseling psychologist, Dr. Judith Osgood says, "Most people are really reluctant to admit, 'My friendships are obsolete and are not meeting my needs.' They start to feel guilty. A girl came to me four months after completing a list of her friends and said she was feeling guilty because she wasn't calling a lot of the friends she had listed. I said, 'It sounds like you don't want to call them.' She finally owned that and said, 'That's right! I'm starting to get involved with other people and the friends I listed seem boring and dry; they're just not making it.' I think a lot of friendships are held onto like many things in life. Things that need to be let go of, so something new can come in, something that's more appropriate to our own growth patterns."

So there's a real value in periodically looking over your friendships in terms of what you are giving and what you are getting. Dr. Eileen Walkenstein says, "In terms of friendship, the giving doesn't deplenish us and the getting doesn't jade us."

NO SIMPLE ANSWERS

In this opening chapter you may find quite a few generalizations and perhaps some rather simplistic statements. As we go along, we'll get more specific. We had to start somewhere, and by now you probably have started viewing your friends in slightly different, or slightly more perceptive ways. Try not to make any final conclusions yet, as these are only the first steps in an exploration of patterns you have spent years building up. There are many ways to view your friends and the way you choose them, and you'll soon find that the picture can drastically change merely by slightly altering the perspective.

For instance, psychotherapist Marta Vago notes one factor that may be both a negative and positive force, saying, "People tend to look for others that in some way complete them. Each of us has strengths and weaknesses, and whether we realize it or not, we tend to look for people who complement us in terms of those strengths and weaknesses. However, that in itself becomes paradoxical, because the very things that we don't have in ourselves are those we want in others, and these may be the very things that often annoy us in the other person."

Ms. Vago gives an example from her relationship with her professional colleague and love-partner, Dr. Bart Knapp: "I'm more structured in my thinking and in the way I relate to time than Bart is, and I know that's an issue for me. This fact that I tend to be too structured causes me problems. I love the fact, I think, that Bart is less structured and less rigid in his time sense. So, in a sense, he complements, he completes something for me when it comes to time. However, his nonstructuredness in terms of time is the very thing that drives me up the wall. So, while I'm looking to complete something for me, at the same time I don't want to complete it. I'm always in a kind of bind, between the devil and the deep blue sea. Do I really want to complete my gestalt, or do I want to hang on to an incomplete gestalt in terms of myself and my strengths and my weaknesses. I think that would be another thing you could ask yourself: What are the qualities that you really treasure in your friend, and what are the qualities that drive you up the wall about your friend? I bet you'd find that in a lot of instances the same quality would be mentioned in both answers."

RESENTMENTS AND APPRECIATIONS

This is an exercise that many psychologists use in group interaction workshops. It may be the best way for you to see if Marta Vago's comment has any validity in your friendship structure. Go over your entire list of friends and list the things that you resent about each of them. Be as totally honest as possible. Then go over the list again, this time listing all the things you appreciate about each of your friends. Look at your two new lists and see whether, in individual friendships, you don't resent something that is very much related to something you also appreciate.

MARK AND CANDY

The thing Mark most appreciated about Candy was her childlike quality. She was playful and sexy, in an innocent childlike way, and carefree, never seeming to worry about anything. The thing that Mark most resented about Candy was her immature attitude, her irresponsible lack of long-range goals, the way she was always late, her messy apartment, etc., etc. Can you see how paradoxical Mark's attitude was? Her childlike attributes entranced him, but her childish irresponsibility irritated him, though they were part and parcel of the same basic personality trait and emotional makeup.

We often try to have our cake and eat it, too, in just this manner. It may not be an easy problem to solve, and we may have to make some painful adjustments in our priorities. But knowing that a problem exists, and has certain contradictory aspects to it, is the first step. Just as knowing who your friends are, and how you feel about them, is the first step in beginning to see how they affect your life and how you might improve or enhance the situation.

YOUR PREREQUISITES FOR FRIENDSHIP

If you were to go about selecting a brand new friend right now, what kind of friend would you look for? What kind of person would he or she be? What kind of relationship would you like to have? Answer these three questions for yourself right now, and save your answers. You may find some of your friendship prerequisites changing or expanding by the time you finish this book. Or you may merely find out how very healthy your friendships are, and how right you are to choose friends the way you've been choosing them.

In his book *Emotional Common Sense*, Dr. Rolland Parker says, "Making and keeping friends is a psychologically important factor in its own right. It creates an atmosphere in which we can avoid the worst effects of stress and its emotional discomforts and also create a pleasant frame of mind in which we can face other problems. Friendship will by itself help to overcome tendencies to deprivation, loneliness, and alienation."

In the next chapter we're going to examine much more closely exactly how you view your friends and how you see yourself interacting with them. But before you go on, sit back and think about what you've learned in this chapter.

Can you complete the sentence "One new thing I've learned about my friends is the fact that ———"? Examine how you feel about this, and then go on.

CHAPTER 2

CIRCLE OF FRIENDS

We all have circles of friends, people who revolve around us and our lives. Graphically seeing this process can illuminate some of our friendship issues and our friendship priorities. Looking at your life in a circular pattern can provide much insight and a fuller perspective, especially when you place yourself in the center of that circle. Most people have only a very narrow view of their existence, and some see themselves almost pushed into a corner, with everything and everyone else relating to them as if in frontal attack. Using a circle process, you can see that you are truly the center of your universe—a most realistic self-appraisal rather than an arrogant stance. For if you appreciate yourself as the center of your world, you will appreciate all other people as the center of theirs. And you will begin to realize that no matter what is happening within your awareness, there is no way you can always be aware of everything happening in the whole circle. If something bad is happening to you, it's probably inhabiting a very narrow slice of the total pie, and it only assumes importance when you focus on that narrow slice to the exclusion of all else happening in the circle. In this chapter we are going to explore and play with some circles, and see what they can teach us about ourselves. As preliminary practice, we'll look at a view of all the things that are important to us in our current lives. In this particular circle, we'll be represented by a dot in the middle, and those things most important to us will be closest to that dot. A typical such Life Priority Circle might look like the circle on page 32.

As you can see, this is the circle of a very active woman. Her husband, children, and career seem equally important, with friends just a little less so. It's important to note that this circle constitutes how she feels about her life *right now*, and her priorities could change at any time.

Now it's your turn. On the opposite page is a blank circle. You are the

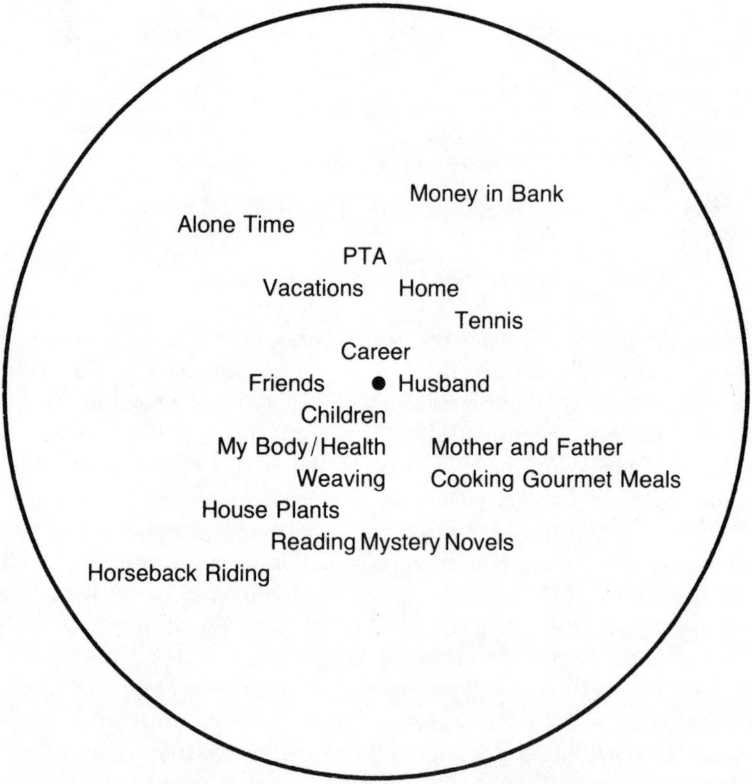

dot in the middle. Place the things most important to you closest to that dot. Try to include everything that involves your interest, pleasure, time, and energy. Since we'll be looking at our friends in detail later on in this chapter, just put them all together in one category of "Friends" for the purpose of this initial circle exploration. You may identify all other people, places, and things by name or general classification.

LIFE PRIORITY CIRCLE

Were there any surprises in terms of those items you placed closest to you at the center of the circle? Looking at the picture presented above, what kind of a person would you say you are? Have your values and

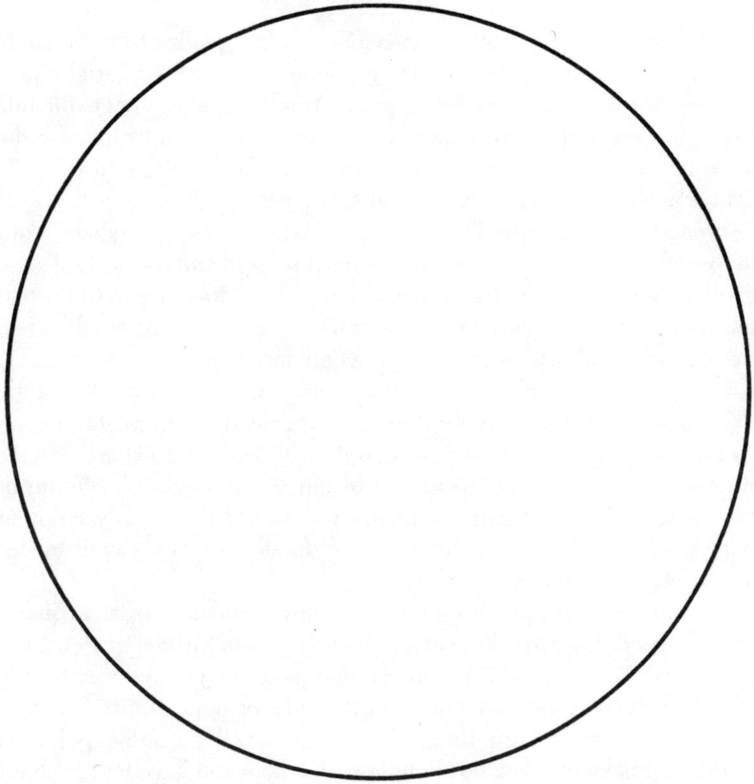

priorities changed recently? Or is this basically indicative of those things you've always felt were most important? And, finally, is there anything you would like to see move closer to the center in the not-too-distant future? Anything you would like to devote more time and attention to?

And where did your friendships go in your Life Priority Circle? How important are they to you? And are you satisfied with that degree of importance?

Another useful tool for further exploration of individual friendships is to see whether you can produce a Life Priority Circle for one of your close friends. This will give you a good indication of whether you really know this friend and his or her priorities in life.

THE FRIENDSHIP CIRCLE

Next we are going to look at our individual friendships in terms of how they fit into our sphere of existence. First of all, realize that the circle you fill in on the next page is indicative of how you are feeling right now. Feel free to modify it at any future point. You'll probably want to include those people you marked as current friends on your friendship list in the last chapter. This circle includes those people you feel are in your life right now. This can include several categories:

Intimate Friendship. Those people with whom you share your deepest feelings, with whom you are most relaxed and comfortable and spontaneous. These are friends to whom you would feel free to express both negative and positive feelings, without fear that this would affect the basic fabric of your relationship. Acceptance would be a major factor in an intimate friendship. Each of you accepts the other's thoughts, feelings, and behavior, even if they dramatically differ from your own.

Limited Friendship. These are people with whom you share specific interests and feelings. Someone, for instance, you might play tennis or go fishing with, and whose company you would thoroughly enjoy at those times. But you probably wouldn't totally reveal yourself to this person or share your deepest feelings.

Potential Friendship. This might be a new friendship, or an acquaintanceship with the possibility of developing into an Intimate Friendship or Limited Friendship. It might include people you have met briefly and liked, though you have not had the time or opportunity for more meaningful contact with them. There may well be some potential friends you have overlooked. People with whom you have had pleasant contact, perhaps an exchanged smile or brief conversation, on a regular basis. Dr. Edna Foa, a Philadelphia psychologist, often assigns her patients the task of looking for specific friendship cues, indications from others that they would like to have some kind of contact, or merely signals from them that they are feeling warm and friendly. Dr. Foa says many people ignore these friendship cues, thus perpetuating the myth that they have no friends and no possibilities for making any.

You might, before filling in your Friendship Circle, choose to make three lists, containing the names of your Intimate, Limited, and Potential friends. You can then place them where you will in the circle, perhaps identifying them with the letters I, L, or P.

Remember, this is not a test on which you are going to receive a grade. There is no "good" or "bad" Friendship Circle. Only you can interpret the results. This is a tool and technique primarily designed to increase personal awareness of the role friends play in your life.

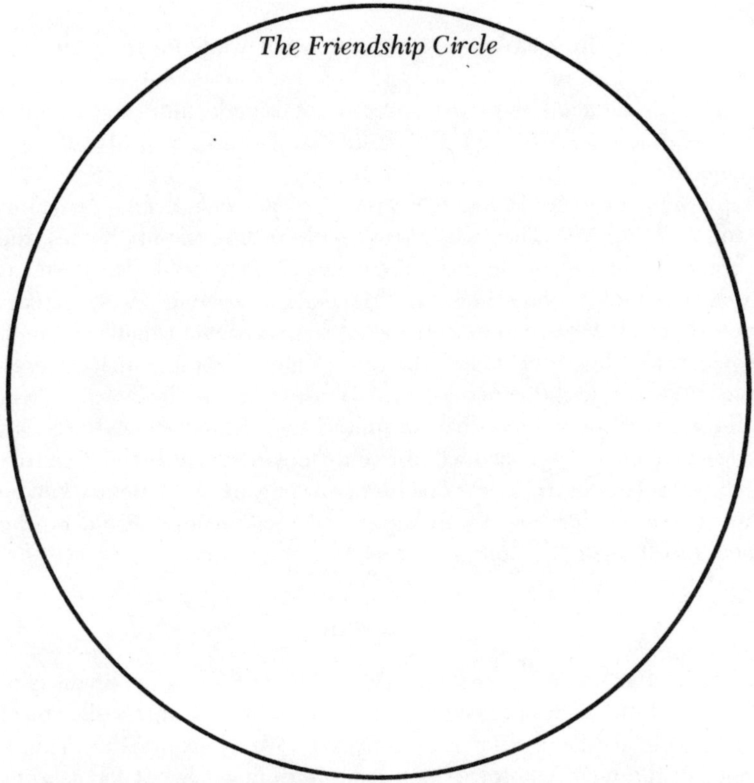

You might choose to fill in your friends' names in pencil so as to allow for easier modification in the future. You might even choose to copy the circle on a piece of blank paper instead of writing in the book.

If you can't decide where to place a specific friend, one useful method is to close your eyes and picture that friend and become aware of how you feel about that friend at this moment.

CIRCLE ASSESSMENT

Now for some preliminary conclusions. Look at those friends you have placed closest to the center. What constitutes the difference between these people and those you placed further away from you? Is it merely the time you spend together? Or are there certain qualities possessed by your closest friends and not by those you keep at a distance? If you had to write three conclusions about you as a person and the kinds of friends you choose just from looking at this circle, what would those conclusions be?

Are you satisfied with the number of friends indicated in your friendship circle? Do you feel validated by the quantity of your friendships?

For some people, friendships are signs of accomplishment, status symbols if you will. The more friends gathered, so the myth goes, the more valuable the person doing the gathering. This attitude, however, usually prevents truly intimate friendship. Someone who gathers friends as if they were points on a giant scorecard will usually refuse to reveal his or her innermost thoughts to any of them. Such "friend-collecting" would indicate deep-rooted insecurity and lack of a positive self-image. Someone who has an unhealthy self-image, who believes himself or herself unworthwhile, would never reveal his or her true feelings and thoughts for fear that his or her unworthwhileness would be discovered. Hence a series of superficial relationships would be the usual result of such emotional attitudes.

ACCESSIBILITY

One of the ways in which people cover up their unwillingness to enter into intimate relationships with others is by creating the illusion of a number of deep and satisfying friendships. We'll look into this in more depth in the next chapter, which deals with fantasy, but for now it's useful to examine a primary manifestation of this illusion/delusion. Usually it's more a self-deception than any attempt to deceive the outside world. But what it can produce is a major obstacle to intimacy, or to the development of either intimate or limited friendships. Look at those friends in your Friendship Circle. How many of them are really accessible? How many of them are really available for personal contact on a regular basis? Place a circle around all the friends in your circle who are nonaccessible, who live out of town and can usually only be contacted by phone, letter, or infrequent visits. Place the letters NA in the circle around their names.

If all or most of those friends closest to you in the circle are nonaccessible, you have created an intimacy block. You are using these friendships, which offer you very limited nourishment, to create the illusion that you don't need other friendships, and thus can rationalize away your unwillingness to reach out to people.

It is fine to have nonaccessible friendships, but this can be a negative factor in your life if they are the only friendships you consider important, or if you allow them to hamper in any way your ability or desire to create accessible friendships.

NEGATIVE AND POSITIVE POTENTIAL FRIENDSHIPS

If you did not include at least a few Potential Friendships in your Friendship Circle, you might want to do so now. Looking at these Potential Friendships can tell you much about how you go about forming relationships with others. For instance, are there any people you consider as potential friends whom you have avoided spending more time with even though they have made friendly overtures toward you? What do you think this says about your willingness to allow new friendships to develop? Of course, if you have all the Intimate Friendships you can handle, and they are satisfying all your needs that can be satisfied by intimate friends, then there is nothing harmful in keeping Potential Friendships just that. What Dr. Herbert Otto noticed, however, was that many people kept their potential friends and acquaintances at arm's length with an attitude that could be summed up in the statement "I don't want to invest myself in more relationships." Dr. Otto says, "You have this attitude among people that relationships represent an investment, and the fear of rejection comes in here, so that very often the rationale you hear when you talk to people about friendship is, 'I've invested all of myself in these friends; I am unwilling to invest and risk in terms of having further friends because I might be rejected.' " Of course, anyone who has really healthy friendships would be *more* willing to freely reach out to others, since rejection would not be a major consideration. If you really have enough friends, and you reach out to some potential new ones, you can have the attitude that it really doesn't matter if these new friendships work out or not, since you are already getting a lot of friendly nourishment and aren't operating from a needy or desperate space.

In our culture, most people seem to have missed the point that rather than close off other possibilities for contact, healthy relationships foster new possibilities and new degrees of openness to others. In friendship or lovership, the process of loving increases the capabilities of the lover, and love is multiplied by just being. If you are truly in a loving, joyful relationship, then you will have lots of love and joy to share, maybe not the time to share as much of yourself with others, but certainly the capability to share fully in whatever moments are available for others.

The positive Potential Friendship is one that truly has the potential for moving up to a Limited or Intimate Friendship. If all or most of the Potential Friendships in your Friendship Circle are people you would *not* consider as possibilities for these other two categories, then they may be acting as an intimacy block, and you have to take responsibility for any friendship deficiency in your life. If there is someone you considered enough to place in your circle, but about whom you would say, "Oh, but this could never be a really deep friendship," then you might be creating an intimacy block for yourself. If nothing else, the energy these Potential Friendships or acquaintanceships take may be just the energy you need to develop new and satisfying relationships.

Psychologist Judith Osgood says, "People very often do not perceive potential friends. We don't think about people as 'this person could be a potential friend.' " Dr. Osgood also feels it has a lot to do with the energy available, saying, "A potential friend is where your energy hasn't gone yet. I think it's hard to open up that energy circle for something new. It's hard to open up space or to be available. A large majority of people keep very closed networks on themselves. If I have time, it's usually going to be used to fill in something I already know rather than be open to something unknown. I think people that aren't known are perceived as 'strange.' The unknown is frightening. Although there are many, many potential friendships that are available to most people, the energy that it takes to approach someone to even start that process going is quite a bit."

It might at this point be useful for you to look at exactly how much time and energy you have available for friendships. Is that time and energy being used as effectively as you'd like? Are you getting a satisfactory return on the amount of energy you are investing? If not, the Friendship Circle can give you some clarifying clues as to where you focus that energy, and how refocusing some of it might change the situation.

TIME CHECK

Figure out exactly how much time you have available and want to spend in friendly interaction. To start out, arbitrarily pick out a figure that makes some sense to you. As we go further along in the book, you may choose to modify that figure. You may find, as you explore your friendships in more depth, that you need to spend more time in this area of your life to receive the nourishment you require from human interrelating. Or, as you focus your energies more sharply, and get more out of the friendships you have, and possibly eliminate those that are destructive and toxic, you may find that you need less time to get what you want and need from your friends. In either eventuality, let's look at the situation as it is right now. Let us say, for example, that you pick ten hours a week for interacting with friends. Then, your Friendship Circle represents ten hours of your week. Look at it now in terms of this time limitation. Does this give you any new awareness? For instance, do you see that you have too many people in your circle, and there's no way to spread your energy among them all in just ten hours? Or do you find that the friends you've placed in your circle cannot possibly fill that much time for you? Whichever is true for you, make a list of the things you'd like to see changed, and how you think they might be changed. If you feel the number of friends in your circle fit perfectly into the amount of time you have for them, then be aware of how this makes you feel.

PLEASURE PATTERNS

Now we are going to look at another facet of our friendships that may very well narrow your circle down still further: the amount of pleasure you get from these friends. Look over all the friends in your circle. For each one, ask yourself the question "Has this friend given me any pleasure in the past three months?" That pleasure may have come from some shared experience you had with this friend, some fun thing you did together. It might be something nice your friend said to you or did for you. It might be a good feeling you had when making contact with that friend. If you cannot honestly think of one pleasurable moment provided in or by that friendship in the past three months, then draw a circle around that person's name, with the letters NP for "no pleasure" in the circle around his or her name.

Be aware of how the results of this exercise feel to you. Don't make a judgment about yourself based on these results. What do you think this looking at how much pleasure you've gotten from your friendships accomplishes?

If you surround yourself with people you don't enjoy, this fact alone

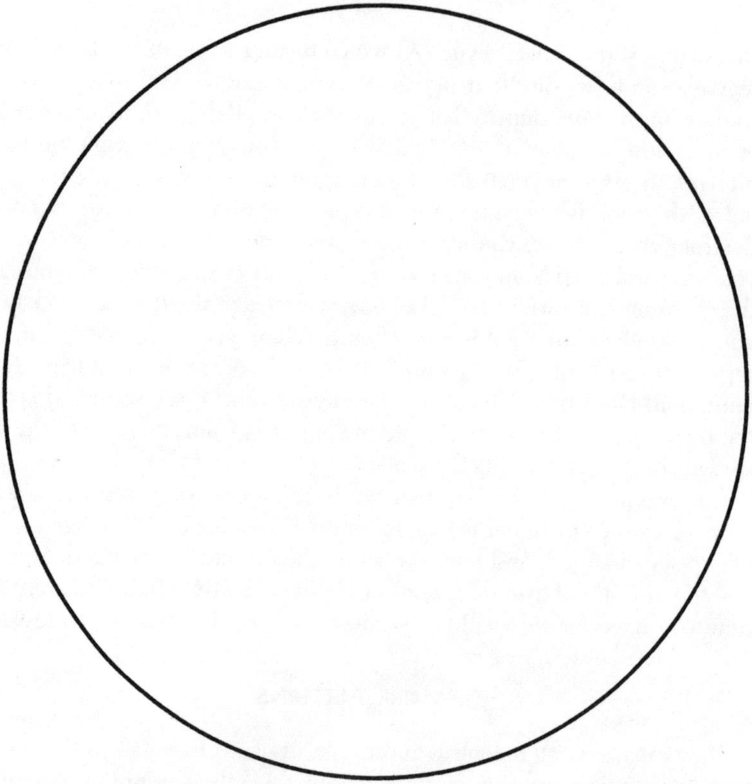

can be a powerful indicator as to how you view yourself. Some of the self-statements that might lie behind such a situation are:

"I don't deserve pleasure."

"If I have too much fun in life; sooner or later I'll have to pay for it."

"I'd bore a really interesting, entertaining person."

"I'm incapable of giving someone else pleasure."

"Pleasure is bad. Work and sacrifice are what count."

"Friends are for helping me get ahead, not to give me pleasure."

"Friends are for helping out in bad times, not for sharing good times."

Look at your circle now, and decide for yourself whether or not any of these statements have any meaning for you.

If you've suddenly realized that none or few of your friendships are really giving you any pleasure, you can begin to use this new awareness as a foundation for building truly supportive and nourishing relationships. Dr. Judith Osgood says, "Most people are really reluctant to admit, 'My friendships are obsolete and are not meeting my needs.' They start to feel guilty." Dr. Osgood created the Friendship Bond Identification Form to help people look at their friendships. This instrument is similar in some ways to the Friendship Circle concept, except it's a little more statistically oriented since Dr. Osgood also uses it as a research vehicle. "I think a lot of friendships are held onto like many things in life that need to be let go of so something new can come in that's appropriate with our own growing." We'll look further into this in the chapter Room to Grow, but for now you might look at whether seeing your friends in terms of how much pleasure they do or don't provide in your life is giving you some indication of whether it's time to reassess those relationships.

CIRCLE SHIFT

In the circle on page 44, let's completely shift our friends around. Those you had put closest to you place on the outer edges. Those who were farthest removed from you, place close to the center dot.

Look at the results of this exploration. Can you see any chance for such a reversal in your life? Would you gain anything at all if this shift were to actually occur? How would such a shift change your life?

THE TWO-FRIEND CIRCLE

In the circle on page pick out just two people. Place the one you feel warmest toward closest to you, and the other an inch or two away.

How would you feel having just these two people in your Friendship Circle? Do you feel that would indicate that you aren't a very worthwhile or lovable person? If you really had an intimate relationship with each of these people, could this satisfy most of your friendship needs? Do you know why you placed the one closest to you in that position? Could you ever see the other person moving into that position of closest friend? If you should lose that closest friend, where do you think a replacement would come from?

The truth is that we can find room in our lives for only one or two really intimate relationships. If one person says, "I have one really close friend," and another says, "I have ten close friends," and they each have only ten hours to spend with friends each week, then obviously the

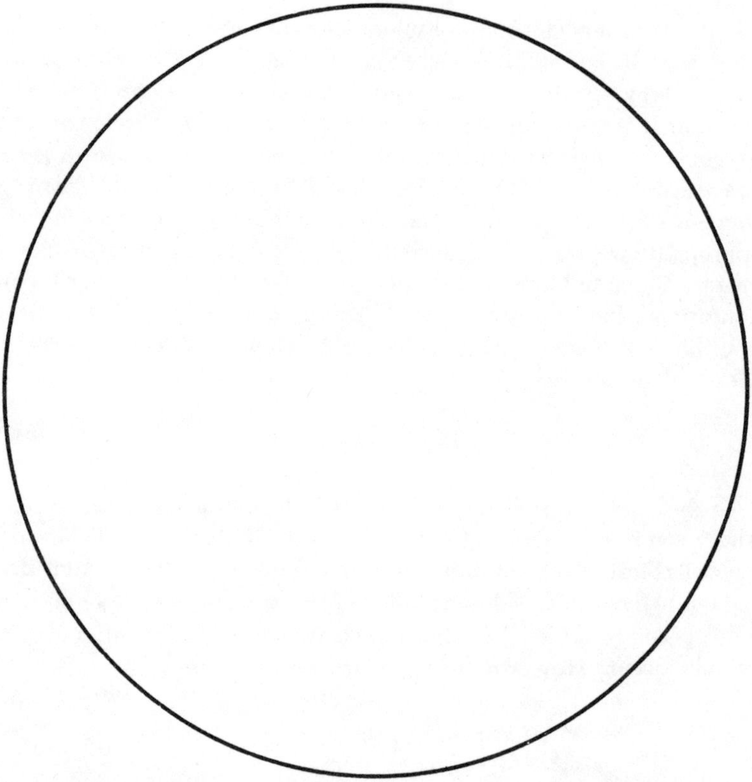

person with ten friends is having different kinds of relationships with them than the person with one friend is having. Psychiatrist Leonard Zunin says, "Most people who are pretty well adjusted have an intimate circle of friends that's usually small, usually less than a handful of close friends. And most healthy people, well-balanced people, I think, enjoy having friends that they have things in common with, shared values, shared backgrounds historically, religiously, racially, and so on, *and* also they enjoy contrasting friends. I think the perfect balance is to have at least one close contrasting friend and at least one close similar friend."

So you might look at the two friends you chose for this last circle in terms of whether one is close to you in background and values, while one doesn't share these similarities. If this isn't the case, would you like it to be? Do you see any advantage to Dr. Zunin's suggestion? If not, trust your own feelings. All through this book you are invited to discard that which doesn't fit you and to use only that which can help you design the life-style that feels best for you.

Another reason for having a circle with just two friends in it is to illustrate that even if you had only two friends left after eliminating those who were not accessible or providing recent pleasure for you, you still have enough to start your friendship growth process with. In friendship, it really is the quality of the experience you share that matters, rather than how many different people you experience. Having a large group of friends may well be preventing you from more satisfying intimate contact with those friends who can offer you the most in support and nourishment.

A FRIEND'S FRIENDSHIP CIRCLE

One way to check out how close a friend is to you, and whether this is really an Intimate Friendship, is to see how much you know about this person's other relationships, and where you fit in the sphere of his or her interpersonal life. So, in the final circle on page 44, place your closest friend in the center, and around that friend place all his or her friends, including yourself in the position you feel you occupy.

What did you learn from this experience? Could you feel comfortable checking out your perceptions with the friend involved? If not, this may also reveal something about the extent of your openness and intimacy in this relationship. Are you happy with your position in this person's Friendship Circle? Are you really sure that's where your friend would place you? Is there any chance he or she would place you even closer to the center? Or farther away? How would you feel in either situation? Imagine each one happening, and experience how these changes would feel to you and how they would affect your feelings toward this person.

How did filling in these Friendship circles feel to you? Do you think they helped you see your friendships more clearly? Are you confused about any of the results or your responses to them? If so, don't force a resolution of that confusion; it may well act as a catalyst for growth as we continue our exploration.

You might choose to return to the basic Friendship Circle from time to time as we examine other facets of friendship and other ways of looking at the friends you choose.

Even after the next chapter, in which we'll imagine our friends in various fantasy situations, you might find yourself changing your mind

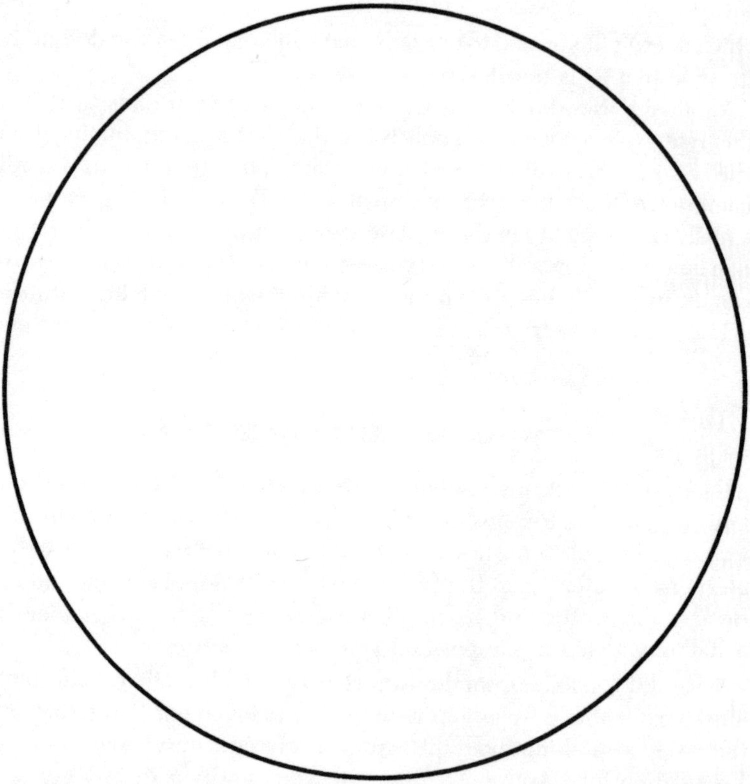

about the position of some of those friends in your circle. Feel free to make those changes whenever they feel appropriate.

Before going on, finish the sentence "One new thing I've learned about my friends is the fact that ———." Look at how you feel about this and move on to the next chapter.

CHAPTER 3

FRIENDSHIP FANTASIES

We all pretend about our friends. We pretend that they are more or less than they really are, depending on our needs. We pretend that they like us more or less than they really do, again depending on our needs. Dr. Herbert Otto, chairman of the National Center for the Exploration of Human Potential, in La Jolla, California, talks about what may be the biggest pretense of them all, which he terms the "Friendship Structure Self-Delusion." This is a basic fantasy that people have about the quality and quantity of their friendships, and Dr. Otto notes, "The subject is so important and they are so deprived that they have to delude themselves into believing that they have enough friends and that they see enough of their friends."

Dr. Otto did several in-depth studies of this phenomenon and found that 80 to 90 percent of those interviewed will answer yes to the questions "Do you have enough friends?" and "Do you see your friends enough?" But on closer examination, these "friends" turn out to live far away and may be physically encountered as little as once a year. Dr. Otto says, "Unless a friendship is maintained through interpersonal contact and exchange on a continuing basis, it's fantastically unreal. It has no basis in reality except on the level of self-delusion. In other words, the individual says to himself he's satisfied, but he isn't meeting his friendship needs on a reality level. I strongly suspect that *most* people are not fulfilling their friendship needs while saying to themselves, 'I have enough friends and I'm seeing enough of my friends.' "

SUSANNAH

Susannah had lots of friends, or so she thought. There were always one or two or three people available to join her for a good time or to come to one of her gourmet dinners. Susannah felt she had a wide circle of close friends who would always be there for her. Then she got seriously ill and had to spend six weeks in a hospital. Most of her friends sent get-well cards, but in the entire six weeks she only had two visitors, and both seemed slightly embarrassed about the whole thing. This was a very painful emotional experience for Susannah, but it did cause her to reevaluate her entire friendship structure, and she eventually formed several deep and lasting friendships.

This kind of experience is hardly unusual. The term "fair-weather friend" is often used to describe such superficial relationships. These kinds of friendships may have their place, but when we delude ourselves into thinking they constitute the reality of our intimate relationships, we are shutting ourselves off from a lot of real relationship opportunites.

These friendship delusions take many forms. Psychologist Dr. Gerald Walker Smith says, "One of the saddest things I've heard in my practice was from a woman who'd been married twenty years to a man who'd finally made it in big business. He was a vice-president somewhere and he left her and got involved with another woman. One of the main issues this woman had to deal with involved the fact that for twenty years all she'd been doing was having a social life with her husband's business associates. As she described the situation, 'These are people I don't want to know. I've been trying to make him a vice-president. Now he's made it and my whole social life has been a sham! It never was. It never had integrity!"

Psychiatrist Dr. Eileen Walkenstein says, "I think the fear of being isolated is very strong in some people. Some people can't stand being alone, and so they enter into a very frenzied round robin of social relationships they call friendships. I had a woman patient who had been seeing me for quite some time, and would tell me that everything was fine in her marriage and that she had a whole big circle of friends and everything was great! Well, ultimately it became very clear that her marriage was disintegrating. Then, in telling me what a marvelous circle of friends she had, she also told me that she didn't dare tell one person in that circle that she was having trouble with her husband. And these were what she described as very steadfast friends who'd do anything for one another and whose friendships had persisted over the years. When I heard that, I said, 'Well, are they really your friends if you can't say this to them?' It was a shocking thing for her to realize that she really couldn't say these things to them and still maintain friendship, that she would have to cut off the relationship with them if she were to reveal some things about herself. I would guess that this woman purposely surrounded herself with these types of people so she could live and support the problems that she had on a superficial level without having to go in and face the crisis. She'd been living in a crisis for twenty-five years, without once really facing it."

Dr. Walkenstein also sees a lot of what she calls "pseudo-friendships," including in this category "Friendships like the pot party kind. People come together and smoke marijuana and really don't know each other or themselves. People join communes who really don't love anybody, including themselves. So, I see a lot of pseudo-reaching from very isolated and isolating kinds of individuals who aren't really making it."

Friends from the past may also be fantasy friends if up-to-date contact isn't really maintained, if all your contacts dwell on the past rather than the present. Eileen Walkenstein describes these as "comfortable old friends with whom I feel very little in common except for some old bonds that are unexplained—just part of past history. Those kinds of attenuated relationships are spread over the years; are always there, yet not in the living flesh, so to speak. I think they are part of some nostalgic kind of longing for comfort that may be more wish fulfillment than real, and may not really nourish either party except in fantasy. There's a lot of baggage that we carry around with us from the past."

Along this same line, Dr. Gerald Walker Smith says, "I think it's awfully easy to get into relationships which are really memories. Look at the camaraderie that occurs when veterans of foreign wars get together. They reminisce about the bombing run on Naples, and it's some of their closest contact with other people, by way of something that happened in 1944."

Again, these kinds of relationships may offer you something, but the danger comes when they become the only kinds of relationships you have, your main interaction focal points.

FANTASY FROM INADEQUATE COMMUNICATION

A lot of the pretending we do about our friends has to do with the lack of real information. Most of the contact we have with our friends is on or near a very superficial level. We really rarely know very much about what they are feeling. Since this creates a gap in our mental/emotional impression file, we automatically fill in the gap with fantasy. The problem is that we often consider this fantasy as fact, and it then gets in the way of our receiving and processing actual information from and about our friends.

This fantasizing can create a lot of confusion in any relationship. It often leads to unrealistic expectations, and these in turn lead to unexpected conflict and confrontation as the expectations lock horns with reality.

HARVEY AND EVE AND JIM

Harvey and Eve were a wealthy middle-aged couple with two grown sons. Their sons both entered the medical profession and thus ended an early fantasy of their parents that involved their growing up and taking over the family business. Their friend Jim was an industrial psychologist who had developed some new techniques for creating happy working relationships between employers and employees and between management and labor. Though his background and interests were in human relations, Jim thought he would go into business for himself, and become a management consultant, setting up his own firm in this field. Harvey and Eve had attended some of his workshops, and brought him in to work with their own employees. Very pleased with the results, they encouraged him in his plans, and even offered to lend him some money to get started. Jim worked hard, but with little success. He just wasn't cut out to be a salesman or businessman. He could create the ideas, and communicate them, but he couldn't sell them to the businessmen who needed his services. He decided that instead of trying to directly contact businessmen, he would put all of his ideas into a book and reach them that way. All through his efforts to set up a business operation, Harvey and Eve had been warm and effusive friends. As soon as Jim decided that business just wasn't his thing, they started to cool off the relationship. Though his book became a huge success, Harvey and Eve remained aloof and unfriendly.

The reality of Jim's lack of business skills came into direct conflict with Harvey and Eve's fantasy image of him as a fellow businessman. The reality of their ulterior motives and expectations came into direct conflict with Jim's fantasy image of Harvey and Eve as his intimate friends. Lack of communication at the beginning of the relationship contributed to the hurt and disappointment each felt. Probably, on a conscious level, Harvey and Eve didn't even know of their heavy emotional investment in Jim's business undertaking. If the three of them could have asked one another, "What do you expect of me?" at the beginning of the relationship, they might not have assumed a friendship existed, or they might have started one with healthier perceptions and more realistic expectations.

CHECKING OUT EXPECTATIONS

Examine your list of friends. For each one, finish the sentence "From ——— ,I expect ———." List all your expectations of that friend.

Go to your list again, and this time finish the sentence "From me,——— expects ———." List everything you think your friend expects of you.

Now check out whether these expectations are realistic or unrealistic. Realistic expectations are those for which you have real factual information to back them up, or those you've checked out and had confirmed by the friend in question. All your unconfirmed and unsubstantiated expectations may not prove to be unrealistic, but they certainly can stand some further examination or discussion with the specific friend involved. In Interpersonal Perception, R. D. Laing, H. Phillipson, and A. R. Lee talk about the experiences, perceptions, and actions that occur when two people encounter each other. They specifically refer to another area that involves unrealistic or fantasy expectations by saying, "My field of experience is filled not only by my direct view of myself and of the other, but *my view* of the *other's view* of me. I may not actually be able to see myself as others see me, but I am constantly supposing them to be seeing me in particular ways, and I am constantly acting in the light of the actual or supposed attitudes, opinions, needs, and so on the other has in respect of me." Here again, the best way to check out your perceptions of what your friends think of you is to simply ask them, and a number of the interpersonal skills discussed in upcoming chapters deal with developing and using this resource. But right now you might find it useful to look at your list of close friends and try to imagine what each one thinks of you as a person and a friend. In Chapter 2 we looked at where your friends would place you in their circle of friends, and this may have provided some perceptions of where you stand in their lives. But how does each particular friend specifically view you as a human being?

WHAT DO YOU PRETEND?

One exercise often used by psychologists and group leaders in the human potential movement is done in dyads. One person asks the other, "What do you pretend?" and keeps on repeating the same question for several minutes. The person being asked has to come up with a different answer each time the question is asked. A sample set of answers might look like this:

"I pretend I'm more confident than I am."

"I pretend I enjoy doing housework."

"I pretend my husband always satisfies me sexually."

"I pretend my children never annoy me."

"I pretend I like my husband's mother."

"I pretend I'm interested in my neighbor's idle chatter."

"I pretend I'm not anxious about this exercise."

It might be interesting for you to play this little game with yourself about your friends. Pick a friend from your list, and come up with as many answers as possible to the question "What do I pretend to this friend?" Then try as best you can to answer the question "What do I think this friend pretends to me?" You might carry this a step further by going on to the question "What do I pretend to myself about this friend?"

FANTASY PROGRAMMING

Chances are you have a rather romanticized image of what a friend really is. Novels, movies, and television have all contributed to this, going back to the books and movies you saw as a child. Can you remember some of your early programming on the subject of friendship? Can you remember a favorite story that illustrated the value and faithfulness of friends? How does this compare to the reality of your friendships at the time and the reality of them now? We often accept the fantasy input as more real than the actual facts, which are telling us something else. We excuse this misperception with a statement that goes something like this: "None of my friends are that special yet, but they will be as we get to know each other better. If not, I'll just have to find new friends who will be that special and that faithful and fulfill that many of my needs." It's really a matter of saying, "While I'm not perfect, I expect my friends to be."

THE POWER OF PRETEND

Dr. Claude Nolte, a humanistic psychologist and author, leads therapy-oriented workshops on a system called The Power of Pretend, based on the things that people imagine to be true and how we can reprogram with positive fantasy images. He notes that one of the things we most fantasize about our friends is how trustworthy they are. "There's an imagined safety factor, a personal safety factor that's involved when you graduate from a superficial friend. Everyone has an image about a 'friend,' and it's this feeling of 'I can tell him anything.' Complete confidence, complete trust. Now, when that person misses and tells someone else something I said in confidence, then I'm in for a shock to my nervous system. My expectations of complete safety, complete trust, are not really realistic. I have an idealized image of a friend."

Can you think of a time when a friend let you down? Look back to the expectation that this friend's subsequent action destroyed. Was it really something you had checked out with your friend? Did he or she really ever promise not to let you down in this way?

The first step in removing the dangers of unrealistic expectations and the things that we pretend about our friends is to simply recognize what these fantasy images are, and acknowledge them to ourselves, taking full responsibility for creating them in the first place. If we can build to a feeling of honest sharing with the particular friend or friends involved, we may at some point want to share these expectations, to check them out. In later chapters, we'll examine a number of techniques designed to accomplish this. Here and now, however, we are looking at our own feelings about our friends and trying to see them in new perspectives.

INITIAL ASSUMPTIONS

Psychiatrist Leonard Zunin is particularly fascinated by greeting behavior, and in fact wrote a whole book on the subject, *Contact: The First Four Minutes*. Dr. Zunin writes, "When you treat an assumption as fact, you are taking a risk. Certainly, the distinction between fact and assumption is often blurred, but a substitution of one for the other may lead to disappointment, frustration and self-deception. You may be right or wrong, but unfortunately, once assumptions are firmly implanted as truth, people usually have a difficult time revising their views."

Think back to the first few minutes you spent with a close friend. Did you have any assumptions about this person? Look at the same few moments at the beginning of other friendships. What kind of assumptions do you usually have at initial contact with someone you subsequently get to know and like? Are all your initial assumptions borne out by fact? Dr. Zunin goes on to say, "The more careful you are in assuming, the sooner you get through to enjoy deeper and more rewarding relationships. You must understand your prejudices and misconceptions of other people and life-styles."

In your imagination, you might relive the beginning of all of your important relationships, as a good way to learn what motivates you to reach out to others, and in what, if any, ways you limit yourself in human interaction.

POSITIVE FANTASY

While fantasy images that get in the way of reality can be a highly negative factor in our lives, fantasy can also be a strong constructive force, putting us more in touch with reality. The difference between negative and positive fantasy is awareness. In positive fantasy, we are consciously using our imagination to gain some new perspectives and possible new insights. Often, the major difference between a healthy emotional state and an unhealthy one is simply knowing the difference between fantasy and reality.

In his book *Fantasy Encounter Games*, Dr. Herbert Otto says, "Fantasy can be a form of direct communication with the unconscious. One of the true functions of fantasy is as a stepping-stone to reality. Use of the fantasy also becomes a way of reaching and expanding deeper levels of the self. Through a study of our fantasy stream we can attain new awareness and self-understanding. We can discover unknown aspects of the self (the fantasy self) and by integrating these aspects with those which are known, bring about a greater wholeness and synthesis of the self."

FLOATING FRIENDS

This is a guided fantasy trip you can take, designed to provide you with some new views of some of your friends, and perhaps some new insights. It will probably be more effective if you either tape record the entire fantasy or have someone read it to you.

To begin, lie down in a comfortable and relaxed position, and close your eyes. Check out how your body feels to you. Are you making good contact with whatever you are lying on? Is any part of your body tense or uncomfortable? If so, shift your position to correct this. The dots in the fantasy instructions indicate pauses. These should all be at least one minute long, giving you enough time to exercise your imagination. You might experiment with pauses of different lengths. Here are your instructions:

Imagine yourself lying on a lovely secluded beach. Your eyes are closed and you are relaxed, and imagining yourself lying on this lovely beach. The sun is shining. The waves are gently breaking. The smell of the sea is in the air. You can even hear an occasional sea gull . . . .(pause).

You are lying on an inflatable floating raft, and as you lie there, the raft is slowly inflating, lifting you above the surface of the sand. The waves are slowly breaking closer. As the raft inflates to its full size, the water comes in and gently lifts you up, and you slowly float out onto the surface of a calm ocean . . . .(pause).

You can still feel the sun beating down on you, as you continue to float, in a completely relaxed position, with your eyes closed. You are aware, however, that somewhere ahead of you there is another raft, with someone else floating on it. You know it is there, though you can't see it. You're not concerned, because you know there's a friend on the raft, even though you don't know who it is yet. Your two rafts slowly approach each other until they are side by side . . . .(pause).

You are now floating alongside the other raft. You slowly turn your head to the side, and slowly open your eyes in your imagination, to look at the person on the adjoining raft. It is a friend. Someone you like very much. You reach out your hand and take your friend's hand in yours. You continue to float on the calm ocean together, quietly enjoying the experience . . . .(pause).

You let go of your friend's hand and allow the other raft to gently and slowly float away from yours. You wave good-bye to this friend, and just as the other raft floats out of sight, you feel a slight bump on the other side of your own raft. It is still another raft, with someone else you like very much on it. You float awhile together, and then say good-bye, as yet another friend floats up beside your raft . . . .(pause).

You suddenly realize that you are alone again, and floating down a river instead of on the ocean. There is beautiful scenery everywhere you look. You can't see it, but down the river a mile or two is a very special island. Waiting on that island is a very special friend who is going to share the island's adventure with you. The river winds and turns and you begin to approach the island where your friend is waiting. It may be one of the three friends you already met on the raft, or it may not. You'll find out when you arrive at the island and begin your adventure . . . . (pause). (This pause should be longer, in fact as long as you would like to continue the fantasy on your own.)

EXAMINING THE EXPERIENCE

It may be useful to repeat this fantasy trip from time to time. You might have found that there weren't enough pauses to suit you, and you can feel free to add as many as you like. Can you remember how you felt when you met each of the friends you encountered during your fantasy? Who was waiting for you on the island, and how did your first sighting of this friend feel? How do these feelings compare with your views of these friends if they are on the list of friends you compiled in the first chapter? How do they compare with what you learned about these friends in the second chapter? Were there any real surprises, for instance, anyone appearing who wasn't even on your list?

You may have learned a lot from this fantasy trip, but don't expect any major revelations this first time, and most especially if you haven't had a good deal of practice exercising your imagination like this.

FANTASY PERSPECTIVES

Another way to use fantasy constructively is to imagine you and one or more of your friends in situations you might not normally experience. This can give you a new way of seeing this friend, in an unfamiliar setting that may alter some of the restrictive views we usually have. In some of these exercises, you'll be asked to choose the friend or friends you want to share this experience with. This can tell you much about which friends you see in certain roles.

Again, let your imagination run free. You'll probably achieve more by doing all of these lying down in a comfortable position with your eyes closed. Take as long as you like. You may want to make snap decisions and just quickly answer some of the questions. This is fine, but you may experience another dimension by also, at some point, repeating the same exercise more slowly, adding more detail, actually imagining yourself living it.

THE MARTIAN

You and several friends are sitting in a comfortable living room. You have just received positive information that one of your friends is a creature from Mars, pretending to be a human being so that he or she can thoroughly investigate this planet. You do not know whether the motivation behind this masquerade is peaceful exploration or something more sinister. Which of your friends would you suspect first, and how would you go about checking out whether they are really human? Can you remember any incident that might have given you a clue that this friend was not quite what he or she appeared to be? How do you feel about receiving this information that a friend of yours is a Martian? Angry? Betrayed? Amused? Do you feel your friend should have trusted you enough to let you in on the secret? Try to imagine the conversation you would have with this group of friends. Would you announce that you know the truth to check their reactions, or would you keep it to yourself, trying to trap the Martian? Play with this fantasy and take it anywhere you like. Don't analyse the experience until it's all over.

SUPERGIFT

You have just inherited a billion dollars, and you would like to buy each of your friends the gift he or she would most enjoy receiving. Decide what this would be in each case, and imagine their reaction at getting it.

How would your friends feel about your generosity and your good fortune? Would any of them resent it? What does this tell you about them? About yourself?

COSIGNER

You are desperately in need of cash, and your credit rating is down, so you need a cosigner for the loan that will bail you out. None of your friends have the kind of money you need, but any one of them can qualify as a cosigner. Which one do you choose?

VD

You have contracted a venereal disease. You're not ready to tell just anyone about this, but do feel a need to share the information with one friend. Which friend would you choose to let know about your affliction? How would you break the news? What do you think this friend's reaction would be?

NUDELY YOURS

You have become a nudist and really enjoy the pleasures of social nudity. You want to share this with one of your friends and invite him or her to a nude party. Which friend would you feel most comfortable inviting? Can you imagine inviting all your friends? Which do you think would come? How would each friend react to the invitation?

THE ORGY

You've decided to go to an orgy for the first time in your life. You are looking forward to this unique experience. It will be private, with a number of warm and attractive participants, none of whom you've ever met. There is no way anyone will ever know you attended unless you tell them. There is one catch, however. You must bring one friend, a member of the same sex as yourself. Which friend would you choose and how would he or she react?

LIFEBOAT

You and eight of your friends are adrift in a lifeboat. Expert calculations have determined that there is no way you can survive without getting rid of three of your passengers. You are captain and have to make the decision as to which three go overboard. All your lives are at stake, and there is no alternative.

After you've made your choice, imagine telling each of the three victims your decision. Would they understand? How would you explain the reasons for your decision?

DESERT ISLAND

You have to spend the rest of your life on a desert island. You may take three friends with you, but no one with whom you are now involved in a love relationship. Which friends would you choose? Can you imagine how you would all relate on the island, who would be the leader, and how you would divide up the various tasks that would have to be performed?

WHITE HOUSE

You have just taken office as President of the United States. The head of the secret service has asked you for a list of friends who may be admitted to see you at any time. You are also asked to compile a list of friends who will be put directly through to you if they phone. Decide which friends you really want to have this kind of access to you, and which ones you would like to isolate and take this opportunity to eliminate. Which friends do you feel would be a positive influence on you in this new role, and which ones would be a negative influence?

THE BIG CHANGE

For as many of your friends as you would like to include in this fantasy, imagine a complete personal transformation. If they are now attractive, they will turn ugly. If they are financially secure, they will become poor. If they are now extroverts, they will shyly withdraw. Only their loyalty and affection toward you will remain the same. How do you see each friend changing? How would this affect your relationship? If you were to change completely, how do you think your friends would feel toward you?

SWITCHING ROLES

You are to become one of your friends, and one of your friends will become you. This switch will last for one year. Which friend do you choose to exchange lives with? How would this big switch affect your lives? Would it affect your relationship in any way? For instance, would you want to be thought of in the way you've been thinking of your friend?

HIDDEN TALENT

Several of your friends have talents they have kept hidden from you. They are very gifted in these particular areas. Can you guess which talent each friend might be hiding? How do you feel about not being told? Would you like to have a talent that you've been hiding all these years? Invent one for yourself, and imagine what it would be like to tell your friends about it.

THE SECRET

Each of your friends has a major secret, one that they haven't shared with anyone. They each decide that you are the only one to whom they want to tell this secret. Imagine them each approaching you individually to tell you. What are the secrets each friend has been keeping? How do they affect the way you feel about each friend?

ANIMAL FRIENDS

Imagine each of your friends as an animal. Try to pick an animal that most closely approximates your individual friends' personalities and characteristics. How do you think each of your friends would feel if you shared this fantasy with them?

SPECIAL PLACE

You are going to take a trip with each of your friends. You get to go to the place they would be happiest visiting. Imagine what these special places are if you don't already know, and how you would feel going there with this specific friend. Are there any places you would not enjoy? What special place would you choose for yourself? Can you imagine going there accompanied by one friend? Which friend would you choose and why?

THE HOSPITAL

You are going into the hospital. You've come down with a slightly contagious, painful disease. Which friends would visit you, if any? Which would you want to come?

NEW FRIEND

You meet a fantastic new person with all kinds of fascinating thoughts, feelings, and activities to share with you. A thoroughly enjoyable and exciting new friend. You get to share this new person with one other friend. Who would it be?

FREEDOM OF CHOICE

You can have as friends any one man and any one woman living in the world today, no matter how famous. Whom would you choose for your two new friends?

THE FINAL WEEK

You have one week to live. Which friends would you choose to spend that week with? Why? What would you do with your final days? Would you want to spend any of the time alone?

CHANGES

If you suddenly became more lovable . . . more popular . . . more wealthy, would you want to change any of your friends? If you could have any friends you wanted, which of your current friends would you want to keep?

FRIENDLY RITUAL

In this fantasy you're going to invent a friendship ritual. What do we mean by a friendship ritual? Well, in many societies, this is quite a normal activity, a part of the everyday routine. In a conversation with the author, Leonard Zunin discussed the process: "In civilized society, where survival isn't our goal, we don't have ritualized friendship. The more we live in a survival society, the more we have ritualized friendship, such as the Indian blood brothers; formalized, crystallized, ritualized friendship. Take the Babenba tribe in South Africa, a very peaceful tribe. If you and I as tribe members want to be friends, this process takes about a year. What we do is, when you come over to my hut, you steal something of mine. I look around and it's gone. I know you took it. Everyone else in the tribe knows this is going on. You don't establish more than one friendship at a time. When I go into your hut, I steal something of yours. We do it gradually, until at the end of approximately a year, everything in my hut is yours. There's nothing there that I own. Everything in your hut is mine, and we don't say anything about it. When you visit me and see all your stuff in my hut, you don't say a word. We can stop at any point along the way, but when the process is completed we go to the chief and there's a special tribal celebration. A ceremony establishing us as lifetime friends, in an Indian blood-brother sense, knowing that we will stand by each other for the rest of our lives regardless of what happens."

Imagine your own friendship ritual, taking any form you desire. Imagine performing this ritual with one of your current friends.

Imagine a modification of the Babenba ritual, in which you and a friend exchange one possession each, a possession that means a great deal to each owner. Which friend would you want to perform this ritual with? What possession would you offer? Can you choose the possession you'd like to receive?

FANTASY CHECKOUT

How much were you able to get into each of your fantasies? Which ones did you enjoy most? Can you honestly say you learned anything new about your friends? Finish the sentence "One new thing I think I've learned about my friends is the fact that ———." Examine how you feel about this.

In the next chapter, you're going to get an opportunity to ask yourself a series of questions that will reveal how much you really know about your friends, and how you really feel about them. Before going on, however, it might be useful to go down your complete list of friends and see whether there is anything you would add or subtract from the characteristics you noted for each.

The chances are you not only saw some of your friends in a new way by fantasizing about them, but also realized how much fun it can be to exercise your imagination. In these times, when everything seems to be prepackaged and so explicit as to leave nothing to the imagination, we don't get enough of a chance to examine the world of make-believe. Using fantasy while being aware that it *is* fantasy can be one of the most fruitful devices of all for expanding consciousness and enlarging your horizons.

CHAPTER 4

FRIENDSHIP REALITY

As we noted in the preceding chapter, there is a lot of fantasy connected with human interaction. But what really happens between two human beings in terms of meaningful contact has to do with reality. The first task, therefore, is to be aware of what is really happening. Much of the material in this book is designed to allow you to see the reality of your interaction with friends: what you are getting from them, what you are giving them, and how you feel about this. But this is only part of the reality. A philosopher once described human relating as "two onions slowly peeling each other." As you build up trust and experience with a friend, new levels of contact emerge. The first important thing that happens involves the sharing of feelings. You are not usually going to be willing to share deep feelings with a casual acquaintance, and the sharing of feelings deepens with the deepening of a relationship. You get to know more about what your friend is feeling as the trust level builds up, just as your friend gets to know more of what you are feeling.

In the next chapter we'll be looking at the way a lot of systems and therapies apply to friendship, including Gestalt therapy. For now, it's useful to note the Gestalt view of human contact, as articulated by one of the nation's most highly respected Gestalt therapists, Dr. Robert Resnick of Los Angeles, in a talk for the 1973 annual meeting of the Association for Humanistic Psychology. Dr. Resnick said "In technical terms, contact can only happen when the excitation at my contact boundary meets yours. Otherwise we have conversation, we have bullshit: 'What time is it?' 'Did you see this?' etc., etc. Contact occurs by putting out verbally or nonverbally, or both, where I am at the moment. And if I happen to be sad, the only way contact can occur is when I'm willing to put out my sadness. That's where I'm living at the moment. It's like being on a trip, and if you're in Oshkosh, that's the only place you can call from. You can't call from anywhere else. If I don't happen to approve of being sad or being angry or being whatever I am, then no contact is going to occur. Contact happens or it doesn't happen when I put out where I am. If the other person is receptive, and better yet, if they're receptive *and* willing to put out where *they* are, then contact can occur. Contact means their boundary meets my boundary, and in Gestalt terms, with an awareness of differences. Without an awareness of differences, you don't have contact. To have contact you have to have at least two things or people, otherwise what's contacting what? And this is contact: Where I am touches where you are, but I'm still me and you're still you, with an awareness of differences."

PUTTING OUT REALITY

What kind of contact are you making with your friends? Before looking at what you know about your friends' attitudes and feelings and values, hopes and aspirations, from what they've put out to you, let's set a realistic foundation by being aware of what kind of reality you are putting out or projecting to your friends. One question you might ask yourself to place this issue of putting out reality into proper perspective in your own life is, "Do I ever pretend to other people that I am happy when I am not?"

Try to think of some recent period in your life when things weren't going too well, when you really didn't feel good, when something was making you feel sad or angry. Did you pretend that you were on top of the world, feeling just fine? Now, there are times when you might choose to do this. There are people to whom you may not choose to reveal your true feelings. Do not put a label of "right" or "wrong," or "good" or "bad" on this, on the degree of honesty expressed by what you put out to others. But realize this: You are not making contact if you are not putting out where you really are. Once you accept this basic psychological truth, once you identify *your* way of interacting with others, then you can be said to be choosing the way you want to be, the way you want to behave. If you *don't* recognize that a lot of your interaction isn't really allowing contact to occur, if you *don't* realize it when you *are* allowing contact, then you are allowing yourself to be a victim of old conditioning rather than acting as a healthy and mature individual making free choices. It's similar to the situation faced by a comedian telling jokes. Some of those jokes are going to be good, and some of them are going to be bad. The good ones are those that make contact with the audience, reaching something in enough of the audience to get a successful laugh. The main and perhaps only difference between a good and bad comedian is that a good comedian *knows* the difference between the way an audience responds to a good joke and to a bad joke. He knows when he is making contact, and when he is not, and can act accordingly in his future performances. Every once in a while even the best comedian is going to come up with a real klunker, just as every once in a while, you're going to engage in bullshit rather than contact. The secret of success is in knowing the difference. If you pay attention to what you are putting out, you will soon begin to know the difference.

PUTTING OUT PSEUDO-PROJECTIONS

Our society is so conditioned and dehumanized that we have a whole ritual that supposedly communicates feelings, but in reality communicates absolutely nothing most of the time. It involves that simple greeting inquiry, "How are you?"

Other words are sometimes used, but the result is usually the same. These words would seem to indicate that the person asking the question really wants to know how the person being asked is, how he or she is feeling, how they are doing in the world, how things are going. In reality the question and the response often fall into the category of polite conversation or bullshit. Think about the last time you asked, "How are you?" Did you really expect an honest answer? Did you really want one? How about the last time someone asked you the question? Did you give an honest answer or did you feel compelled to manufacture a reply you thought would be acceptable to the person asking? This is not to say that an honest answer is always the right answer or that the person asking really wants to know. But again, be aware that an honest answer is the only way real contact can happen between you and the other person. You are operating in a healthy and self-supportive way when you decide for yourself whether you really want to make contact with this other human being, and then base your answer on that decision. For example, an acquaintance whom you have no desire to know better or have as a friend asks, "How are you?" You might choose to reply, knowing that this is just a polite ritualized inquiry, "OK." If, however, an intimate friend asks, "How are you?", you might reply, "I'm feeling pretty good, but I'm a bit worried about my job. It's been producing a lot of tension, and I really find myself getting uptight." The first reply wasn't a lie, but it certainly wasn't making contact. You may have decided that this person didn't want to really know how you were, and you may have chosen not to put out what you were really feeling, or where you really were. But if all your responses to "How are you?", to intimate friend and acquaintance alike, fall into the automatic "OK" category, you are missing many opportunities for genuine contact. And it isn't how much information you put out, but whether what you do put out is really coming from where you are at the moment, that determines the authenticity of your communication with other people. Of course, a lot of the bullshit comes from more than just the words you use. Putting on phony smiles and effusive attitudes also falls into this category.

CONTACT VERSUS BULLSHIT

For purposes of further self-exploration, we'll use these two labels. *Contact* will mean honestly putting out some information that indicates where you really are at the moment. *Bullshit* will be mere polite conversation, or an attitude designed to cover up your feelings. Let's look at ten common sentences and see if you can determine which category each falls into.

1. How did you like Sunday's game against New York?
2. I'm feeling lonely, and I'd really like some company tonight.
3. Nice weather we've been having, isn't it?
4. I remember playing that game as a kid. Boy, does that bring back memories!
5. Fine. How are you?
6. There's somebody I'd really like to get to know.
7. I'm busy tomorrow night.
8. I'd love to spend an evening with you, but I promised I'd have dinner with a very good friend tomorrow night.
9. Where do you live?
10. I really like talking to you.

As you could probably easily tell, all the odd-numbered sentences were *bullshit*, while the even-numbered ones were *contact*. Most conversation falls into the *bullshit* category. And people then wonder why they aren't getting close to other people!

A lot of the salesmen-oriented success books promote *bullshit*. They tell you that you can get people to like you by lying to them, by flattering them, by pretending to feel what you don't really feel. The best salesmen have always been people who genuinely like other people, who express honest feelings, who are even willing to risk hurting someone else's feelings to tell them the truth. Dr. Jerry Greenwald, a Gestalt therapist, says, "The way a lot of people relate to friends is what I would call 'Dale Carnegie—How to Win Friends and Influence People,' and for me that approaches what I call toxic behavior. A lot of people relate to friends in terms of 'what does this person want so I can get him to like me, so I can get him to be my friend?' They might be quite successful at that. There was a movie I saw in which a salesman had a large collection of lodge buttons on the inside of his coat, denoting his membership in various organizations. Whenever he met someone, a customer for instance, he'd find out what club that person belonged to and pull out the appropriate button, and come up with the secret handshakes and grips and so forth. So he would just orient himself to the other person, and win him over as a customer or, you could say, friend. For me, that may work very well in making a superficial contact, or in being a good salesman, but it would limit the depths of the friendship, because a person doing this is really not being straight, he's really not communicating who *he* is, and someone doing this would have a lot of trouble removing this superficial, unreal material as the friendship goes on. That in itself can become a disruptive thing. You begin with these phony patterns, then you say, 'Well, when I first met you I wanted to impress you, and now I really like you, and I really want to be friends, so I want to tell you that I was conning you when I was doing this or that.' For me, if I were on the other end of that, I'd get suspicious, and ask, 'Well, now how will I know when this guy is not conning me? How am I going to know when he's not playing any more games with me?' "

One way to check out for yourself whether you are guilty of this sort of phony communication is to honestly determine your first priority in reaching out to other people—is it really to communicate with them or is it to make them like you? A main prerequisite of a healthy self-image is an attitude that it's not important that everyone like you, that as long as you put out who you really are, you will attract people who can and will respond to that true projection. It's indicative of perhaps the primary conflict between belief and feeling that we humans have, that we often expect every single human being we encounter to like us, and treat each human interaction as if that were a definite possibility. The conflict comes because at some intellectual/emotional level we know this is impossible. Our experience shows us it is impossible. If someone were to ask you, "Do you think it's possible for every human being you meet during your entire life to like you?", how would you respond? Most people say something like, "No, of course not!" And yet, perhaps because of our cultural conditioning that puts such a strong value on being liked, at some level of our emotional being we *do* expect everyone to like us, and suffer pangs of sadness, disappointment, frustration, and anger when it doesn't happen. Since, in any normal life, it's bound *not* to happen many, many times, we can thus set ourselves up for a lot of unpleasant feelings. None of which are necessary! And when we expect someone to like us, we may very well be tempted to cover up the truth about ourselves, for fear he or she will discover that we aren't really likable. It becomes a vicious circle. Judy meets Harriet. Judy wants Harriet to like her. So Judy covers up her real feelings with the superficial, unreal material described by Dr. Greenwald. She's making *bullshit*, not *contact*. She begins to manipulate by putting out to Harriet what she thinks Harriet wants to hear. Her sole purpose is to get Harriet to like her, not to let Harriet know who she really is. There are only two possible results to this. If Harriet is someone who really can't be a good and nourishing friend to Judy, then chances are Judy's *bullshit* will create a pseudo-relationship that can only be destructive and time-consuming to both parties. If Judy put out who she really was, and Harriet didn't respond to that, then Judy could make contact with someone else who might respond, rather than wasting all that time with Harriet. On the other hand, if Harriet is someone who can really be good for Judy as a friend, then this valuable human resource will probably go unrealized. For Harriet to be a real friend to Judy, she has to respond to who Judy really is. If Judy doesn't put out who she really is, then Harriet can't do that responding. Thus, a real friendship opportunity is lost. If Harriet is the kind of person who would respond favorably to who Judy really is, it's highly unlikely she would *also* respond to who Judy is pretending to be. Even if she did respond to the *bullshit*, it would tend to limit the relationship since, with the passage of time, it would become harder and harder for Judy to replace the façade with the truth. The premise offered here, therefore, is that the only way you can have a real friend and real contact is by putting out who you really are. Anything less will either attract someone without much to offer you, or deter someone who can be a good friend, or limit a relationship to superficial interaction without real communication.

JARGON AS JABBERWOCKY

The primary definition of "jargon" used to be "gibberish." Now that has moved to a secondary definition as more and more professions, businesses, and psychologies create their own languages. This is useful when used to communicate in academic, therapeutic, or professional and scientific circles. But much of the jargon filters down to social usage, creating a new means of separating one person from another. In social situations, people who would never be so discourteous as to speak a foreign language in the presence of someone who didn't understand it, think nothing of using jargon, which is usually just as unintelligible to those unfamiliar with it. Also, the use of jargon is almost always involved with thoughts rather than feelings, and once someone spends a lot of time using jargon, it becomes very difficult indeed to return to simple, honest language. Simplicity is the key to expressing feelings. There is no way, no matter how many words you use, no matter who you are, to express more feeling than the simple words "I love you" convey.

Self-help and pop-psychology books, and this book falls into both categories, are often the catalyst for jargon spouting. With the recent emergence of Transactional Analysis as a powerful therapeutic tool, and the many books on the subject, it is not uncommon to hear bits of conversation like "You're speaking from your Natural Child!"; "That's an old script of yours"; or "I'm collecting brown trading stamps." When one understands the concepts behind these bits of jargon, they can be very useful in analyzing behavior. But they do not enhance communication when used in social situations. And it's not unusual for someone who has just read a book or attended a class or workshop involving a psychology that has its own jargon to spout out sentence after sentence of the stuff. In an article, in *New Times*, the issue dated October 31, 1975, author R. D. Rosen coined the term "Psychobabble" for this type of jargon. Rosen notes that people are often using this jargon to create the impression that they are being honest and really communicating. He cites such sentences as:

"Are you getting in touch with yourself?"

"Going through some heavy changes?"

"Are you going to get your act together?"

"I'm sort of in a weird space."

"It's a real high-energy experience."

The problem with this kind of phony candor is that with constant repetition, the words became meaningless. They are also a way of hiding real feelings and depersonalizing communication. If you say to someone, "I really like your vibration," you might be trying to tell them you like them, or you like the way they make you feel, or you are feeling empathy towards them, or you are attracted to them physically, etc., etc. The problem is simply that you are not communicating with this person when you use such jargon. You may as well go ahead and use Lewis Carroll's Jabberwocky, and say to them: "Twas brillig, and the slithy toves did gyre and gimble in the wabe." If you remember Alice's response to the poem in *Through the Looking-Glass*, she said, "It seems very pretty, but it's rather hard to understand! Somehow it seems to fill my head with ideas, only I don't know exactly what they are!" Compare this with a sentence that someone might use in Psychobabble: "I'm really feeling your energy, and I can tell you've been through some heavy stuff, but have really got it all together now." Couldn't you see Alice making the exact same response to this sentence as to the Jabberwocky?

In his brilliant book *How to Meditate*, Dr. Lawrence LeShan talks about what he terms " 'Vibrations,' 'Energy' and Other Cheap Explanations of Things." He notes, "The word 'vibration' is used frequently in very confused ways. Frequently these are ways that sound beautiful and useful until you really begin to try to think about what the person using them really is describing. Then you wonder if he is crazy or if you are so uptight and conventionally bound in your thought processes that you cannot see all the lovely realities that everyone else, nodding their heads in agreement and admiration, obviously can. Usually you are tempted to follow the example of the courtiers when the Emperor's new clothes were being displayed and agree that you can see the chakras, Kundalini forces, etheric bodies, energy streams and God knows what else. You are then involved in beautiful poetry and have completely confused it with reality. Unfortunately this does not lead to the advancement of knowledge or to your own growth and development."

Of course, it's easy to fall into this trap, and to believe that you are experiencing *contact* rather than *bullshit*. But the only way to communicate with a human being honestly is to communicate what you are really feeling toward that person, in personal terms, not pat phrases, not jargon or Jabberwocky or Psychobabble. Robotlike patterns of communication foster robotlike emotional patterns. Robots can be programmed to produce huge quantities of jargon, huge quantities of words. What they can't do, and what you as a human being can do, is respond on a feeling-level to the unique person you are contacting by putting out something real from the unique person you are. All else may as well be meaningless gibberish. In fact, in group therapy sessions, psychologists often use an exercise called "gibberish," in which two partners pair up and speak to each other in nonsense words, trying to express feelings. The idea is to get away from logical-rational thinking and logical-rational words, and get into feelings. In this context, gibberish can be used to express emotion. It's a useful exercise, but it is not communication. If you frantically try to express anger by saying "Boorswich Toomey Cullswigger!" and waving your arms, the person you are addressing will get the idea that you are angry, but won't have any way of knowing why, or what it has to do with him, or why you are choosing this moment to express that anger, or what you want him to do about it.

As with all forms of *bullshit*, jargon, Jabberwocky, and Psychobabble are at the very least a form of laziness, at the worst a means of avoiding contact and hiding feelings.

THE EXCHANGE OF INFORMATION

All of this isn't to say that it isn't useful to sometimes communicate things other than feelings. You can develop more intimacy and deeper sharing with a friend who lets you know what he or she thinks about various ideas, values, events, objects, and people. The interaction between two friends involves a lot of what boils down to the simple exchange of information. For example, if you have had a friend for some years, chances are you have experienced some rainy weather together. If you have no idea how your friend feels or responds to rainy weather, then you have not been exchanging this kind of information, have not been paying attention. While feelings are the most important part of friendship communication, they are not the only part. Always talking about your deepest emotions would get rather tiresome. And there are times when it isn't appropriate. If you are canoeing down a river, it probably isn't the ideal moment to share feelings. You would get much more out of the experience by merely experiencing it. Even the feelings evoked by the canoeing itself would probably best be shared after the fact. But the experience itself provides you with information about your friend. If nothing else, you would probably know whether or not this friend enjoys canoeing.

BALANCE

The idea is to have a balance of interaction. Some of this will involve feelings, some of it thoughts, some of it shared experiences, in the healthy friendship. The more actual knowledge we have about a friend, and his or her biographical history, emotional attitudes, values, hopes, and aspirations, the more connections we can have together. The more ways in which you are connected to a friend, the more you are going to trust that friend enough to reveal yourself to him or her. In our often superficial culture, much interaction involves the making of judgments and relationship decisions on the basis of insufficient information. Obviously there is no way you can know all there is to know about another human being. Nor would you want to. Unless, of course, you chose to subordinate yourself to one other person, to become, for instance, a James Boswell to some Samuel Johnson. It is perfectly normal, therefore, for you to have insufficient information about a friend. But be aware that this is the case, that you do not know all there is to know about this person, no matter how long you've known him. Overenthusiastic information can, in fact, get in the way of productive and satisfying interaction. If you have an hour to spend with a friend, and you spend that hour asking that friend questions instead of *being* together, you have not had an hour of relating, but merely an hourlong interview. A relationship starts out with little or no information and a lot of fantasy. As the relationship grows, so does mutual knowledge of each other.

THE BIOGRAPHY

One way to explore how much you know about a specific friend is to write a brief biography of that person, just as if it were an entry in *Who's Who*. You might warm up by doing a brief biography of yourself, including your likes and dislikes, your talents, your background, education, and professional experience, your love life, your goals in life. Take about ten minutes to do this. Then do it for a best friend. See whether you can clearly determine the difference in the amount of knowledge indicated in both biographies. Obviously you know more about you than you do about any other person. Is this evident in your biographies? Imagine you are a third person, completely objective. From looking at both biographies, which person would you most admire and want to get to know?

Do a few more biographies, including all the people closest to you. How do you feel about how much you know about these people?

FRIENDLY QUESTIONS

The following fifty questions are designed for you to ask yourself about an individual friend. Some of the questions are followed by brief comments which are aimed at clarifying the specific area concerned and giving you some insight into your relationship to this person.

1. *What is the single most important quality this friend has added to your life?*
   This can tell you which values you might have in common with him or her, and what you look for in this specific relationship.
2. *Is there another city in which your friend would rather live?*
   Sometimes friends won't share the fact that they are not happy in the city they're now living in, for fear that a friend might not choose to engage in intimate relating if the mutual accessibility is only going to be temporary. Friends have thus voiced amazement when someone picks up and moves to a distant city, even though this may have been the person's desire for many years.
3. *Would your friend ever consider going on a vacation just with you?*
4. *Is there something both you and your friend would like to learn, perhaps a new skill?*
   One surefire way of developing a deeper sense of connection is to learn something new together with a friend. The eventual accomplishment will give you something more in common, while the act of learning can be a more powerful shared satisfaction.
5. *Does this friend have a stronger need for people or for privacy?*
   Of course, only in an intimate friendship would you even know about the other person's privacy needs. And even in deep relationships of long duration, many people are unwilling to share this powerful need, for fear of hurting the other person's feelings. We'll discuss this more in a future chapter, but be aware for now that a privacy need is a personal thing, and has nothing to do with the person you may have to disappoint in order to fulfill that need.
6. *Do you feel this friend usually puts out where he or she really is?*
7. *Is there anything your friend would be willing to die for?*
8. *If you had an incurable and terminal illness, how do you think this friend would respond?*

Many people are deeply disappointed at the response of their friends to illness, and this often has to do with not being aware of the friend's true nature and commitment to the relationship prior to the illness.

9. *Is your friend more serious about life than you, or less so?*
10. *Does your friend feel closer to you now than at the beginning of your relationship?*
    You might be aware that most people tend to project their own feelings onto their friends at one time or another. Check out whether you are really looking at how you think your friend feels or are merely projecting the fact that you do or don't feel closer to that person now.
11. *Could you be separated from this friend for a year without it affecting your affection for each other?*
    Some friendships, with strong foundations of trust and mutual caring, can easily survive moving from accessibility to nonaccessibility, and perhaps back to accessibility again at some later date. Noted social scientist and group leader Emily Coleman says that she likes the fact that some friendships are interrupted and then may be reinstated at some later date. Ms. Coleman also says, "Sometimes our friends aren't just right for us at a certain period in our life. But to be able to come back to them again when the time is right for them and right for us, I like that. To be able to come in and tune in quickly even though maybe I haven't seen them for a number of years."
12. *Is there any time your friend would rather be with you than with an attractive member of the opposite sex with whom a romance is possible?*
    We'll look at this in more depth in the chapter Friends and Lovers, but it might be useful to see how much you now know about your friend's reactions to this kind of situation. In one survey of college women, a large percentage said they usually spent time with their female friends only when they had failed to obtain dates with men. This could be an underlying source of tension within a same-sex friendship if one or both people involved have a feeling that they are suitable companions only when nothing romantic or sexual is available.
13. *Does your friend read more or less than you do?*
14. *Can you name a book you either know you both have read and*

enjoyed, or one you think you would both enjoy reading?

15. *How does your friend feel about his or her family?*
16. *Who is your friend's favorite relative?*
17. *What kind of childhood does your friend describe?*
    This can be a powerful area of sharing, and very useful, especially if there are major differences in the childhood backgrounds of you and your friend. One exercise often used in human interaction groups involves two people sharing the physical attributes of the house they spent the most time in as a child. They each draw the house, and the room in which they spent the most time, and describe what they liked to do in that room, and how it was furnished.
18. *What were your friend's first sexual experiences like?*
19. *Is this friend currently being sexually fulfilled?*
    This can be an indication of how much honest sharing goes on in this friendship. If you don't know anything about your friend's love life, then there obviously is an area in which such communication and sharing has been severely restricted.
20. *Does your friend most often try to please others, or does self-pleasing come first?*
    If your friend is into self-pleasing, chances are he or she has a strong and healthy self-image. You can learn something about your own self-image by discovering how you feel about your friend's self-pleasing. If you feel you are being deprived by this, it might indicate some unhealthy self-concepts on your part. The healthiest friendships result from two people pleasing themselves and being able to take mutual pleasure in that event.
21. *Can you think of a time when this friend was particularly sensitive to your feelings?*
22. *What is your friend's favorite recreational pastime?*
23. *Can you think of one thing your friend really likes to do, but that you don't?*
    This goes back to Dr. Bob Resnick's statement earlier in this chapter: "Without an awareness of differences, you don't have contact." Do you feel compelled to share all your friend's activities, or can you enjoy your friend's enjoyment of something you don't care to participate in?
24. *Can you think of something really important to your friend, but not so to you?*

25. *Can you remember a time when you felt free to ask this friend a favor, and the response you got, and how you felt about that response?*
Many people find it difficult to ask for favors, especially when they really have a strong need. In a truly intimate relationship, each person would most likely feel comfortable asking the other for what he or she wants.
26. *What is your friend's favorite possession?*
27. *What present could you give this friend that would produce the most pleasure, assuming you had unlimited funds?*
28. *What is your friend's favorite food?*
29. *Does your friend believe in a supreme being?*
30. *What was your friend's first job? Was it an enjoyable experience?*
31. *How does your friend feel about his or her current employment?*
One of the main manifestations of a healthy self-image is doing work that is pleasing. Dr. Abraham Maslow's concept of the healthy individual, whom he terms "self-actualized," includes the fact that this person usually is doing work he or she thoroughly enjoys. In fact, the distinction between work and play is often blurred in these well-balanced individuals. Work provides them with much of their pleasure and excitement and passion in life. If all the friends you choose hate their jobs, you may be reinforcing your own weak self-image by surrounding yourself with others in similar predicaments.
32. *If you are not now so engaged, could you see yourself and this friend in business together?*
33. *Is your friend happy about his or her body and consider himself or herself attractive?*
34. *What one word would your friend use to describe his or her current life?*
35. *Would you describe your friend as a warm person?*
36. *What is your friend's major disappointment in life?*
37. *How would this friend react to your deciding to end the relationship?*
38. *What would cause this person to decide to end the relationship?*
39. *Can you imagine this friend doing something shocking to you?*
40. *Can this friend accept a no from you?*
41. *How does your friend feel about the current state of affairs in national politics?*

42. *Can you think of some area in which your friend has conservative, traditional views?*
43. *Can you think of an area in which your friend's views are liberal and permissive?*
44. *Would your friend rather travel by boat, plane, train, car, bicycle, or foot?*
45. *Are there some things you could never say or reveal to this friend?*
46. *Can you imagine something your friend could never say or reveal to you?*
47. *How does your friend feel about cheating as a means of getting ahead?*
48. *If an armored car went by and $200,000 fell out, would your friend keep it or return it, and if he or she returned it would the motivation be honesty or fear of being caught?*
49. *What is the main thing your friend is getting out of the friendship?*
50. *If you met right now as strangers, would your friend choose to begin a relationship at this point in your lives?*

These fifty questions do not constitute a quiz which you can pass or fail, but perhaps they've given you some awareness of the quality of the friendships you've chosen to explore with them. You may have found some areas on which you may want to focus in future communication with a friend. Don't feel something is wrong if you can't answer some of the questions. Very few friendships involve such a high level of exchange of information as to permit the answering correctly of all fifty questions. A friendship is a growing process and, if things are moving along at a healthy pace, you will know more next year about this person than you know today. Don't be impatient. As in life itself, the satisfaction is not in any end goal of total knowledge, but in the gathering of that knowledge through the experience of living, sharing, and growing.

Acceptance of a friend can be a beautifully gradual process, just as self-acceptance can be. In *I Ain't Much, Baby—But I'm All I've Got,* Dr. Jess Lair says, "We do not know what we should be. We do not know what we should do. And we do not know what we are very well. And the answer, it seems to me, is that what we are is kind of like an unfolding of some mysterious thing. The excitement of life is partly waiting to see who it is and what it is that we are. And in my experience we cannot see to the heart of ourselves. We cannot see the path that is best for us."

What Jess Lair is saying, in effect, is that it's healthy and desirable not to know all there is to know. And if this is true about yourself, it is even more so about a friend. So by all means know as much as you can know in the experience of friendship, enjoy the getting to know, but don't expect to know it all, and don't feel inferior or incompetent if there is a lot you don't know, even about your best friends. Just enjoy how much more there is left to discover!

Finish the sentence "One new thing I've learned about my friends is the fact that ———." Examine how you feel about this, and go on to the next chapter.

CHAPTER 5

SYSTEMATIC PERCEPTIONS

One of the major premises of this book is that you have much to gain in the way of useful insight by examining your friends and your friendship patterns. There are many tools which can help you in this process, including those which lie at the core of a number of recognized and established "systems" of therapy and/or self-development. This chapter is aimed at focusing attention on some of these tools, but by no means is an attempt to present a complete description or comprehensive review of the actual systems. Each could fill the pages of several books and, in fact, a number of books have been written to this purpose. The author has chosen to use editorial judgment in narrowing down the possible useful techniques. You are well advised to use similar editorial judgment to explore those which seem useful in looking at your friends, and to discard those which don't. In using this editorial judgment, pay close attention to your feelings as well as to your intellectual inclinations. If something doesn't "feel" right, have no qualms about discarding it. Too often we accommodate ourselves to ill-fitting concepts merely because they seem to have some substance, or appear in a book, or are suggested by someone we respect. The primary, and probably the only criterion that can lead to real growth, it simply to ask: "Is this fitting for me? Does this make sense for me?"

WORDS AS LABELS

All the systems described in this chapter are merely ways of labeling human behavior, ways of marking the road map of your life, so that you will have some better idea of where you have been and where you are now, and perhaps even where you are going. These labels are particularly useful in identifying places you constantly revisit in your emotional life. Without labels, you could conceivably repeat certain experiences over and over again without knowing that you are doing so. In terms of friendship, this kind of repetition can often lead to hostility and alienation, without understanding its source or origin.

ILLUMINATION NOT ALWAYS NECESSARY

We don't always have to know or understand everything that is part of our lives. You may have some friendships that are totally nourishing and healthy and satisfying, so that there is no real need to carefully examine the dynamics of these relationships, unless you would like some guidelines for the future. Chances are, however, you have some friends who are not giving you very much, not adding anything to your life. This sort of situation deserves more exploration on your part. What in you attracts such people and/or finds them attractive?

Then, of course, you probably have friendships that are somewhat satisfying but have the potential for much more nourishment. These too are worth exploring in more depth. As we consider the various approaches and techniques, try them on for size, find the one that casts the brightest light on your particular situation.

THE GESTALT FRIENDSHIP

We start out with one of the most potent and controversial of all the new therapies, Gestalt therapy, as evolved by Dr. Fritz Perls. Applying some of the Gestalt concepts to friendship is not very difficult a task, for they apply beautifully. Especially the main focus, which is simply awareness. In fact, this entire book could be said to be a book about Gestalt friendship. The premise here being that the more aware you are of and about your friends, and of your responses to them, the more able you are going to be to make real choices in your friend relationships.

Gestalt therapist Dr. Jerry Greenwald says, "Any awarenesses a person has about how he's relating to his friends, what he does with them, this would tell him something about how he relates to himself."

FRIENDSHIP AWARENESS

Few people really focus on their awareness of their friends. One way to do this is simply to ask yourself, "What am I aware of about this friend?" Just make a list, as long a list as you like. A sample one might look like this:

I feel good when I'm with her.
She always listens to me.
We really have good times when we go to dinner together.
She has excellent taste in clothes and furniture.
We seem to like the same books.
I always feel relaxed and comfortable in her home.
She's always the first person I think to call when I'm inviting people over.
I miss her if we don't communicate, at least by phone, every couple of days.

You could make this list now, and then see if you will want to add items to it as we explore more facets of friendship. In fact, thinking back over the first four chapters, you may already be able to come up with some new awarenesses.

The most important awareness, of course, is how you feel about this friend. One way to check this out is to think of the person and fill in the sentence for yourself: "As I think of ———, I feel ———." You might also choose to do this little exercise the next time you are face to face with this friend. You can also make a mental list of all the things you are aware of when you are in close proximity to this friend. For instance, how does your body feel, relaxed or tense? Do you feel comfortable looking directly into this person's eyes? Do you find yourself being protective of yourself when you're around this friend? Do you feel you must keep parts of yourself hidden from this person? Do you feel this person might misunderstand or take advantage of you if you were completely open and vulnerable? Do you feel a sudden spurt of energy and aliveness whenever this friend comes near? Do you feel a warm tingle of anticipation when you are about to see this person? And a nice glow of satisfaction after you've been with this friend? All of these are emotional awarenesses.

Dr. Jerry Greenwald says, "Any kind of awareness of any relating experience would be valid in other areas, too." For example, you might feel the same tingle of anticipation before seeing a friend as you do when you are about to go on a trip or do something creative. The absence of this tingle might tell you that you really aren't looking forward to what is about to happen.

THE REALISTIC NOW

Gestalt awareness always happens in the present. In a therapy session, you might be remembering the past, or fantasizing about the future, but the therapist will always invite you to experience and perceive these feelings as they are happening now. Though you may not be fully in the present when remembering or fantasizing or worrying, these activities are setting off emotions which you can be aware of. Realistically, to look at what is happening right now, you would have to say you have no friends. For, while you are reading these words, you are not interacting with a friend. And the friendship only really happens during that interaction. This isn't to say that you can't have real feelings about your friends when they aren't present, but true awareness would include the information that only direct action involving these friends is real, and all else involves, to some extent, fantasy or remembering.

JENNIE AND MARGO

Jennie and Margo are friends. At this moment, Jennie is very upset because Margo had been planning to go on a vacation with her boyfriend, and he decided not to go at the last moment. Margo went by herself, and was very depressed about it Thursday night when she spent some time with Jennie. She left Friday on her trip, and it is now Sunday, and Jennie is worried about her. What Jennie doesn't know is that Margo met a wonderful man Saturday night, and is now ecstatically enjoying the initial stages of infatuation. The feelings Jennie is experiencing are real ones, but the Realistic Now situation is that she isn't having current contact with Margo, and isn't privy to real information. What may occur is that Jennie will resent Margo when she returns all aglow from her vacation. That resentment will stem from the fact that Jennie suffered needlessly, and was feeling very loyal as a friend because of this suffering empathy. But Margo didn't need Jennie to suffer for her, and the truth is that even if she had been alone and depressed during her entire vacation, she still wouldn't have needed Jennie to suffer on her account. She might have appreciated some caring empathy on her return, but there was no way Jennie's worrying about Margo could possibly do any good for Margo when she and Jennie were not interacting.

A Realistic Now approach would also save a lot of wasted energy used in assuming that you know what a friend's response is going to be to a specific situation. You never really know until it happens. You may not be able to totally eliminate all feelings of concern, but an awareness of "I'm a little apprehensive, but I realize that I have no way of really knowing how this is going to turn out, and I will wait until the event before I actually choose my response" will promote much more realistic and fulfilling relationships.

A Realistic Now approach to your friendship interactions also involves an awareness of consequences and of how what you do will affect the friendship environment. If you have a friend who is allergic to cigarette smoke, and you choose not to smoke when with that friend, this is a choice based on your past experience. You don't have to light up each time you come in contact to check out whether your friend is still allergic. You can assume that this act will have the same results based on the knowledge you have of the consequences you have noted on past occasions. This knowledge, in effect, gives you responsibility for your environment, as well as for your own responses. All knowledge is really a series of images received and stored by the computerlike capacities of your brain. If you have smoked in the past, and have seen and heard the responses of your friend to this action, then you have built up images of those responses, which has constituted "learning" what the consequences of these actions will be.

THE GESTALT PRAYER

Somehow people have gotten the mistaken notion that Gestalt therapy says you are only responsible for yourself. The Gestalt concept is that you are only response-able, able to respond, for yourself, but you are responsible for the consequences of your actions. A lot of the misunderstanding stems from the often quoted Gestalt Prayer, created by Dr. Fritz Perls, the father of modern Gestalt therapy. It goes like this:

> I do my thing, and you do your thing.
> I am not in this world to live up to your expectations
> And you are not in this world to live up to mine.
> You are you and I am I
> And if by chance we meet, it's beautiful.
> If not, it can't be helped.

The last line is usually left off when the prayer is reproduced on posters, perhaps because of the more romantic nature of the line that precedes it.

Dr. Robert Resnick, a noted Gestalt therapist, said in a talk, "Those lines, in my opinion, have taken the weight of more psychopathy and more bullshit than anything else I know of. The translation, for those who want to use it to do what they want, and call it Gestalt therapy, is, 'I do my thing, fuck you! I want to get to that door, you're in my way, I step in your face. I'm just doing my thing. I'm not in this world to live up to your expectations that I'll ask you to move. Fuck you! Goodbye!' Or: 'I'm not responsible for that person, I'm responsible for me. I'm not responsible for their bleeding. I punched him in the nose, it's my thing.' And with such righteousness! The Gestalt Prayer is a metaphor, a direction, one of millions that are possible. It may fit you. If so, enjoy it. But that's not what Gestalt therapy is. When Fritz wrote it, he prefaced it with 'The Gestalt Prayer, perhaps a direction.' Much more of the meaning comes out for me, and as I remember Fritz talking about it, in: *If I please me and you please you, and enough of the time we please each other, then we have an overlap, and a real core. I'm never going to please you totally. Hopefully, you'll never please me totally. That would be like being with myself. But, if when I please me and you please you, there's enough overlap where we please each other* . . . and it doesn't mean one hundred percent. If you expect one hundred percent, then all relationships, as far as I'm concerned, are doomed. There is no way you're going to have a hundred percent. If there's enough there, you have a core, and it's a solid core, not based on game-playing, not based on bribery and blackmail. Based on I'm pleasing me, and it also happens to please you enough of the time, and vice versa. Then we have something good. If we don't have something good, and we start from the beginning with I please me, and you please me, we'll find out very quickly we don't have anything. And we won't mess around for eight years trying to 'work on it.' Trying to make the relationship better than it is, different than it is, which means game-playing, phony contracts, and sabotage. Where I'm not really pleasing me, and you're not pleasing me either. "Another common distortion of the Gestalt Prayer comes in the literal translation of Perls' metaphor: "and if by chance we meet, it's beautiful. If not, it can't be helped." The word "chance" here is used as a linguistic symbol for: Do we substantially please each other when we are pleasing ourselves? This includes struggles, dreams, yearnings, forgivings and, it is hoped, over some time period. It does not mean I end a friendship if one day you look at me cockeyed or bark in irritation. The relationship itself is not brought into question every time there is a dissatisfaction. Part of the value of a protracted relationship is having a mat to fight and to make up on and to enjoy the richness of being different from each other."

PLEASING ME AND YOU

Before we look further at the Gestalt Prayer and its distortions, you might find it illuminating to look at your friendships in terms of what Dr. Resnick sees as its real premise. Are most of your relationships based on a mutual self-pleasing? Can you say about a friend, "I please me. You please you. And, in doing so, enough of the time we please each other." Or do you find yourself always trying to please your friends, or they're always trying to please you? How do you feel about whichever is true for you?

Dr. Jerry Greenwald, also a Gestalt therapist, says, "The Gestalt Prayer is incomplete. When Fritz Perls wrote that, he simply wrote that poem, he wasn't saying that was his whole philosophy. There were plenty of times when I worked with him when I saw him tell people, 'OK, I'm going to help you.' And he had a lot to say about taking responsibility for when you're poisoning someone else. I think it's up to each of us in a friendship to take some responsibility for when we are putting too much on the other person. If, in a friendship, you keep asking for what you want, and you keep getting 'No!' from the other person, the other person is willing to take a stand and say, 'No, I don't want to do that with you or for you,' that's not the end of the experience. It's the end of that unit of the experience. After a while, when the other person has to keep on saying, 'No, no, no, no, no . . . ,' this has to have a wearing effect on the overall relationship."

ARE YOU HEARING THE NO'S?

You might look at your friendships in terms of whether you really hear the response of your friends. Can you think of something you keep asking for, even though your friend keeps refusing you? Can you see where this has a wearing effect on the relationship? Are you willing to take responsibility for that effect, or are you blaming it on your friend, and his or her stubbornness in refusing you?

JEFF AND STEVE

Jeff kept trying to get Steve to go camping with him. He tried to convince him how nice it would be to be out in nature, how healthy it would be for him. But Steve didn't want to go camping, and the more Jeff insisted, the more Steve resisted. Jeff got angry at what he considered Steve's stubbornness, while he didn't even consider that his insistence was stubborn. The point is that Steve had a right to decide for himself whether or not he wanted to go camping, no matter how much he may have been missing by not going. Jeff was not respecting his feelings; he was not hearing Steve.

Psychiatrist Leonard Zunin doesn't like the lines, "And if by chance we meet, it's beautiful. If not, it can't be helped." He says, "I think both are extremes, and both are fallacious and ridiculous points of view that are not founded on fact. I think there is evidence to point out that there has to be a spark between two people, something that we can't quite define. The skills allow that to blossom. You *must* know the skills of interpersonal communication. It's important to do certain exercises. It's important to build upon that spark. And the more you know, and the more you're aware, the more you can allow that to blossom. But if that spark isn't there, you can bang your head against a brick wall until it's bloody, and nothing will ever happen."

Thus, if you allow yourself to express yourself freely, you might ignite a spark, whereas if you hold yourself in, that spark will never be ignited, because that other person will never really see you. And so, the spark that might have happened doesn't happen. One thing you might look at in your friendships, particularly those that aren't going the way you would like them to go, is whether there was a real spark there from the beginning. Or, as Dr. Zunin suggested, are you beating your head against a wall? Or did the spark happen, and you just didn't take advantage of this opportunity?

Another factor is whether you know what a spark between two people feels like. Have you ever felt that special little tingle when meeting someone for the first time, something that said to you that this could be a good relationship? Dr. Zunin suggests that you might even let the other person know when you feel this, checking out whether they are also feeling this connection. He adds, "It takes an attitude of receptivity, feeling that spark, and then working on allowing it to blossom through the interpersonal tools."

TOXIC VERSUS NOURISHING

Dr. Jerry Greenwald originated the Gestalt concept of "toxic," or unnatural behavior, and "nourishing," or natural behavior. Dividing all behavior into these two categories can give you some simple guidelines. It's an easy way to enhance awareness. He says, "We relate to other people essentially in the same way that we relate to ourselves. The only difference is that we do things to ourselves we wouldn't dare do to anybody else. At least, most of us are more toxic to ourselves than we usually feel free enough to be with other people."

So, toxic or nourishing relating usually has to do with your own attitudes, and the attitudes of the other person, rather than necessarily what you actually do with each other. In his book *Be the Person You Were Meant to Be*, Dr. Greenwald outlines a number of toxic versus nourishing relationship patterns. A few examples of questions to ask yourself:

TOXIC ATTITUDE: Do I believe that the way other people relate to me should live up to my expectations—particularly when they are reasonable?

or:

NOURISHING ATTITUDE: Do I believe it is their right to relate to me as they choose?

TOXIC ATTITUDE: Do I allow others to manipulate me for fear of rejection if I do not comply with their demands?

or:

NOURISHING ATTITUDE: Am I willing to say no when I feel manipulated and take my chances that the others will accept me anyhow?

TOXIC ATTITUDE: Am I usually on my own trip, ignoring the reactions of others (boredom, restlessness, irritation, etc.)?

or:

NOURISHING ATTITUDE: Do I feel in touch with the other people and aware of their reactions?

You might check out your responses to these three sets of questions, particularly as they apply to your current friendships. If you are interested in exploring these concepts further, read Dr. Greenwald's book.

You might even rate your individual friendships as to whether you see them as toxic or nourishing right now. What should you do if you find you're in a lot of toxic relationships? Dr. Greenwald says, "The first step is awareness, of course. This is basic Gestalt. The first step in change is to really, on a gut level, see where you are, see what you are doing. Also, being aware of what you really do get from a relationship."

Dr. Greenwald has come up with what he terms "antidotes" for toxic behavior. In terms of toxic relating, he cites the importance of mutual awareness and respect for each other's integrity, saying, "Respecting the other person as an individual is perhaps the best antidote or preventative for toxic relating. Not intruding on them. Not violating their space, in all kinds of ways. Their psychic space, their individuality, their freedom. Really respecting them as another human being. Not using any kind of power or manipulation against them to get them to do what you want. Perhaps relating to people in terms of how you would relate to and respect an infant. You would not take advantage of an infant just because it's a helpless, dependent little human being that hasn't got any power. In other words, integrity in a relationship, to me, is in the opposite direction from all kinds of manipulation or power plays or coercion."

Can you see yourself respecting your friends as if they were helpless infants? How would this change your relationships? Would you like to be treated with this kind of respect and gentleness? Remember, also, that this is not a hands-off policy. Babies are touched and cuddled much more than the average adult. So, perhaps if you respect someone's integrity, you are also going to be willing to reach out and care for them.

An experiment you might try is to imagine yourself as a baby the next time you interact with a friend. See if this friend would be mistreating you if you were an infant. Then switch this fantasy and imagine that your friend is a baby. Are you being as tender and caring of this friend as you would be of a helpless little baby?

It may sound silly to you, but then many of the ways we relate to each other are silly, wasteful, painful, and destructive.

A SENSE OF WHOLENESS

The word "gestalt" means wholeness, completeness. One way to experience this in a friendship is to experience all the parts of yourself in that relationship. To look at this friendship and see whether you are allowing your whole self to be involved in it. Or are you limiting the parts of you this other person can see? The happiest and most fulfilling friendships seem to be those in which both people are experiencing as much of themselves as possible. Of course, you probably wouldn't have the time or energy to relate your whole being to every single person you call a friend. But, to those friends you call intimate, do you allow all of you to be seen? Do you trust them enough to allow them to see you clearly?

Again, having many superficial friendships may give you an excuse to avoid the kind of openness that true intimacy requires. Dr. Jerry Greenwald says, "If a person, throughout his life, has ten or twenty really good friends, people they really feel solid relationships with, I think this is about the limits of what anybody can handle. And I don't know what he would do if they all lived within three miles of him. He might really love each of them as a friend, and want to be with each of them, and I doubt if he would have that much time and energy to share with that many friends."

MORE THAN SELF-AWARENESS

Over and over again, throughout this book, self-awareness is stressed as the single most important factor in emotional health and growth. But it is not the only factor. Dr. Robert Resnick comments, "It is very important to be aware of what I do with this environment, how I am reacting to this environment, how I am dealing with it. Just being in touch with self-awareness is not enough. Fritz Perls often asserted that self-awareness was only half the story. World awareness completes the situation. With self-awareness alone I can contemplate the interior of my navel and be oblivious *to* and deprived *of* what the world has for me and what I have for the world."

In Gestalt terms, you have to deal with the Realistic Now situation, or the "is" situation. Dr. Resnick says, "Whatever is, is. At any given moment. And it doesn't matter if it's an ocean, or an unreasonable son of a bitch, or a sunset, or a school system, or another person. Whatever is, is. At that moment, that's what it is. What some people want to do is change the 'is,' and then respond to it. This, to me, comes under the heading of miracles. I have a cup of water in my hand. If I want it to be a tuna fish sandwich, there is no way I can first change it to a tuna fish sandwich before I respond to it and then eat it. I can eat it as water, or I can put it down, or throw it, or a whole number of other things, but I can't change it from what it is to something it isn't, so that then I can respond the way I want to respond. If I deal with the water as it is, I can then probably get to my sandwich."

How you respond to the "is" situations in your life is how you get the results that occur. If you are unhappy with the results, the only way to change is to change your response to the "is."

LIZ AND HELEN

Helen was a prude, and very uptight about her own sexuality. Her best friend was Liz, who had a rather uninhibited view of sex. Helen spent most of her time berating Liz about her morals, trying to make her see the error of her ways. Liz didn't let this bother her, as she enjoyed Helen's company and was amused by her evangelistic zeal. Helen was on a course that was doomed. There was no way Liz was going to change what, for her, was a healthy and satisfying way of operating in the world. The only thing Helen could change was her response to Liz. She could ignore her behavior, or try to open her own mind in this area, or end the friendship. She stayed stuck in an unhappy situation because she wanted to change the "is," or Liz, rather than her response to that "is."

And, in this case, the "is," strictly speaking, isn't only Liz, it's the choosing of Liz as a friend by Helen. As Dr. Resnick says, "The 'is' is not only the friend, but the act of choosing the friend. The friend will be in existence whether I see him or her or not. What I do is the 'is' I have choices about." So Helen has created the "is" by declaring that Liz is her friend, and how she responds to this choice, this "is," is how she gets the consequences she is complaining about.

All emotional situations would be resolved so much more quickly and easily if people realized that their responses are what counts in this world. It really doesn't matter what the other person is doing, but it *does* matter how you respond to what they are doing. As Bob Resnick says, "I can't be 'aware' of my friends. I can be aware of my experience of them, my reactions to them."

In the case of Liz and Helen, another friend might very well find Liz's sexual attitudes a positive asset. So it is not what Liz's attitudes are that is creating the problem, but Helen's perception of those attitudes and the way in which she responds to that perception.

If you imagine a friend has mistreated you because of something he or she has said, it is not what is said that has created the bad feeling. It is your response to it. Your friend may have had no intention of mistreating you. You may have misunderstood him or her. But if you sulk, and never share your feelings of being mistreated with that friend, never give the person a chance to give his or her view of the situation, you are going to continue to feel bad, and it will be your fault. Your response to what you think was said, and what you think was meant, is creating the bad feeling. Not the friend. Even if the friend meant to mistreat you, it is still your response to that mistreatment that causes you to feel bad, not the mistreatment itself. You can only make yourself suffer, no one else can do it for you.

Look over your friendship list and your Friendship Circles. Be aware of how you respond to the "is" of each friendship. That response is what causes the results or consequences related to that friendship. If you are happy with those results, fine. If not, then examine your response and see if there is any way you could modify it.

BLAME AND CREDIT TO OTHERS

In our culture we tend to blame others for all the unpleasantness that befalls us, and give others credit for all the good things that happen to us. But in the final analysis we are each responsible for our own happiness. It is our own responses to the situations which emerge in our lives that determine whether we are going to be happy or suffer. It is very difficult to accept the responsibility for this, but it is the only way to start living a full and healthy life. And when you begin to see your friends as people, here to fulfill themselves, not to make you happy or make you suffer, then you can begin to relate honestly and without fear.

GET RID OF YOUR "SHOULDS"

Fritz Perls saw us divided into two ego states that cause a lot of trouble. He called these Topdog and Underdog. He also called them two clowns, and blamed them for the self-torturing process. The Topdog in your personality makes demands, and tells you what you should and shouldn't do, threatening you with dire results if you don't comply. For example, your Topdog might tell you that you should always remember the birthday of a friend. The Topdog might threaten you with the loss of a friendship if you don't remember this ritual, warning you that you will be rejected, unloved, and maybe even the catastrophic threat that *you* won't get a birthday card from this friend.

The Underdog manipulates you by playing weak and powerless, blaming everything on circumstances beyond your control. The Underdog would respond to the above situation by saying such things as, "I'm sorry I forgot your birthday. I'm a terrible person and I don't know how you can ever forgive me." Or: "It isn't my fault I forgot your birthday; all sorts of terrible things happened to make me forget." Or: "Oh, didn't you get my card? I mailed it out two days ago." Dr. Perls saw these two states always vying with each other for control, creating an inner conflict. They are both very dependent on your having a system of shoulds in your personality makeup. Things you think are absolutely necessary to be a good and loved and successful person. A person without shoulds may have responded to the forgotten birthday card situation by saying, "Hey, I just wanted to tell you I still love you, even though I forgot your birthday!" Can you see the difference in these responses?

The problem with shoulds is that they lock you into very rigid behavior that may not be appropriate to the reality of the situation, and may not be based on what you honestly feel about it. If you are attracted to a member of the opposite sex, and your should system tells you that it isn't nice to be forward, chances are you are going to feel frustrated at not being able to do what you would really like to do. Your common sense and feelings tell you that it's perfectly all right to make a polite approach, but your should system tells you any approach is not the act of a "nice" person.

FRIENDSHIP SHOULDS

Do you have any shoulds about what constitutes a good friend? Make a list, with the heading: *A Good Friend Should Be.* How many things do you honestly believe a good friend should be? A sample list might look like this:

A good friend should always be there when I need him.
A good friend will stick by me no matter what.
A good friend will always understand me.
A good friend will not do things that hurt me.
A good friend will like all the things I like.
A good friend will think of me before he thinks of himself.

Do any of these shoulds ring a bell for you? Do you see where they could be destructive? They can damage a relationship because, rather than seeing what a good friend is, the shoulds lock you into rigid expectations of what a good friend has to be. So, even if you are satisfied in a relationship in which all or some of these things are missing, you are not going to be able to stay a friend to this person, since you have judged him unworthy by virtue of the fact that he isn't meeting all your should expectations.

Instead of shoulds, you can just see what this person is really like, and for each individual these features will be unique. If you are in a trusting friendship, one in which you each feel comfortable revealing yourselves, you might check out what your individual shoulds are.

Once again, a warning: *Don't overdo all this checking out, so that you end up spending more time analyzing relationships than living them.* These are tools to use or not use when it feels appropriate. Don't wear them out. In his book *Gestalt Therapy Verbatim,* Dr. Fritz Perls stated it very pointedly: "The 'trouble' with people who are capable of reviewing every second what the situation is like, is that we are not predictable."

TRANSACTIONAL ANALYSIS IN FRIENDSHIP

Transactional Analysis, as developed by Dr. Eric Berne, is perhaps the fullest of all the new therapies, the most complex, the one with the most depth. Some of the popular books on the subject have led people to believe that it is much simpler than it is. True, TA does provide some very simple guidelines to behavior, and it is easy to understand, perhaps the easiest of all the therapies, but it is not basically a simple therapy. You cannot read one book on the subject, or attend one weekend workshop, and be a TA therapist. Yet, many people are misled into believing this is so. This is not to say that learning some of the terminology and techniques isn't very useful, but it is important to realize that you don't know it all, and it would take years of study to know all there is to know about TA.

In this brief examination of TA, therefore, please understand that it is just an attempt to use some of the methods and approaches, and not an attempt to explain it all. If you are interested in further information, read some of the books. TA therapists seem to most often recommend *Born to Win* by Muriel James and Dorothy Jongeward, which also incorporates Gestalt exercises, and *Scripts People Live* by Claude M. Steiner. Both are available in paperback.

As part of our overview, it is necessary to include a prime facet of TA, the ego states of Parent, Adult, and Child. The Parent ego state involves all behavior that was programmed in from outside sources, usually one's parents. In your Parent ego state you might say to a friend, "That was a stupid decision you made."

The Adult ego state involves reality and rational objectivity. In your Adult ego state you might say to that same friend, "I wonder if your decision is going to get you what you want."

The Child ego state usually involves old behavior from childhood, and impulses that come naturally to a child. In the same situation as the above examples, in your Child ego state you might say to that friend, "No! No! You can't do that, I won't let you!"

The complexities occur when different ego states are communicating, for example: Parent to Child, Adult to Parent, etc. And the difficulties occur when an unexpected response is forthcoming from any of these transactions. Complementary Transactions are those in which the communication from a specific ego state gets the predicted response from a specific ego state in another person. For example, you might say to your friend from your Child ego state: "Let's go out tonight and really have some fun!" Your friend might respond from his or her Child ego state: "Great! Let's do it!" This was the predicted response, one that would lead to a mutually agreeable act, and so all is well.

Crossed Transactions are those that involve an unexpected response to the initial stimulus. As TA therapist Marta Vago puts it, "In a Crossed Transaction, the response that I expect to my stimulus is not what I get. It's like a shorting of circuits, there's a momentary break-off in communication." Using the above example, you might still say to your friend from your Child ego state, "Let's go out tonight and really have some fun!" But your friend may respond from his or her Parent ego state, "Don't be silly, we have too much work to do!" You have just experienced a Crossed Transaction, and chances are you won't like it very much, and won't like your friend very much for this unpredictable response. Thus, a conflict occurs.

If you have a lot of these unpredictable responses in your friendship transactions, it may very well pay you to read *Born to Win*, and learn some more about the interrelationship of the various ego states.

STROKING

We all need to be touched and recognized by others. Eric Berne called this need a "hunger." This hunger can be appeased by what TA terms "strokes." These can be actual physical strokes; for example, a friend might hug you. Or by some other form of satisfying recognition, such as a friendly gesture, or compliment, or anything that would say to you, "I see you, I think you are worthwhile, I like you." You cannot live an emotionally healthy life without some positive strokes, which can vary in degree from simple friendly greetings to intimate physical contact. Recognizing this need you have can help you be more aware of what you want from a friendship, and what you can give to this friend.

LIST THE STROKES

Pick one friend and see if you can identify the strokes you have received from this person and the strokes you have given to him or her. A sample list of strokes might include:

She really listens carefully to what I say.

She always hugs me when we get together.

She compliments me on my accomplishments.

She encourages me in what I want to do.

One useful idea might be to keep a Stroke Journal, listing all the strokes you receive and all those you give to others. If you can't think of any positive stroking you have received lately, look over your list of friends and decide who might be most able to give you some strokes. Then discuss it with that person and see if he or she would be willing to do this. One of the ways in which we avoid getting some of the strokes we need is by not being able to ask for them.

The next time you are with a friend, make it a point to give him or her at least one positive stroke.

The more you stroke, the more strokes you will receive.

DISCOUNTS

Strokes are units of recognition. There are also units of non-recognition called "discounts" in TA. A discount is someone either not paying attention to your feelings, or putting them down in some way. In a paper for the *Transactional Analysis Journal*, Aaron Wolfe Schiff and Jacqui Lee Schiff wrote, "The person who discounts believes, or acts as though he believes, that his feelings about what someone else has said, done, or felt, are more significant than what that person actually said, did or felt."

Most people are guilty at one time or another of discounting in their interpersonal interactions. Some typical discounting statements:

Why are you so sad? That's a silly reaction to the situation.

You ought to be glad you've got a job, so stop complaining!

You on a diet? Don't make me laugh! You'll never lose weight.

You think that's bad, wait until you hear what happened to me!

Can you think of a situation in which a friend discounted you? One of the most destructive forms of discounting is that in which one person indicates to the other that his feelings are unacceptable, insignificant, unworthy of attention, or silly under the circumstances. If someone tells you that something that happened makes them feel a certain way, you have no right to tell them it shouldn't. Even if their reaction is an unhealthy or excessive one, it is an honest reaction, and they are entitled to it. Trying to talk them out of it will only create resentment and confusion, and is usually the act of a manipulator.

JUDY AND ELAINE

Judy tells Elaine, "I am really dissatisfied with my life and I'm thinking of asking Phil for a divorce." Elaine responds with, "How could you think of possibly leaving that wonderful man? He's everything any woman would want! Kind. Generous. Attractive. He makes a good salary, and has given you everything you ever wanted!"

Elaine obviously thinks her opinion of Phil is more valid than Judy's, even though Judy has not said anything against Phil, just put the situation in personal terms of her own dissatisfaction. Elaine has not acknowledged Judy's feeling of dissatisfaction, and has made it a statement of, "If Phil isn't a rotten person, you should be happy."

This kind of trip has been laid on many women who are just discovering their own individual personalities, realizing that the values that led them into marriage are no longer meaningful to them, and that they want more out of life, even though their husbands don't beat them, or do terrible things to them, and in fact are often pretty good to them in many ways. These women usually face tremendous discounting pressure from friends and family, and rarely can find support for their decision. The fact that many of them still go through with the decision bears powerful witness to their strength of character and determination. But going against the tide can be a lonely experience, and it often seems that just when they need it most, they are not getting any kind of stroking at all. This is also a good time for a complete reevaluation of one's friendship patterns and structure. If none of your friends would be willing to listen to you or consider your feelings if you should make some dramatic change in your life, then what do you think this tells you about the friends you've chosen?

DRAMATIC CHANGES

One way to check this out is to imagine some dramatic changes occurring, and imagine how your various friends would react. Would they discount your feelings, or even refuse to listen to your reasons for making these changes? This is not to say that they have to agree you are making a wise decision. They are entitled to their opinion, but do they grant you the same right? Some of the changes you might imagine:

—You decide to give it all up and move into a commune with forty-five other people.

—You shave off all your hair and have a ring put through your nose.

—You become a Zen Buddhist.

—You give up your career and start making sculpture out of automobile scraps.

—You give up any relationship you are now in, and move in with two attractive members of the opposite sex.

—You start vigorously campaigning for a controversial third-party political candidate.

—You decide to join the CIA as a field agent.

—You give up your job and start collecting welfare.

—You reveal yourself as the author of the best-selling pornographic novel, who has agreed to star in the movie version.

Do you think your friends could handle these changes without discounting you? Would most of them try to convince you of the error of your ways? Or would they say, "I trust that you are doing what is right for you, and I still want to be your friend." In other words, do you have to stay in your current role and avoid change in order to keep the friends you now have?

OK FRIENDS

Dr. Eric Berne formulated four basic existential psychological positions. These have to do with your attitude toward yourself and your attitude toward others.

I'm OK, you're OK.

This position constitutes emotional health. If you view your friendships from this position or attitude, chances are they are healthy and rewarding. You are saying, in effect, that you like yourself and you recognize the value of others.

I'm OK, you're not OK.

This is the position of those people who blame everybody else for all their problems. This can be a very unhealthy position, and can even lead to paranoid behavior. Viewing your friendships from this position would mean that you have rather poor opinions of all the people you call friends, and are probably not willing to trust them enough to allow a truly intimate relationship.

I'm not OK, you're OK.

This is also an unhealthy position. In friendships, it leads to separation. It's indicative of someone who feels circumstances are beyond his or her control, that he or she is the only one who has problems, the only one who isn't perfect. It's a position of isolation from others or dependency on others.

I'm not OK, you're not OK.

This is perhaps the most hopeless position of all. This is the kind of person who could be totally alone in a crowd, feeling he or she has nothing of worth to contribute to anyone else, and feeling that no one has anything worthwhile to give to them.

In *Born to Win*, James and Jongeward say, "People with the first position feel 'Life is worth living.' With the second they feel 'Your life is not worth much.' With the third they feel 'My life is not worth much.' With the fourth they feel 'Life isn't worth anything at all.' "

Can you identify some of your friendships according to these psychological positions?

TA therapist Dr. Bart Knapp, of Philadelphia's famed Laurel Institute, says, "One of the complaints that many people come in with is that they don't have friends. And this seems to be a two-edged sword. On the one hand, the fact that they don't have friends, their experience of not having friends, allows them to see themselves as being in a *not OK* position. And being in a *not OK* position, they're not able to get friends, they're reluctant to take the chance. So it's a sort of paradox. They lock themselves into this position. If people don't feel good about themselves, about where they are, they can use not having friends to establish that, to get that feeling. And then that feeling in turn feeds into the system, so that they end up not looking for friends."

Dr. Knapp's colleague and codirector of the Laurel Institute, Marta Vago, says, "Many friendships are based on a playing out of the existential position of *I'm OK, you're not OK*. There are societies and clubs that are built on this position. The local Democratic club, for instance, is banded together on the idea that Democrats are *OK* and non-Democrats are *not OK* . Some of the people in the encounter group culture feel people who have been through encounter are *OK*, and people who haven't are *not OK*. There are also many circles of friends which are built on espousing the same constellation of *OK* values. It's *OK* to be rich, or it's *OK* to be poor. Or, the flower children. They were *OK*, and everybody else who wasn't wearing jeans and handing out flowers to people were *not OK*. Many friendships are based on these bonds of *OKness*, where the definition of *OKness* tends to be extremely rigid and quite confining. Sometimes even when they espouse openness and flexibility, the flexibility and openness actually pertain only to their own circle of friends."

Dr. Knapp adds, "It's a situation where an organization starts to talk about 'we' and 'they.' Also, in individual friendships, or couple relationships, it's 'us' against the rest of the world."

Marta Vago goes on, "Many friendships are built on the 'we' and 'they.' In TA terms, the *we-ness* provides mutual stroking. I stroke you by calling you *OK*. And you stroke me by calling me *OK*. And we'll stroke each other by calling him or her *not OK*. The more cliquish a circle of friends is, the more you'll find the 'we' and 'they' dichotomy. If you challenge this clique on their definition of *OKness*, they'll become extremely defensive and they'll start giving you all kinds of scientific and pseudo-scientific reasons why they are *OK* and the rest are *not OK*. Any person looking at his or her friendships needs to examine what some of the *OK* values are that he or she shares with friends, and what are the *not OK* values that they frown upon and play 'ain't that awful' around. Whenever you find yourself in conversations such as: 'Isn't it terrible that the Joneses . . . ,' 'Isn't it awful that . . . ,'what you're into is a mutual stroking of *I'm OK, you're OK,* and *they're not OK.*"

WE AGAINST THEY

Are any of your friendships based on this mutual stroking discussed by Ms. Vago and Dr. Knapp? Do you feel more comfortable with a friend when you have someone you can mutually look down on? Is your circle of friends a rigid and narrow clique that really doesn't allow any new people to enter? Which values of what is and isn't *OK* do you share with which friends?

Ms. Vago asks a question you might ask yourself: "Are the kinds of friendships that you're into now mean that one of the people in the friendship has to be *not OK?* Either you have to be *not OK*, so the other person can be helpful to you, or the other person has to be *not OK*, so you can be helpful to him."

Dr. Knapp illustrates this by saying, "This can be visualized as leaning. The person who is *OK*, who is helpful in the relationship, in effect is leaning on the person who is helpless. Just as much as the person who is helpless is leaning on the person who is helpful. And if the helpful person says, 'I'm no longer going to be helpful,' that leaves the helpless person no one to lean on in the relationship. Conversely, if the helpless person suddenly, one way or the other, finds out, 'I don't have to be helpless. I am *OK*. I can carry my own load,' that leaves the helpful person no one to lean on."

Marta Vago reports on an interesting phenomenon that at times may take place in Alcoholics Anonymous. "At a time when there are no drinking alcoholics in a particular AA chapter, when there are only the alcoholics who are dry, who are on the wagon, and there is nobody to rescue in that chapter, one of the dry alcoholics may start drinking again so there will be someone to take care of. Which is a beautiful indication of how the helpers *need* the helpless to make them feel *OK*."

This issue of dependency is one of vital importance in exploring your friendships. Dependency is probably the single most destructive force in a one-to-one relationship. In their book *Beyond Success and Failure*,

Willard and Marguerite Beecher note: "Only the free and equal can cooperate. It is obviously impossible for a master and a slave to cooperate with each other. Neither is free of the other, and the behavior of the one is strictly limited by the behavior of the other. There is no dominance-submission, superiority-inferiority, leader-follower or parent-child relationship based on dependence that does not deny and destroy personal initiative and prevent true cooperation from taking place. Since cooperation can take place only between equal partners, neither of which has abdicated his own initiative to the other, it is so rare that we seldom see it. But there is no relationship that is fit for a human being short of full cooperation. There is no such thing as a good master or a good slave."

DEPENDENT VERSUS INDEPENDENT FRIENDSHIP

The dependent friendship is one that mutually enslaves, and therefore prevents each individual in the relationship from reaching his or her full potential. This may involve one person dependent on the other, or two people mutually interdependent, and thus unable to function fully outside the relationship. A nourishing, independent friendship is one that fosters individuality for each person, with each person accepting the other's differences and encouraging the other's personal growth.

DICK AND MICHAEL

Dick and Michael were inseparable friends. They were both twenty-five, and went everywhere together. They worked together as maintenance men at the local airport. They usually took their vacations together, and often double-dated. Dick was very happy with his life, but Michael wanted more for himself than a job as an airplane maintenance man. He wanted to go to flight engineering school. Dick kept trying to talk him out of this, and was threatened by this ambition of Michael's, which he saw as endangering the relationship. It would be a night school program, involving four nights a week. Four nights when Dick and Michael were usually together. It was more important to Michael to get some education and improve himself than to spend those four nights playing and relaxing with Dick. But the relationship was important to

Michael, too, and he didn't want to risk its coming to an end, so he kept on putting off his decision. Meanwhile, at a subconscious level, he was blaming Dick for his not getting ahead. And Dick was feeling this hidden resentment, so that their times together were no longer as much fun. They were both trapped in their interdependent roles. This kind of friendship always evokes resentment and stagnation.

KAREN AND JANET

Karen and Janet were two attractive women in their early thirties. They had gone to college together and been friends ever since. They were both teachers, in the same high school. Karen was single, and Janet had been married and divorced. Karen was very happy in her job and enjoyed her family, and the man she was dating. Janet was becoming more and more frustrated and felt ready for a major change. She was presented with an opportunity to work for a year in Europe. She was hesitant about leaving her familiar surroundings and her best friend. Karen said, "Look, Jan, it's only for a year, and it's the opportunity of a lifetime! You know it's just what you need right now to clear the cobwebs out, and I can always visit you during the summer. And you might even meet a mysterious and romantic foreign agent!" So, with lots of encouragement and bantering back and forth, the interaction between Karen and Janet helped Janet make a positive decision for herself, and she took the offer. Karen did get to Europe for the summer, and liked it so much she moved there herself when Janet got a chance to renew her own contract. This mutually supportive relationship fostered individuality and presented each person with new opportunities for growth and personal exploration.

RACKETS

Many dependent and interdependent friendships involve what are called "rackets" in Transactional Analysis. These rackets are behavior and feeling patterns people repeat in order to manipulate others and indulge themselves in feelings of guilt, inadequacy, fear, and resentment.

TA therapist Marta Vago says, "Many friendships are built on complementary rackets. Some TA therapists recognize two basic racket positions. One is 'helpless' and the other is 'helpful.' Many friendships are built on the premise that one person sees himself as 'helpless' or plays 'helpless,' while the other sees himself as 'helpful' or plays 'helpful.' In a friendship between Susie and Mary, Susie always is fraught with problems. She cannot manage. Her husband is a bum. Her children are nasty. And her mother-in-law is a bitch. One of the ways she relates to Mary is by calling Mary up and saying, 'Oh, Mary, Mary, I'm so helpless! I don't know what to do with this. I'm very upset! I can't deal with my children. I can't deal with my husband. I can't deal with my mother-in-law. And everything's driving me crazy.' Then Mary says, 'Oh, poor dear, why don't you get a baby-sitter? Why not talk to your mother-in-law . . . blah, blah, blah. . . .' To which Susie says, 'Yes, that's a good idea, but it won't work because . . .'

Ms. Vago's colleague, Dr. Bart Knapp, notes, "Anything that Mary suggests, Susie has an answer of why it won't work."

And Marta Vago continues, "But while Susie's being helpless and Mary's being helpful, they're maintaining their friendship. Nothing ever gets done, of course, because Susie's not going to take Mary's suggestions. After all, if she took Mary's suggestions, she might be able to solve her problems, and then she wouldn't have an excuse to call up Mary. If Mary gets tired of giving helpful suggestions, and either withdraws or gets angry because she feels she's being taken advantage of, then Susie will get very annoyed and will act on her annoyance by getting angry back at Mary, or will sulk. And Mary may hear from other friends later on that Susie has been telling mutual friends, 'I don't know what happened to Mary. She used to be so nice, but she's not nice anymore because she doesn't seem to care about all my trials and tribulations.' At the point where Mary opts out of being helpful, she is actually breaking the 'rules' of the friendship, and Susie gets very upset, and it may mark the end of the friendship."

Dr. Bart Knapp adds, "I guess it's necessary to look at Susie's being angry, or sulking, as the final hook that she is tossing out, the final bait to hook Mary. The penultimate response before they split. Once more, in either case, Susie is saying, 'I'm helpless, you're doing something to me, and I want you to make it all right.' And if Mary continues as she has in the past, if she doesn't remember that she's breaking out of this role of being helpful, she's very likely to fall back into it. In effect, Mary has now done something that Susie's responding to, so Susie's problem is no longer outside of the relationship, it's now within the relationship."

Marta Vago concludes, "So while Susie starts out by complaining to Mary about all the injustices in the world that have been piled on her, as Mary becomes impatient with her own helpfulness, there occurs a here-and-now replay between the two of them of what Susie's experiencing outside the relationship. A replay of Susie's feeling helpless and unappreciated, and not cared for. Putting the responsibility on Mary to solve it, rather than looking at herself to see why she has all these trials and tribulations. Now, Mary has to prove her friendship, and the only way she can prove her friendship is by constantly helping out Susie. By definition, then, at the point where she stops being helpful, she's not being a friend. These things can get very very sticky. The more a friendship is based on one person being 'helpless' and the other being 'helpful,' the more threatened the relationship is if either one of them switch. If, let's say, Susie decides one fine day that she isn't helpless anymore, let's say through therapy, Mary then may be out of a job. And if Mary stops being helpful, in a sense this puts Susie out of a job."

This example really lies at the heart of a major friendship obstacle, or at least an obstacle to a healthy friendship. TA helps illuminate the issues in many ways. For instance, when Susie stays in her role of "helpless" and Mary stays in her role of "helpful," they are engaging in a series of complementary transactions, each responding the way the other expected them to. If Mary announces she isn't going to help Susie, you have a cross-transaction, one in which the response is an unexpected one.

In terms of the existential positions, Susie is saying to Mary, "*You're OK, I'm not OK.*" And Mary is agreeing with her by being helpful, saying, "*I'm OK, you're not OK.*" As soon as Mary says she can't help Susie, she doesn't know the answers, she doesn't know what Susie should do, she's changing the rules of the game.

"HELPLESS"-"HELPFUL" FRIENDSHIPS

Can you see where either you or your friend ever play "helpless"-"helpful" in any of your relationships? Of course, sometimes you are going to ask for help or advice; sometimes you are going to feel down, unhappy, angry, and seek the comfort a good friend can provide. Can you see the difference between these occasional requests and the kind of pattern evident in the preceding example of Mary and Susie's friendship? If this leaning of one person on the other becomes a habit, it quickly diminishes the friendship into a series of manipulative maneuvers that have little to do with two human beings caring for each other. So look over your list of friends and decide for yourself whether this kind of dependency exists in any of these relationships. If it does, one way to change the rules of the game is to come up with unexpected responses. The next time a friend asks you for help, and you really feel you can't provide it, simply say, "I'm sorry, I can't help you with that." If this disrupts the friendship, or if your friend becomes angry and upset, chances are you were in a "helpless"-"helpful" trap.

Think about how you would feel if you asked a friend to help you, and the friend said, "I still care for you, but I just can't help you now." Would you want to end the friendship, or could you understand your friend's position? Are all your friendships based on the premise that a friend will always give you what you want? Or do you have relationships that allow both persons to please themselves first, and if they can also please each other, then they do so. You can clearly see here the connection between the Gestalt concept of "I please me, and you please you, and if enough of the time, we please each other. . . ." It's the exact opposite of a "helpless"-"helpful" relationship.

FRIENDSHIP SCRIPTS

There are four main areas of application in Transactional Analysis. They are Structural Analysis, which explores the individual's personality, feelings, and thoughts; Transactional Analysis, which looks at the individual's transactions with others; Game Analysis, which looks at transactions, or "games," with ulterior motives; and Script Analysis, which explores and defines the specific life scripts that people live out in their daily dramas.

There will be no attempt here to present a comprehensive picture of Script Analysis on these few pages. But briefly, you may have a greater understanding of your friendship patterns and the ways in which other people relate to you if you understand that each of us lives by a certain set of preconceived notions known as a life script.

Our scripts start at birth, since we are born into certain ethnic, cultural, and societal conditions which require certain standards of behavior and carry with them certain traditions. If you are a Jewish male, for instance, your life script will include circumcision at infancy. Your parents add to this script by giving you certain direct and indirect information. By the time you are ready to start making decisions for yourself about your life, and how to go about living it, you are already preprogrammed with a lot of dialogue and stage direction which tend to narrow your choices.

For example, most of us have some idea of whether or not we want to fall in love and get married, and to what type of person, before we ever begin to go out with members of the opposite sex. Your parents may have invited you into a script which calls for the earning of lots of money, drumming into you over the years the desirability of this path. So, rather than deciding on a career that could give you satisfaction, you pick one that is most likely to bring the greatest financial rewards. Or, if you are a woman, a career may not even be part of the script. Marriage and family are featured, with no allowance for alternatives. The problem with scripts is that they don't let you freely choose the path that feels best for you. Scripts always involve three existential areas: who you are, your role in life, and who everyone else is in relation to you.

In friendships, scripts come into play mainly in this third area. Much of this scripting may have come from the way your parents related to their friends. Also, the destructive gender-role stereotypes probably had you playing mainly with members of the same sex, so that even today you may not feel comfortable having a member of the opposite sex as a friend on a nonsexual basis.

SAM AND CAROLE

Sam and Carole worked in the same office. They really enjoyed each other's company. Neither was sexually attracted to the other, and they each had fulfilling love relationships with others. Sam would have liked to spend some time with Carole outside the office, but was afraid she would get the wrong impression, and he didn't want to hurt her feelings by letting her know he was not sexually attracted. She would have liked to invite him to dinner, but was afraid he would think her too forward, and didn't want him to think she was offering sex with dinner. Two potential friends, locked into their stereotyped scripts, never got to give each other the nourishment they were each capable of providing.

SWITCHING ROLES

Each of us, from time to time, puts on a performance. You are not always playing the same role. When you attend a social function, you may put on another face and take on another role than when you are at work or at home.

TONY

Tony was a hard-driving, aggressive executive. At home, he was gentle and loving. Those friends he made through his job tended to be aggressive, and the things shared with them included basketball games, bar-hopping, and playing cut-throat poker. The friends he made in his role as a home-loving father and husband tended to be in similar roles, and they shared picnics with the family, quiet games of Scrabble, listening to music, going out to dinner, etc. It was as though Tony were two different people. Two different stages, home and work, and so, two different scripts. And the friends from each conformed to the script demands. But Tony's friendships were mostly superficial in both areas. For example, he never invited his friends from the office to his home, and he never got to see their quiet side. His friends from home were people he never let see the aggressive part of him. He kept each set of friends separate, but also, in effect, he was keeping them separate from the whole person he actually was. This whole person could not emerge, and the way in which he chose friends and related to them encouraged and supported this fragmentation in his personality.

The danger of rigid scripts is that they don't allow you to experience who you really are at all levels of awareness.

If you rigidly live a very specific script, chances are your friends will all be supporting players rather than costars. Even if you look for costars, you won't be able to find any emotionally healthy individuals willing to live someone else's script.

Realization that you are living out certain preconceived scripts can lead you to examine whether the script of the moment really fits in with who you are at the moment, and if it doesn't, you can make script changes.

Check out whether you have chosen your friends to support you in a specific script. If so, then when you change your script, or become aware of it, you may very well have to leave these friends.

Marta Vago notes, "One thing that happens almost invariably as we work with people in treatment is that the friends they had when they entered treatment are not the friends they have by the time they leave treatment. This is a very clear indication of how good therapy can influence the way the person comes on in the world, and because of that, how they will hook up with different people. So someone, let's say, who's been playing 'helpful,' and collecting all the nogoodniks in the world in order to rescue them, as they stop playing 'helpful,' all of a sudden they find that their friends are no longer helpless, poor people who can't make it on their own. So the friendships very often change. And people often express great concern that, 'My God, I used to be so friendly with all these people! I've known them for years. I just can't be around them anymore.' Often they feel guilty about the fact that they don't feel as close to these old friends or as comfortable with them. And it takes a lot of working through to recognize that they don't necessarily need the same friends anymore. They don't need to have the same kinds of people around for their own sense of *OKness*. So, very definitely, friendship is a barometer of where you are with yourself. When you have had a shift in the kind of people you're having as friends, you can assume that some basic personality change has taken place."

BASIC PREMISE

Since the basic premise of this book is that your friends are a direct reflection of your emotional status, let's isolate that last sentence from Ms. Vago:

> *When you have had a shift in the kind of people you're having as friends, you can assume that some basic personality change has taken place.*

FRIENDS AND CHANGES

A useful exercise in self-exploration will be to see how the changes in the types of friends you choose coincide with basic changes in your personality and life-style. Make a list, dividing your life into different areas, perhaps four or five in all. This might be according to chronological age, to major personality shifts, or to major changes. Then list some of the friends you had in each area.

A sample list might look like this:

Age 1–12 Friendly and playful. Jim. Terry. Sid. Marvin.

Age 12–19 Shy and nervous. Sid. Harold. Mark.

Age 20–30 Learning. Starting to relate to women. Jules. Sid. Richie.

Age 30–35 Creatively successful. Hammond. Stephen. Neil. Charles.

This is just one way of doing it. Choose a way that makes sense to you. The idea is to see what kinds of different friends you may have had during different stages of your life. It's useful to put down some personality description for yourself during that period. At times you might see a direct relationship between the shift in friends and a change in your personality and emotional needs. In the chapter Room to Grow, we'll explore this relationship more thoroughly. But be aware that there is no need to feel guilty when you find yourself needing to move on to new friends. This is a natural and healthy development, coinciding with change and growth in your life.

LIVING LOVE FRIENDSHIPS

Ken Keyes, Jr., is a philosopher and teacher, author of the *Handbook to Higher Consciousness*, an underground bestseller, and founder of the Living Love Center in Berkeley, California. He calls his system simply Living Love. While it is a system aimed at moving people toward higher consciousness, in the Eastern tradition, it also incorporates some of the basic tenets of humanistic psychology and a very rational-logical approach. Living Love sees all problems, all suffering, as being the direct result of our "addictions". And that the task in growth and becoming happy and healthy is to upgrade as many of these addictions as possible to "preferences," where you can still want these things in your life, but don't get angry, upset, sad, and depressed when you don't have them.

Keyes sees the primary addictions as having to do with security, sensation, and power. If you have a *security addiction*, you might find most of your time and energy devoted to a running battle with the outside world in order to get what you want for your personal security, whether it be food, shelter, money, or whatever. A person who is caught up in a security addiction might tend to choose only those friends who could fill some kind of security need.

If you have a *sensation addiction*, you are mainly concerned with providing yourself with more and better pleasurable sensations and activities. For many people this would focus on sex. For instance, a person hung up in this area might only choose friends who could provide access to desirable sex partners. Other sensation addictions might involve food, music, etc.

If you have a *power addiction,* you are mainly concerned with dominating people and situations, manipulating and controlling. A person caught up in a power addiction would probably surround himself with people whom he could easily control or dominate.

Keyes says, "Usually, what you've done is simply picked friends because they enhance your security, sensation, and power trip. You're not really tuning into a human being so much as just seeing in that human being what you desire from that human being to help you in your security, sensation, and power trip. Seeing in a human being that which will negatively affect your security, sensation, and power trips would lead you to try to stay away from that human being. What most people are after in a friend is someone who's caught up in the same games and addictions. We select our friends because they're on the same brand of security stuff, and we feel we understand them. Or the same type of sex trip, the same type of power trip, and all of this is just staying trapped. It's not enough, it's not deeply satisfying."

SECURITY ADDICTION FRIENDSHIP

Let's look at the friendship of Jerome and Kevin. Jerome has a serious security addiction. He is striving to get ahead, and his moderate income and lack of material possessions causes him a great deal of distress. He really likes Kevin, but Kevin is broke and happy. Jerome finds this intolerable. Kevin's uninhibited attitude about money drives Jerome up the wall, for he sees it as the most dangerous form of irresponsibility. Also, of course, if Kevin doesn't have money, and seems to have a good life anyway, this endangers Jerome's whole life theme. Jerome gets so uptight around Kevin that they no longer can be friends. He now seeks someone whose main goal in life is, like his, the achievement of wealth.

There is nothing wrong with wanting a lot of money. Where it becomes emotionally destructive, and an addiction, is when the absence of a lot of money creates discomfort, anxiety, and uptightness. For example, suppose you want a great deal of wealth, and from the age of eighteen you really worked toward this, not really having a moment of satisfaction until you finally are successful at the age of thirty-eight. That's twenty years down the drain! And there's a good chance that the financial success won't ever make up for those lost years. You can't usually start enjoying life at thirty-eight if you haven't had the practice and experience of ever enjoying it before. Which is why many people who achieve financial success after great sacrifice, and the sublimation of all other needs, usually continue to work primarily at making money the rest of their lives. It's all they've learned to do. How much more sensible a course if you decided at eighteen to go after financial success, but also to savor life fully on the way. But you have to believe that is possible, and back to TA, you may have a "script" that says financial success comes only after great personal sacrifice and a lot of hard work with no pleasure.

GIVING UP FRIENDSHIP DEMANDS

Your addictions will make you demand certain things from your friends. Ken Keyes, Jr., likes to talk about unconditional love. Reaching out to people without conditions, without demands. He says, "The way you have friends is by giving up the demands that separate you from people. If you don't have friends, the problem is totally in your head. The whole problem of friendship simply lies in giving up these boxes that you're enclosed in, these emotion-backed demands. I'll only have friends, real friends, to the extent that I give up my inner demands for security, sensation, and power. That's what makes us go into illusory friendships. You create friends in your own head, you don't find them out there. It is your addictions that determine whether, in the drama of life, you will see a person as a friend or not. And the course of that friendship is totally determined by the interweaving of your addictions and the other person's addictions. The game of friendship is simply to continually give up everything that separates you, every demand that separates you from flowing in love and oneness with your friend. And what you're giving up is simply that which keeps you from enjoying friendship; you're not giving up anything worthwhile. Furthermore, the giving up is not an external action, it's an internal one. Suppose, for example, your friend has difficulty sleeping, and he or she likes to call you up at three o'clock in the morning, and you get uptight over that because you really like your sleep. What you give up is that part of your programming, your conditioning, that makes you irritated when that person calls. You get into a space where you can love that person regardless of when they call. You don't get angry or convey hostility when that happens. At the same time, you are very free to say to that person, 'Look, I really don't like your calling me up, and I guess if you keep doing that, whenever I really need a night of sleep, I'm just going to take my phone off the hook. It just doesn't seem to fit my pattern to have you call me late at night, so don't call me.' What you have given up is this emotion-backed demand that triggers hostility and anger, fear and jealousy, and all these negative emotions, but you are still free to communicate in a loving way, 'Say, I don't like this way of doing it, I'd rather have it the other way.' The beautiful thing is that human beings, when it's done openly and honestly like this, are remarkably accepting of whatever drama, however unusual it may be, that you want to play."

Do you demand certain things from your friends? Make a list headed I Demand from My Friends. Complete this list as honestly as possible. Remember, none of us is ever free of all of our addictions, as defined by the Living Love system. We have our whole lives to work toward turning them into preferences. This work can be a joyful experience, as can be all growth. Understanding that you do have certain addictions can make every instance in which you feel uptight a real learning and growing experience, for each uptight feeling can be a message to you to pay attention, for here is an addiction you can work on.

Ken's ideal of friendship may seem hard to achieve, but for many people who have experienced the Living Love system through Ken's books, at workshops in Berkeley and around the country, and at the Consciousness Growth Intensives at Cornucopia in Miami, based on his work, it works well. Ken says, "It's my experience that as long as you have an addiction, a demand, a need for other human beings to make it in life, it won't work, it won't be enough, because you will grasp them too heavily. You will manipulate them because you will view them as the source of your happiness. You'll have to control them, just to keep them close to you. You'll have to make sure they don't start doing things that upset you. You've destroyed their freedom. And all of this tends to make the friendship deteriorate into a barter/game type of relationship, which has in it the seeds of disillusion. It's only when you don't need friends that you truly are tuning in to every possible meaning of friendship. You can't be addicted to friendship, otherwise you grasp it and destroy it. As long as you have to have friends to be happy, it won't work. When you don't need friends, you live in an ocean of friendships which is completely satisfying. The game is to feel a loving friendship with everyone, regardless of whether they're doing the dance that you're doing. It's playing games if you only feel close to people who are doing the waltz. The thing is to just tune in and love everybody, behind all the dances that we are trapped in. Love everyone unconditionally, but of course you'll dance with the people who want to do the dance that you're doing. In other words, if I'm doing the waltz, and if you want to do the waltz, then we'll do the waltz together. Otherwise, you do the polka, and I still love you just as much as if you're waltzing, but we won't be spending as much time together."

ACCEPTANCE

This is the key word. Acceptance. Being able to accept other people, even though they aren't doing the same things you are doing, even if they aren't doing what you want them to do. You may choose to spend most of your time "dancing" with the people who are doing the dance you are doing, but if you shut out all the other people, you are putting strong limitations on your own potential. Do you think of yourself as an accepting person? Can you really accept a friend who is in a different space from you? If you are in a profession or a white-collar job, can you even consider making friends with a waitress or a truck driver? As a research project, a well-known psychologist, who wishes to remain anonymous, took a job as a garbage collector. He found himself in some deeply satisfying relationships with other garbage collectors, people whom he would never have considered associating with in his role as a psychologist. And the garbage collectors would never have associated with him if they had known his real role. He came to the conclusions that most people paint themselves into these small corners of existence, and thus build their own prisons of isolation from all who don't fit in with their narrow preconceptions of what is acceptable.

The Living Love system makes a lot of sense to a lot of psychologists because it *is* so rational-logical. It doesn't ask the impossible. It merely suggests that you can be happier if you start giving up your addictions and demands, not the things you are addicted to, but the addiction itself. If you are addicted to a Rolls-Royce you own, then you are constantly worrying about it being stolen or dented. When you give up that addiction, you can just enjoy the car, and you can also still take every precaution necessary to ensure its safety.

Whenever a friend seems to cause you anxiety, realize you are causing yourself the anxiety because of some addiction you have. As Ken Keyes, Jr., puts it, "No one can upset you. No one can irritate you, no matter what they do. They can only direct certain energy toward you, which you pick up with your forms of perception, and feed into your brain, or biocomputer, and then, if you have addictions that make you reject those patterns of energy, you proceed to trigger uptightness, anger, fear, jealousy, or whatever. So no one can get you uptight; it's only you that can get you uptight. If you are taking in the other person's energy, what they say and do, and you are experiencing it with love and oneness, then you just get high together. And there's nothing that anyone can do involving you, when you are perceiving their patterns, their actions, their words, that you can't use in one way or another to help yourself grow. We're all here to help each other grow into higher consciousness. The way in which we interact is a part of helping each other grow."

GROWING FRIENDSHIPS

Is the way you interact with your friends helping you grow? There are many ways to look at this. And they all sort of fit together. The Gestalt concept of each person pleasing himself in a relationship really fits in with the *I'm OK, you're OK* existential position of Transactional Analysis, and they both are highly compatible with the Living Love concept of addiction-free friendship and unconditional love. Now it's up to you to decide how to best use whatever awareness you have picked up from these initial explorations into these therapies and systems. Any one of them can give you insight, but what you do with that insight is up to you. Of course, just learning that you are operating with certain negative behavior patterns can make you more aware, and modify your future behavior. Growth, at best, is a gradual process. You may choose to explore the three approaches more thoroughly. Check the annotated bibliography for the names of books to help you do this. This chapter has been filled with a lot of material, a lot of words. Don't try to absorb them all at once. You may choose, in a leisurely fashion, to go back and review some of these concepts, and see how they apply to your specific situation. It's a good idea, whenever you are anxious or uptight in a situation involving a friend, to come back and see if you can pick up some guidelines, to at least understand why you are feeling the way you do, and how you might move toward alleviating that anxiety or uptightness. Remember, all such negative feelings are self-induced because of your expectations, demands, and life scripts. These can all be changed or eliminated. It is all up to you.

Finish the sentence "One new thing I've learned about my friends is the fact that ———." Examine how you feel about this, and go on to the next chapter.

CHAPTER 6

FROM MANIPULATION TO FRIENDLY ASSERTIVENESS

"Many friendships are not really friendships at all, but manipulations." With this statement, Dr. Gerald Walker Smith points to a major problem in human interaction. A lot of energy that could be applied in nourishing ways to relationships is instead wasted on either trying to manipulate other people or in trying to prevent oneself from being manipulated.

Someone trying to manipulate a friend is really making several self-statements:

1. *"I don't have what I want, and can get it from my friend."*
2. *"I can force my friend to give me what I want."*
3. *"I cannot openly ask my friend for what I want."*

Statement one is part of the pervasive cultural belief that says we get happiness from external sources. It is indicative of the same conditions that produced our current pill-popping mania, the concept that "I can't help myself, and therefore must get what I need from other things and other people." In one of the most provocative opening sentences ever to appear in a book, Dr. Eileen Walkenstein, in *Beyond The Couch*, said, "Listen, we're living in an age in America when everyone wants to suck a tit and not enough mamas are offering." One of the main factors inherent in the emotional makeup of any manipulator is a feeling of impotence.

Statement two is one of the great misconceptions of human relations. The fact is that you can never force another person to give you what you want without either giving up your own power or integrity, or damaging the relationship, or damaging yourself to such an extent that you won't be able to appreciate what you want when you get it.

Statement three leads to one of the basic ways in which all manipulators operate. By lying. Without lies, there can be no manipulation. Sometimes the lie is subtle, other times gross, but it is always there. This is perhaps the basic difference between manipulation and

Friendly Assertiveness, which is simply being able to ask for what you want directly and openly, without resorting to games, lies, and manipulation. A poor sense of self-esteem lies at the root of the manipulator's problem, since he or she feels that asking openly for what is wanted would produce refusal on the part of the friend, quite often because the manipulator doesn't feel he deserves to get what he wants. Dr. Everett Shostrom, in his book *Man, The Manipulator*, says of these people, "The manipulator is a Junior God who tries to run his life and others by control and manipulation. He has a deeply rooted attitude of distrust in himself and others." Also, the person who can't be open in asking for what he or she wants is reflecting an inability to be open in sharing any kind of feelings, which constitutes a formidable barrier to healthy relating. People often manipulate because asking directly for what they want might reveal deep feelings they are unwilling to reveal, either because they feel their friends would find those feelings unacceptable or because they themselves find their feelings unacceptable.

Not asking for what they want is often how people with poor self-images avoid the risk of rejection. Not declaring what they don't want is another way nonassertive people fall into manipulation, and into lying.

Some manipulative sentences:

"I can't make it Tuesday night, I have an important business meeting."

This is the kind of manipulative excuse-lie that often occurs between people. The person making that statement may just feel like being alone on Tuesday night, or another friend may be suddenly available and that friend is higher up on the friendship priority list, or any of a dozen other reasons that have nothing to do with a business meeting. If a friend does this to you, what he or she is saying is that you can't handle the truth, you won't be willing to accept that your friend has other priorities, that your friendship is contingent on not being refused what you want unless business or illness or some other "valid" excuse intervenes. If you *have* been unable to accept your friend's honest statements in the past, you may have triggered the manipulation, but the person who lies is always responsible for the manipulative act.

"Would you like to go see the John Wayne movie?"

If you've used sentences like this one, start realizing that they are dishonest. First and foremost, *you* want to go see that movie, so you really want to make a statement, not ask a question. Something like "I want to see the John Wayne movie, and I would like your company, so would you be willing to go with me?" Can you see the difference between the two sentences? Again, it's the difference between manipulation and Friendly Assertiveness. It may seem an unimportant difference, a very slight change in semantics, but words have tremendous emotional impact on us, and the use of the language is the way you often express emotional strengths and emotional weaknesses. By not declaring your wants straight out, and trying to disguise them as concern for the other person, you degrade both yourself and your friend. It can also lead to the kind of game-playing that has you making trivial situations major issues in your relationship. Saying, in effect, "If you were my friend, you would want to see the John Wayne movie with me."

"*Oh, maybe Thursday night. I'll give you a call if I can see you then.*"

Consistent unwillingness to make specific time commitments is another favorite manipulator's ploy. Or consistently being late for appointments, or consistently canceling appointments. All of these are saying to you that the manipulator believes his or her time is more valuable than yours, and you have nothing better to do than wait around. It is one way those people who feel impotent or powerless maintain an illusion of power over others. And if you buy into the manipulation by going along with it, then you sustain that illusion, and even reinforce it. You encourage their manipulation by allowing them to perpetuate the illusion. These are people who care for their own comfort and convenience much more than they care for you as a friend. It's almost as if they are saying, "I'll spend time with you if I have nothing better to do." You may also be perpetuating your own illusion of inferiority by allowing yourself to be manipulated in this way.

These are just some of the subtle ways in which many people manipulate others. Most of us are manipulators at one time or another. Chances are you have been guilty of some form of manipulation every time you have tried to get something you wanted from another person without believing it would be as much to their advantage as to yours for them to grant your request.

"YOU'VE GOT IT, I WANT IT"

Among the many interpersonal exercises in his book *Awareness*, John O. Stevens has one called "You've got it, I want it." You might try playing it with some of your friends. You sit down with a friend, and one of you imagines the other has something he or she wants, without saying what that something is. The partner who is imagining he or she has this something responds to the other partner's demand of "I want it" perhaps by initially replying, "I won't give it to you." The person who wants it keeps on asking for it, and the partner who has it keeps on refusing, maintains this dialogue for four or five minutes, back and forth. Then you switch roles. It's a game designed to show you how you go after things and how you respond when other people are going after something of yours. It's an excellent way to see whether you operate through manipulation.

Think about the last time someone you know had something you wanted, or could provide you with some nourishment or service you desired. How did you go about asking for it? Directly? Honestly? Or did you use dishonesty and subterfuge? You might look over your entire list of friends, and see how you operate in this area. Also, how your friends go about asking for what they want from you.

There are a lot of variations on the "You've got it, I want it" theme. Here are some of the possible ways you might be interacting with your friends on this issue:

"You've got it, I want it."
"You've got it, I deserve it, I want it."
"You've got it, I don't deserve it, I still want it."
You've got it, help me learn how to get it for myself."
"You've got it, I've got it, let us share."
"You've got it, I've got it, let us each keep our own."
"I've got it, you haven't got it, and you can't have it."
"I've got it, I'll help you get it for yourself."
"I've got it, you can have it if you do what I want."
"I haven't got it, you haven't got it, let's look for it together."
"I haven't got it, you haven't got it, let's suffer together."

Can you recognize any of your attitudes or responses, or those of your friends, in any of these existential statements?

A WAY OF LIFE

Manipulation can be a way of life, living a script that says if you don't control others, they will control you and prevent you from getting what you want. Some of the ways in which the manipulator lives this script are very indirect, and cannot always be immediately identified as manipulation. These include:

Suffering manipulation. The suffering manipulator uses guilt by seeing to your comfort at the expense of his or her own. This person might use statements such as "Don't worry about me, do what you want." Or: "It's all right, I don't expect any thanks." Or: "Go enjoy yourself, I'll find something to do." This is often the way a manipulative parent controls children. There's the old story about the son who married a girl of a different faith or color, and phoned his mother to tell her and to announce that he and his new wife would now be looking for a place to live. The mother says, "You don't have to do that, there's plenty of room for both of you right here at home." The son is amazed at her acceptance of the situation, and says, "How can you say that? You're always complaining about how crowded the house is." The mother responds, "That's OK, you can use my room—because as soon as I hang up, I'm going to go stick my head in the oven!"

Emotion-stifling manipulation. This person manipulates you by cutting off your emotions, thus discounting your feelings. This may include such statements as "Don't cry, it's all right, there's always a silver lining." Or: "Why are you so angry over such a silly little thing?" Or: "Sad? How can you be sad when there are so many beautiful things in your life?" The emotion-stifling manipulator tries to tell you that your feelings are insignificant, not worthy of expression and, finally, that he or she is not willing to hear them. Usually this type of manipulator is also the kind of person who cannot express or fully experience deep feelings of his own. A father telling his son "Don't cry, grow up!" is also manipulating through this form of control.

Baiting manipulation. There are all kinds of ways manipulators use to get you hooked, to get you involved in their problems, to get your attention, to distract you from your own issues. This includes the person who is always interrupting his own sentences. For example: "I think that we should really do something wild and— Oh, never mind!" You respond, "What? What should we do?" And he says, "Never mind, it's not important." And he either never tells you or springs it on you after you've built up so much anxiety that you're hardly likely to reject the idea. This baiting manipulator likes to control all conversations, and will often interrupt your thoughts or change the subject to maintain control. Another favorite stunt this person uses is to pretend not to hear you.

One of the nation's top therapists, Harry Sloan, will announce to a therapy group that he is going to give instructions for an exercise only one time, so they had better listen. Otherwise, he says, there will invariably be someone who asks him to repeat himself, and thus gets the attention of the entire group. Another form of baiting manipulation is to do something outlandish, or say something shocking, or wear something different or blatantly revealing. If you are someone who is somewhat uncomfortable about your body and nudity, then a woman friend can manipulate you by wearing a dress that exposes a good deal of her breasts. Or, if you are sensitive to four-letter words, someone can manipulate you with very blunt language. Or, if you are rather shy and modest, a friend can manipulate and embarrass you by shouting in public or by trying to get you to join in a wild dance. And the manipulator using these techniques can then make you feel guilty for your discomfort, saying, "You're just not with it; you're old-fashioned; you've got to loosen up and enjoy yourself!" And you might agree with him, but that doesn't take away from the fact that you have been manipulated. This person has, at some level, intentionally caused you discomfort or embarrassment in an area in which he knows he feels more comfortable than you do.

Undeclared expectations manipulation. This lies at the core of the difference between manipulation and Friendly Assertiveness. It's a situation in which your friend has certain expectations about what you are going to give or do for them, and doesn't tell you what they are, and gets angry or sad when you don't deliver. In effect, this person is saying to you, "If you cared for me, you'd be able to read my mind." These expectations quite often involve what the manipulator sees as certain rigid standards of behavior for a friend. These self-statements might include: "A friend will call at least twice a week" or "A friend will never be too busy to see me" or "A friend will always feel warm and loving when I need it." But the undeclared expectations are left undeclared, and you are hooked into feeling guilty when you don't live up to them. And you really don't have the opportunity even to choose whether or not you want to meet these demands, because you usually don't find out about them until it's too late, at least according to the manipulator!

NOT ASKING IS MANIPULATION

Thus, not telling someone you need something from him can be one of the most destructive forms of manipulation of all, to both parties. The manipulator doesn't get what he or she wants or needs, and the manipulatee, to coin a new word, gets to feel guilty or becomes the target of hostility and resentment. Dr. Leo Buscaglia, author of *Love*, and creator of the Love course at the University of Southern California, covered this issue with a story he told in a talk entitled "What Is Essential Is Invisible to the Eye."

> There are people in this room, I know, who are dying of loneliness. You know, we have a fantastic façade: We don't need. And we really don't know how to tell people we *need.* God, don't you sometimes think about the people you could save, if they could only let you know? How can we turn on to them? I remember in Love class, one of the most significant things that ever happened was one night when a dog walked in. You know, a crazy old stray dog walked into Love class! And we don't ever turn anyone out of Love class! But this dog came walking through, and an amazing thing about it, as I watched, every single person in that room loved that dog. They patted him. And his tail was just wagging away! He was telling everybody, "Boy, is this neat! I found the kooky classroom I've been looking for!" And they were holding him. One thing, though, they were trying to hold that dog, and you know the wonderful thing about it? The damn dog wouldn't let them hold him! He'd stay there just long enough to be hugged a little bit and split, to the next one, to the next one, to the next one, sharing everything with everybody. It was outrageous! Watching the dynamics, you know. And all of a sudden one of the girls yelled, "Dammit!" You know, we pay attention to feelings like that! And so we turned around and we looked at her. We said, "What's the matter?" And she said, "Here I am, sitting here, dying of loneliness to have somebody touch me, and nobody touches me. A stray dog walks in and everybody touches him!" And one guy says very simply, "Well, maybe it's because you haven't told us that you need us." And I know some of you are saying, "We shouldn't have to!" You know, we're not mindreaders! We might be great carers, but if you're going to walk around looking like the Rock of Gilbraltar, no

one's going to take a pickax to get to you! I always say, if you want to be loved, you have to be *lovable!* You have to show your vulnerability. So you know what this girl did? She got on all fours and she crawled through everybody! And everybody touched her! We're not so bad. Maybe we have to let people know that we *need.*

Some people manipulate others into reinforcing their own poor self-images, sometimes by playing helpless, as noted in the overview of Transactional Analysis in the last chapter. This could be called "passive manipulation." As soon as you are sucked in, as soon as you agree that this person is helpless, you have been manipulated. And some relationships involve two people playing this game, sometimes in some sick alternating rhythm. Dr. Gerald Walker Smith says, "I think that some grossly parasitic relationships last a whole lifetime because they stay in balance like two people on a teeter-totter, both of them sucking on each other at the same intensity. Therefore the relationship seems great. The problem with that kind of relationship is that it's quite fragile. If one of them starts to grow or change at all, the relationship can't stand it."

DEHUMANIZING MANIPULATION

Manipulators often don't have real friendships. In fact, it could be said that there is no such thing as a manipulative intimate friendship, since manipulation prevents intimacy and promotes distancing. Dr. Marjorie Toomim, a clinical psychologist in Los Angeles, says, "Some people use their friends as objects, and they eat them up, wear them out, and then they find somebody else to feed them. The names of their friends are interchangeable, and the process is always identical. They need to fill a certain need, and it doesn't matter who the person is that fills it. It isn't a person anymore, it's an object. Or, at most, a friend at a very minimal level."

One way you can check out whether you are using any of your friends as objects is to look at whether you really need this specific person, with this specific kind of personality, to fill the needs being filled by this friend. Or would any warm body do? Do you acknowledge the uniqueness of your friends? And appreciate it? Or could they all come off the assembly line, like a bunch of programmed robots? In fact, for a lot of people, many of the friends they have might as well be robots. They won't hear their feelings, and won't share their own. They avoid all real warmth and human contact. So another question to ask yourself is whether there are any of your friends that could be replaced by a sophisticated robot and still satisfy the needs you are letting them satisfy.

"BEING NICE" MANIPULATION

One of the prime ways in which people manipulate others, as well as allow themselves to be manipulated by others, is by avoiding the honest declaration of an opinion or a feeling in order not to hurt someone's feelings. The simple truth is that everyone doesn't have to like or love you, and the only way you are going to avoid hurting people's feelings is by either letting the whole world manipulate you or by becoming a hermit.

JEANNIE AND DAWN

Jeannie and Dawn worked for the same plastics firm. Jeannie had several close friends, and was living with the man she loved. Dawn was divorced and lonely, and didn't have any close friends. She wanted to be Jeannie's friend. Jeannie felt sorry for Dawn, and every time Dawn suggested they do something together, she'd come up with an excuse, ending with something like "Maybe some other time." What Jeannie really felt like telling Dawn was "I'm sorry you don't have any friends, but I have a full life and I just don't have time to be your friend." But Jeannie was afraid that this would upset Dawn, that Dawn couldn't handle this truth.

Now let's look at the real truth. Jeannie was manipulating Dawn, in the worst possible way. She was wasting the most precious possession of all: Dawn's time. By not being straightforward she allowed Dawn to keep on focusing on her as a potential friend, thus cutting off opportunities to approach and become friendly with other people. Dawn assumed that Jeannie did want to be her friend, but outside forces and circumstances had prevented its happening so far. This was a false assumption, a lie if you will, fostered by Jeannie's manipulative actions. Granted, Jeannie was operating from good intentions, but manipulation can occur even with good intentions. Jeannie was using Dawn to enhance her own image of herself as a "nice person." If she were honest with Dawn, it might temporarily create some disappointment, even sadness, but this would soon end, and Dawn would go on with her life, no longer tied down by her attraction to Jeannie. But Jeannie would not be able to think of herself as that nice person. So, in effect, Jeannie would suffer more from Jeannie's honesty than Dawn would. And deep down, at some subconscious level, Jeannie is aware of this. The nicest thing you can do for someone who is attracted to you, and who isn't a person you are able or want to spend time with, is let them know the truth, so they can begin immediately looking for someone who is willing to meet their needs.

How would you feel if you were a gold prospector, and you started digging on some land, near the land of an old prospector whom you greeted each day, and after six months of digging and finding nothing, the old man says, "Some fellows dug all that land up years ago. I could've told you there wasn't any gold there, but I didn't want to hurt your feelings or make you think you had poor judgment in picking a site"?

You'd be pretty angry at the old man, right? And no wonder! He could have prevented your wasting six months, six months in which you could perhaps have found gold at some other location. Can you see the analogy? So, if someone is digging for the gold of friendship in you, and you know there isn't any gold for them there, and you don't tell them because you don't want to hurt their feelings, you are missing a real opportunity to do them a lot of good by preventing them from wasting time, allowing them the freedom to dig elsewhere.

Oh, sure, someone you tell the truth to may not like you anymore, but so what? If you don't want to spend time with them, what do you care if they like you or not? But it's amazing how many people are hung up on having the whole world like them, even though they wouldn't want to relate to the whole world. This kind of attitude creates stagnation, indecision, and weakness. Look at the records of political figures who tried to be loved by everybody.

WAYS TO AVOID MANIPULATION

The best way to avoid manipulation is to use Friendly Assertiveness. Don't be angry or hostile, simply state what you want and what you don't want.

Deal with your feelings, and do what feels right for you, not what you believe other people expect of you, not what you think you should do, not what will get the other person to think you are nice.

And be aware of your emotions. Be aware of what you really want. You don't have to tell the whole truth, you don't have to be brutal, but let the other person know that you are going to do what you want to do, and if it comes to a choice of one of you being disappointed, you would rather it not be you! Jeannie could have told Dawn she didn't have time in her life for a new friend, which was the truth, without elaborating that she wouldn't find Dawn a suitable friend under any circumstances.

SITUATIONS YOU COULD HAVE AVOIDED

Look over your list of friends, and remember for each one a time in which you did not do what you really wanted to do, or a time when you said yes when you would have liked to say no. Remember the circumstances of these interactions as vividly as possible. Imagine how it would have turned out if you had used some Friendly Assertiveness. Would the friendship have ended? Would you have felt better? Would it have avoided misunderstandings that still persist?

Be aware that every time you don't honestly express yourself, you may be guilty of manipulation or control. At the very least you are depriving them of something that is indispensable to a real friendship; honest feedback. Even something so subtle as getting a compliment can produce manipulative behavior.

If someone says to you, "I like the way you look tonight," can you just respond with "Thank you" or do you have to tell them something nice in return? Or, even worse, do you say something like "Oh, I don't look so hot," thus making them feel both a liar and a fool? If you respond with a simple "Thank you" to a compliment, then you are exhibiting sensitivity equal to that of the person paying the compliment. You are acknowledging that you have similar taste, since you also like whatever it is your friend is complimenting, or you wouldn't be doing it. If, instead, you say, "Oh, it's not much," you are putting down your friend's taste and perceptiveness, and questioning his or her sincerity.

One of the best ways to insult somebody is by not graciously accepting an honest compliment.

And if you feel awkward and embarrassed about receiving compliments, then accept this as an indication that you need to work on your self-esteem. If you want to return a compliment, do it at some later point, after the glow of this one has been absorbed. Don't dilute a friend's compliment with one of your own. It's not a competition!

BEING APPRECIATED

And you know something? People really appreciate it when you don't allow them to manipulate you. Psychologists have found that people feel much warmer and more comfortable with assertive friends, friends who declare their boundaries, who say right out what they want and what they are not going to put up with. It saves a lot of time and energy that can be devoted to the nourishing parts of the friendship.

Counseling psychologist Dr. Judith Osgood says, "I've often had friends that I felt tried to manipulate me. One woman friend asked me for a ride to the airport. At the time I was living in San Diego, as she was, so I didn't know she meant the airport in Los Angeles. When she told me, I said, 'Well, I don't want to drive to Los Angeles. I prefer that you fly.' She got very upset with me, and she said, 'Well, what kind of friend are you? If you were going, I'd drive you.' Which is the kind of pressure that often gets put on people. I said, 'If I have to do what you want in order to be your friend, then I'd rather not be your friend.' She was really taken aback, and then realized what she'd been doing, and was extremely grateful. She said, 'I'm really glad you said that. I had no idea that I was pressuring you like that.' And we talked about it, and we're still friends. It's that kind of taking a stand, and not allowing manipulation, that leads to a healthy friendship. Because that attitude of 'I can say yes to you and I can say no to you; I don't have to please you all the time'—that's where the real deep appreciation comes from. When I know that I can't control you, and that you can't control me, yet we still really care about each other. I don't have to sacrifice myself to be your friend; I can be me and be your friend. And that means sometimes being with you when you want me to be, and it also means not being with you sometimes when you want me to be. Usually real friends get beyond expectations, and that's why real friendship has an enduring quality: there aren't any strings."

JUST ASK

Do you think your friends would appreciate you if you were to refuse to do something they wanted you to do, as long as you let them know you still cared for them and wanted to keep the friendship? This also is part of Friendly Assertiveness—reassuring people that you like them, even if you won't do what they request. Ask them. Ask a few of your friends whether you could say to them, in a pleasant tone of voice, "Hey, I really enjoy our friendship, but I really don't want to do that for you, and so I'm going to turn you down, but I hope it won't affect our friendship." You may be surprised at their willingness to accept a refusal from you.

WON'T INSTEAD OF CAN'T

Be honest when you refuse. Say, "I won't," or, "I choose not to do that right now," instead of "I can't do that." You can do anything you want, but you have certain priorities, and certain preferences, and you exercise your choice over these.

BETTY AND GEORGETTE

Betty and Georgette were good friends. Betty asked Georgette to baby-sit for her on a Thursday night, since her baby-sitter was sick and she couldn't find a replacement, and she had a date she really wanted to keep. Georgette said, "I'm sorry, I just can't do it. Something really important is happening that night, and I can't miss it." Betty accepted that explanation and finally made other arrangements at the last minute. Later she found out that Georgette just stayed home and watched television that night, and she was furious. As she saw it, she had been lied to. In a sense, she had been. Luckily, the two of them were in an encounter group together some weeks later, and the group was instructed to share any resentments they had toward other group members. The therapist had aimed the exercise at bringing out resentments that had built up over the two-day workshop, but Betty used the opportunity to voice her resentment of Georgette's "lying and letting me down" several weeks earlier. Georgette responded by admitting that she had misled Betty, but felt very uptight over the behavior of Betty's four-year-old son, and just didn't enjoy his company. Betty was able to accept this, and said that at the time she would have found this a good reason for Georgette to refuse her request. Georgette could have avoided a lot of pain, hostility, and expended energy if she had merely said, "I'm not going to be able to help you. I really don't want to spend an evening with a small child, and doing so would make me feel uncomfortable." Direct refusals are always better than wishy-washy excuses.

ACCEPT YOURSELF

Realize you are not all-powerful. You cannot meet all the needs of any one of your friends. So from time to time you are going to have to disappoint them. This is the reality, even if you believe that friendship means never turning down a request for help. Life just doesn't work like that. We have a limited time allotted to us. We have certain priorities and, if we're healthy and mature individuals, we are going to take care of our own priorities first.

Social scientist and group leader Emily Coleman, says, "For me to be able to relate to friends, I have to be able to set my boundaries. I have to be able to say no to friends before I can really open up to them. I have to be able to feel as though I am not being used by them. It's very, very important to me to have many different kinds of friends, because there's no one friend who can fulfill all of my needs. I like to have some friends I can learn from, and some friends I can teach things to. I like to have some friends who are more serious than I am; I like to have some friends who are more playful than I am. I like to have friends who are different from me in a number of respects. Then we have to be flexible, and both of us have to be able to ask what we want from each other, and say what we don't want from each other. I know someone is a close friend when I can tell him or her what I don't want. There are a lot of people I can tell nice things to, but when I can tell someone what I don't want, I know that's a friend I can trust, or else I wouldn't try that with him or her. It's difficult for me to give negative feedback, and I don't usually bother unless it's a friendship that's worth developing. I think that, for too much of my life, I had superficial relationships because I couldn't set my limits, I couldn't say what I didn't want. And now, as soon as possible, I try to say what I don't want. I don't blast anybody, but the way I feel is that if this is a friendship worth developing, I've got to be able to say negative things, and by saying those negative things, the friendship is sort of tested. It either goes someplace deeper after that or, if they can't take it, then that's the end, and I don't have to waste much time with them."

TAKING THE RISK

Actually, Emily Coleman is talking about risking. Risking offending a friend by setting boundaries. Avoidance of risk can always lead to stagnation, boredom, stunted growth, and superficial friendships. Taking risks always leaves you feeling more alive, *whether you get what you want or not!* And it is the only sure way to allow true intimacy. After all, what is the worst thing that could possibly happen if you tell your friend exactly what you want? It's simply that this friend will say he or she can't deliver, and perhaps you should look elsewhere. If you don't ask for what you want, you are still not going to get it from this person. But if you don't ask for what you want, you also won't get it from a person who might be willing to give it to you, *if* he or she knew you wanted it!

Right now, think of something you would like to ask a friend, something you have been unwilling or afraid to ask for up to now. Imagine that you are asking this friend for this something right now. Imagine your friend's response. In fact, why not imagine both responses? Picture this friend giving you what you want. And then picture him or her refusing you. Check out what the difference is between the feelings evoked in these two images. And think about this: Is the feeling you would experience if you were turned down any worse than the feeling you have when you don't ask?

PRIVACY NEEDS VERSUS INTIMACY NEEDS

One of the great conflicts in human interaction is based on a simple truth: *There are times when we need people and there are times when we need to be alone.* We all know this, but for some strange reason we find it difficult to accept this truth when it comes from a person who chooses to be alone at a time when we want him or her to be with us. This refusal to accept another person's privacy needs often leads to manipulation and attempted coercion as the person who wants company tries to convince the person who wants to be alone that "it's more important for you to respond to my need than to yours."

In her book *Making Friends with the Opposite Sex,* Emily Coleman says, "In seeking to live a richer life with others, it is necessary to learn to make and break contact; to get close and to move away. Contacts need to be broken so we can feel them when they are made, so we can be aware of our own separateness and identity, and so we can spark and be sparked by many, getting a balance and variety of emotional nourishment. Contact even with those we love best of all must be broken frequently to tune in on ourselves, and to give us freedom to move from one relationship to another, one situation to another, and to recharge our batteries, getting new ideas, feelings, thoughts and facts to integrate into our personalities."

Can you accept this idea? More to the point, can you accept a friend saying to you, "I need to be alone right now, so I can't be with you"? If you're not sure, run a scene through your mind in which a friend says this to you, at a time when you would like that friend's companionship. This goes to the core of whether you see your friend as an object to be manipulated to meet your desires, or as a person to be respected and appreciated for his or her individuality.

And honest communication is important. You may even find out that both your needs can be met. Perhaps your friend has privacy needs, but would be willing to spend part of the time with you. Or you may even find that, if you share a real need at an honest emotional level, your friend may be willing to postpone the time alone. Needs aren't always equal in intensity. You may need company more than your friend needs to be alone, and a good friend may be quite willing to respond to your request, if you make it openly, not through manipulation.

SOLITUDE VERSUS LONELINESS

If you consider being alone a negative, unpleasant situation, then you may tend to try to manipulate others into giving up *their* time alone. The person who appreciates his time alone, who uses this solitude in healthy, nurturing ways, will be able to appreciate this need in others. In his book *Portraits of Loneliness and Love*, Clark E. Moustakas writes, "I came to realize how often at crucial times a person moves forward not through therapy or friendship, but rather when he is utterly alone. In naked isolation and loneliness the potential for growth and change exists, the desire to live and to be joyous again is reborn."

You also foster manipulation when you don't acknowledge or accept the importance of sometimes being alone. If every time you just want to be alone, and a friend wants your company, you feel you have to invent a more "important" reason for refusing that friend, then you are manipulating yourself and inviting manipulation in return. And if you can't accept the need of your friend to be alone, you invite that friend to come up with invented excuses instead of the honest "I need to be alone right now."

Psychologist Judith Osgood says, "In my therapy work I focus a great deal on balance. You need to have both a time to be with people and a time to be alone, and most people don't take enough time to be alone. And people often assume that if they have friends they won't be lonely. I tell them that's not necessarily true. Sometimes loneliness is a result of being lonely for a part of yourself, and getting involved in friendships is an avoidance of whatever it is in you that you're wanting to develop. For example, one thing a lot of us are looking for is our own creativity, the feeling that we are a resource. A person who begins to spend time alone starts to get a greater sense of what it is that's emerging. If you're always spending time doing things *with* people, without time to let something incubate inside, the inner self has no chance to emerge. Sometimes friendships are an escape. I think some people are relieved when someone calls while they're alone. They say, 'Ah, I don't have to be with myself.' "

Are you afraid to be alone with yourself? Do you use your friends to avoid this? Dr. Gerald Walker Smith says, "If I can't be alone, that's a real danger sign." This is something that quite often happens after divorce or separation. Dr. Smith talks about his own experiences: "It was a critical decision for me, at the time I went through a divorce, when I finally got to the point where I decided that I would much rather be alone and deal with my aloneness than just go out and find somebody to be with. For a long time I couldn't stand being alone. It would just spook me. I would do anything to avoid being alone. I would go to almost any kind of meeting just to be with people. And I was in a very sad emotional state when I was in that position."

If you are afraid to be alone, you might very well use your friends to avoid the necessary self-confrontation. Dr. Marjorie Toomim tells about one patient of hers who did just that: "This woman can't make it in a love relationship, and she uses her friends to support her constantly. When she feels bad, she has a list of ten to twenty people that she calls. She calls them to find out if they love her. She uses these people to make some human contact, because otherwise she has none. She only relates to people who won't disappoint her when she needs that support. And mostly she just shows them one side of herself, the needy side, the helpless side. She doesn't ever get angry with them. She really doesn't trust them with herself, which is one reason she doesn't have a love relationship: she just can't trust anybody. She is controlling with her friends, and to some extent she is controlled by them. She asks them what to do, and she gets so many suggestions that she gets confused, so she doesn't do anything that anybody tells her to do, and does what she was going to do in the first place, which was nothing. She is using her friends, exploiting them."

ALONENESS ENRICHES

There are times, even when it may be painful to do so, when you really can only grow by being alone, and you are exploiting friends and putting onto them the delegated responsibility for your lack of growth when you ask them to fill that time for you. We have all had those beautiful alone moments, but rarely remember this when we feel lonely and unloved. Psychiatrist Eileen Walkenstein says, "Aloneness can be a very feeding experience. I have a patient who, for therapeutic reasons, had to split from his wife and she from him for a few weeks until they worked something out independently of each other. She was describing the first evening she was alone. She had been married for twenty-five years and had never spent a night alone by free choice. This was a mutual choice, since they decided that they were going to be alone for these few weeks to work something out. She said it was storming that night, and the view from her window was magnificent. The lights of the storm on the bay. She felt the drama unfolding in front of her, the marvelous natural phenomenon of the storm, thunder and lightning, and the colors on the water. She said her husband and she had never shared that. Even though they have a good relationship, a very good friendship and relationship. But it was not very alive. This separation was an attempt for each one to bring more aliveness back to the relationship. Well, her description of her aloneness was most magnificent. In a sense, she was very companied, even though she was by herself. She had the whole world coming in, and she was receiving the whole natural world at her windowsill. So, that's aloneness. Aloneness is a time for being, for creativity. It's very difficult to create when you're distracted by somebody else's creativity or by somebody else's pull in some other direction."

ACCEPTING YOUR FRIENDS' PRIORITIES

Alone time is just one of several priorities that may be important to you and your friends, sometimes taking precedence over the friendship itself. Friendly Assertiveness means being able to tell your friends when there's something else you really want to do or someone else you really want to be with. If you are viewed as a possession rather than a person, then the friend may resent you. Accepting the personhood of a friend means accepting that there are other priorities, other needs, other desires that have to be fulfilled, often outside the friendship.

Dr. Judith Osgood talks about one situation in her life: "This weekend, I had really wanted to see my dearest friend in San Francisco. I wanted to see her very much. But she told me, 'There's something else I really need instead. I was looking forward to seeing you, but that's changed, and I really need to do something else.' I could tell her I was really disappointed, and that was OK with both of us. I was being responsible for the fact that I had to deal with the change in my expectations. I had expected to see her. What I see wrong in fulfilling all of each other's needs is that as soon as I say yes when I mean no, as soon as I do something I don't want to do, I start to feel resentment, and there's some kind of limitation that starts to happen. It's a pattern that begins. I start to be accommodating, and I start to focus on what the other person is wanting instead of being able to communicate what I want. I really try to teach and live that whether I get what I want or not is not important, it's whether I'm aware of what I want, and whether I can state it, without expecting that I'm always going to get it. Knowing that I can accept having what I want or not having it, and this seems to be a real freeing thing for me."

BEING ABLE TO ASK FREES YOU

It feels good to ask for what you want in Friendly Assertiveness, even if you don't get it. The act of asking is separate from the results of your request. You can feel good asking, and then you respond with a new feeling when the other person responds. If the other person grants your request, you get another good feeling. If not, you may feel disappointed, but that doesn't take away from the good feeling you got by being able to ask for what you wanted! If you don't ask for what you want, chances are you won't get it. And you also won't have the satisfaction that comes from just being able to ask.

FEAR AS MOTIVATION

The main reason people won't ask for what they want, whatever it is, is that they are afraid they'll be rejected, that their friends will find their request unacceptable. For instance, Dr. Osgood says, "A lot of people want to spend more time alone, and are afraid that if they do they won't have any friends. A fear that if you spend time with yourself, your friends won't be there when you need them. There's a strange norm: You've got to spend a lot of time with your friends or they won't be there."

It is useful to be aware of your fears in this area. Every time you hesitate to assert yourself, to ask for what you want, to say what you don't want, answer the question *What am I afraid will happen if I do what I want to do?*

Dr. Edna Foa, a psychologist with the Behavioral Therapy Unit of Temple Medical School's Department of Psychiatry in Philadelphia, sees manipulation occurring when a person feels a want is either socially or legally unacceptable, and is therefore afraid to state it openly. She says, "I see all interpersonal relationships in terms of what we give to the people we interact with, and what we receive in return from them. There are many things we can exchange, some of them symbolic, some of them more concrete, like money, presents, goods. We also exchange love. We can also indicate, verbally or nonverbally, that we respect a person we interact with, and in this situation we are giving him status, so we are exchanging status. What we get back can be a thank you or it can be love. You can exchange information for status. For example, if someone tells you something, and you say, 'That's very interesting—I really enjoyed hearing that,' you are giving them respect, or status, in exchange for information. There are legitimate and illegitimate exchanges. Manipulation involves an illegitimate exchange. When you are giving a resource, it is usually exchanged for another, equal resource. When you give love, usually it is exchanged for love. When a person gives love in order to get money in return, this is an illegitimate exchange. Suppose you have a friend who says, 'Look, I'm going to give you all the love you want, but I want money for it.' You would find that this is an illegitimate request. If a person wanted to get money in exchange for love, or give money in exchange for love, he would not openly make this request because it would be rejected, so he has to manipulate. Calling something a manipulation really means that the exchange is not acceptable. What the person wants in return for what he gives is not acceptable, and so he doesn't state it openly. If you had someone you didn't particularly like invite you to dinner, and spend a lot of money on you, and you know this person wants love from you, you would feel very uncomfortable, because love has to be given for love."

WHAT DO YOU WANT IN EXCHANGE?

Can you honestly list all the things you want in exchange for your friendship? Pick a friend and think about all you want from this person, all you expect from him or her in exchange for your being a friend. Is there a price on your friendship that would be unacceptable if you were to state it openly to your friends?

MUTUALITY OF NEEDS

The healthiest and most rewarding friendships occur when there is equality in the quantity and quality of exchanges desired and offered. You cannot have a true friendship if it consistently means more to you than to your friend, or vice versa. For, if this is the situational reality of your relationship, one of you will be less willing to take risks in communicating than the other.

SAM AND ED

Ed had been very lonely before meeting his new friend, Sam. Sam liked being alone, and didn't really need a friend, but he enjoyed Ed's company. Ed was often afraid of telling Sam when he wanted to see him, for fear that he would be putting too much of a burden on Sam's good feelings for him. This, then, was a relationship doomed to stay stuck, Ed never getting what he really wanted from Sam, and so never sharing his really deep feelings; Sam never knowing that his attitude was instilling this fear in Ed. The situation itself may have been unchangeable, but Ed's response to it could have been a much healthier one. He could have simply told Sam that he had a need for more human contact. Sam might have replied that he was getting enough human contact from the relationship, in which case Ed could then have looked for some more friends, perhaps even with Sam's help in a cooperative effort.

Of course, the healthiest situation would be to not have any needs at all, but a lot of wants. Dr. Gerald Walker Smith says, "If I need the person more than he or she needs me, then there's trouble. Friendships have a much better chance if there are as few needs as possible and as many wants as possible. If the needs are really wants, the friendship has a much better chance than if the relationship is weighted down with needs." This fits in with Ken Keyes, Jr.'s, concept of addictions outlined in the last chapter.

MIXING NEEDS

If you want something from a friend over and beyond what he or she is offering, it's easy to slip into manipulation, and very difficult to use Friendly Assertiveness. For instance, your friend may enjoy fishing with you, and you may want to spend time with this friend's family on holidays because you don't have much of a family. If you don't openly ask for what you want, namely more of a family connection, you may very well try to manipulate your friend into inviting you.

Gerald Walker Smith tells of a healthy friendship interaction he has with Michael Murphy, the cofounder of the famed Esalen Institute, where Dr. Smith sometimes leads workshops. "I play golf with Mike Murphy. If my need were strictly to fraternize with Mike, and golf were a medium for doing that, then I'd be in trouble. But that's not the way it is. We're out there to play golf and we don't talk about many things other than golf. Which is kind of fun. I'm very careful not to talk about Esalen, because that would be using the friendship in a way that I think is inappropriate."

WHICH PARTS OF YOU IS THE FRIENDSHIP NOURISHING?

One way to check out whether you may be in a situation that could involve manipulation is to look at which part of yourself is being nourished by this friendship. If it is an unhealthy part of you, then it's probably a manipulative friendship. If, for instance, you are reinforcing and nourishing the part of you that is afraid to be alone, rather than confronting yourself and dealing with the issue, then you are involved in manipulation, and it would be nearly impossible to use Friendly Assertiveness in this relationship.

Dr. Marjorie Toomim says, "Let's say I am very passive and quiet, and the only people I connect with are very active, bossy, dominant, loud, outgoing, and outspoken. What I am doing is not using the more active part of myself. I'm externalizing that part of me. You live through your friends. And it may be that you are attracted to that kind of outspoken person, but you don't like them, in which case it may be a disowned or disliked part of yourself. I have one patient who has fights with all her friends. She says, in fact, 'A friend is somebody you can fight with!' And what she is doing is putting part of herself out there that she doesn't like, and criticizing it all the time. So a friend for her is somebody she can project onto. And she fights herself in the person of this friend, and tells the friend how lousy she thinks she herself is."

DESTRUCTIVE VERSUS CREATIVE USE OF FRIENDS

We all use our friends. The difference between manipulation and Friendly Assertiveness is that you openly let your friends know you are using them when you are being assertive; you hide this fact when you are manipulating. Also, the negative or destructive use of friends usually involves dynamics mainly focused on the using, with no other depth to the relationship. The only contact is when one friend is using the other, or when both are using each other simultaneously. In healthy using, therefore, there is more to the relationship than the act of using. Whereas in unhealthy using, that's the main reason for the relationship—it's more than just a fringe benefit. Also, in a healthy relationship the using is out in the open, with the user saying to the friend, "I care for you, and since you can provide me with the need, I will use you to fulfill it if you are willing." Dr. Gerald Walker Smith agrees: "I think the best way of using friendship is if the person's up front about it; if they say, 'Look, I want to use you.' Then it's not manipulative."

HOW TO USE YOUR FRIENDS IN HEALTHY WAYS

In any friendship, each person is going to have some interests, talents, and skills different from the other person's. An exchange or barter of these, done openly, is one good way to use each other constructively.

CHRIS AND HARRY

Chris was a writer and lawyer. Harry was a Senator. They met at a news conference, when Chris was doing some free-lance reporting for a television station. Harry needed a speechwriter. Chris needed political contacts, for this was where he wanted to aim his career. They made an open agreement to share their resources, and became good friends. Chris wrote the Senator's speeches, got to know his way around Washington, and eventually became involved in running for political office on his own. The friendship lasted well beyond the period of mutual using.

This might be another difference between constructive and destructive use of friends. If you are using your friends in manipulative, unhealthy ways, you will probably drop them as soon as that particular need is filled.

SHORT-TERM USING

As long as it's done honestly and openly, however, there is nothing wrong about fulfilling certain needs at certain periods in your life through specific friendships. Certain major crisis periods can produce intense mutual feelings, which may or may not last once the crisis has ended. Patricia Peabody, of Miami, talks about one such brief but intense friendship. "There was a girl who lived in the same apartment building when I was pregnant for the first time. She was also pregnant with her first child. The joy, the doubt, the thrill, and the pain we were experiencing created a strong bond between us. She made what she called 'hatching jackets' for me, and I decorated her nursery for her. The long daily walks we took, to keep our obstetricians happy, were a source of great enjoyment for both of us. She was the one who gave me encouragement and timed the pains until my husband arrived for the dash to the hospital. She was the person I most wanted to see after my baby was born. She eagerly listened to every detail of my experience with empathy no one else could duplicate. Four weeks later, when her baby was born, I sat all night in the waiting room, as nervous as the father. My friend and I moved away from that apartment building to different kinds of lives. Somewhere, in the moving about of young families, we lost each other, but we'll never really lose that friendship. I know she thinks of me at least once a year, about the time I think of her: when our oldest children celebrate their birthdays."

Many women report similar deep feelings of attachment forming during pregnancy, sometimes with the woman sharing their hospital room. Often the two women go their separate ways, but they get a lot of healthy use out of each other.

Someone once said, if you really want to know about life and love, ask a poet. Ric Masten has unusual insight into people and their behavior, since as a sort of strolling troubadour for the Unitarian Universalist Association he appears at colleges and Unitarian churches all over the country, and stays at over a hundred different private homes each year. Ric says, "Whenever I have a problem, something that's really bugging me, I will look over my friends and think which one I'd like to go talk to about it. I never really have to go, because I chose the friend I chose because I know what his answers are going to be. So I pretty well use my knowledge or feelings about my friends to fight my way out of my own problems, without actually having to go to them, though very often I do go. We all want to be used. I love to be used well. I hate to feel that I've been used poorly."

One way in which Ric Masten feels friends can use each other well is by providing new perspectives to each other. He says, "I'm blind to my own beauty and the beauty of Big Sur, where I live, but I have a friend who helps me see that beauty, and I wrote a poem about her:

when sybil comes
she comes with doors and windows
and you can see your mountain
through her eyes
when sybil comes
she draws aside the curtains
and the lilac and the lupine
take you by surprise

your vision
has been clouded
your eyes no longer see
then sybil comes
and as she looks around
you will find the ocean
right where
it used to be
with tiny freighters
steaming up and down

when sybil comes
the cobwebs turn to flowers
and you will see

your gardens are in bloom
when sybil comes
we'll have
children in the morning
and gypsies in the canyons
all the afternoon

then out
on the veranda
we sip our burgundy
and sit
and watch
the sun begin to fall
you've seen
a million sunsets
but each time sybil comes
you realize
you haven't seen them all

when sybil comes
she also brings a parting
and something would be lost
if she should stay
and so it goes
the sunlight and the shadow
the coming
and the going
and today.

Ric explains the final lines further by saying, "Sybil can't live at our house, because then she becomes too close. Sometimes someone becomes more than a friend, they become family, and you lose a friend that way very often." In this particular situation, if Sybil became too close, Ric would lose her fresh perspective on his home environment. On the other side, Ric notes, "There are those people who come into our lives and help us to see our own ugliness because we give them some kind of importance." And he illustrates this:

have you ever had
someone coming

you wanted to impress
too much

a guest
who had you running
to wash
and scrub
and straighten
up the place
until you
could see clearly
what an awful
mess of squalor
you really live in

someone coming
who had you aware
of spotted rugs
and torn upholstery
and dishes
that were chipped
and didn't match
scratched tables

someone coming
who had you
angry at the kids
for ancient crayon marks
and BB holes
who had you
picking up a yard
that could have
been a garden
cursing weeds
that should've
been a lawn

someone coming
who had you
hating yourself
and that

cramped ugly
little kitchen
where your
weeping
sullen wife
is banging
pots and pans around
burning
a tasteless dinner
that will go
with the
cheap wine
she says
her cheap husband
bought

have you ever
let someone
who hadn't even
arrived yet
rob you of
all your magic
and then
later
in the evening
had a
sunset happen
made you
feel ashamed
well
that makes
two of us

A good example of how catastrophic expectations help us magnify our supposed liabilities. Ric adds, "A friend is someone I care enough about not to clean the house. Because I know they aren't coming to see the house, they're coming to see me."

Do you have friends you can use to see new beauty in yourself and your environment, or do your friends help you focus on the ugliness? And remember, it may well be your perception of those friends, and the importance you give them, that causes you to see the ugliness. They may just be coming to see you and not the house you live in.

FRIENDLY POTENTIAL

What can happen in a healthy friendship is that you can each help the other to discover new beauty in your lives. Psychologist Herbert Otto sees one of the responsibilities of friendship being to awaken your friends to new potential in their lives. He asks, "What potentials do your friends have that you see in them, that they may not have discovered themselves? I know any number of my friends have a lot of potential in certain areas. It's always been hell for me to confront them, but I have confronted them. I have a good friend who is a gifted clinical psychologist, and he's a genius of a metal sculptor. He did two or three really fantastic things and then dropped it and went on to something else. In many friends that people have, there are aspects of the friend's potential that they may not be fully aware of, but confrontation and really stroking them, and making them aware in a very clear way that there *is* something there that can be developed further can make a hell of a difference. I see it as my responsibility to do the confronting. Then, what they do with it is up to them."

Do you know of some potentials your friends have that they haven't fully experienced? Look over your list of friends. See if you can figure out a way to encourage them to make better use of some of their talents by your support and nourishment.

FRIENDS AS CHARACTERS IN OUR BOOKS

Our lives are like great books stretched out before us. Parts are finished. Parts unfinished. And we are the editors. We decide what goes in and what gets taken out. Our friends are characters in our book, and there may be too many of them, or there may not be enough of them, or there may be just the right number. But perhaps they are not being developed as characters to the fullest extent. We are in charge of that, too. There is no way we can write about these friends in our book and fully describe them. All we can do is write our perception of them. The sides of them they allow us to see. The sides they show us. To a great extent, we are responsible for whether or not that is enough. If a friend shows you a limited amount of himself, you have the right to say, "Hey! I know there's more to you than this, and I want to know it. Show me some more!" This may be scary for your friend. But if you are using Friendly Assertiveness, and sincerely asking that more be revealed, and conveying that you are willing to accept whatever *is* revealed, because this is your friend, then more will be unfolded. And your book will have more depth, as will your life.

Finish the sentence "One new thing I've learned about my friends is the fact that ———." Examine how you feel about this and go on to the next chapter.

CHAPTER 7

CREATIVE RELATING

We all need other people in our lives. Sometimes, with our emphasis on self-awareness and individual freedom, we lose sight of that basic emotional fact. Let's see if we can clarify just what we mean by "need."

In the foreword to his book *Coming to My Senses*, John Robben said, "We all need to know we're not alone." In fact, many psychological studies have shown that infants will not grow or develop properly if they are not given loving attention. You know yourself how very important other people are in your life.

In his book *Love*, Dr. Leo Buscaglia says, "We need others. We need others to love and we need to be loved by them. There is no doubt that without it, we too, like the infant left alone, would cease to grow, cease to develop, choose madness and even death."

Dr. Darwin E. Linder, professor of psychology at Arizona State University, says in his book *Psychological Dimensions of Social Interaction*, "Whether we have an instinctive need to be with others or have learned through experience that people mediate valuable outcomes, social contact becomes for most of us a necessary part of existence."

Dr. Harry Stack Sullivan, author of the classic *The Interpersonal Theory of Psychiatry*, stated, in effect, that all things that damage us and all things that enrich us have to do with our relationships with others. So the professional experts in human relations agree with what has probably been your conclusion through your own life experience: *We need other people.*

How, then, is this different from the "neediness" deplored in interpersonal concepts? Well, if you are a healthy and mature individual, you will acknowledge that other people are necessary to your growth and existence. If you are a needy, dependent individual, you will be desperately seeking others to reaffirm you, to love you, to accept you, and however many people become a part of your life, it will never be enough. Perhaps the main difference is the motivation. The healthy individual recognizes the need, but operates from a place of self-support, reaching out to others as it feels right to do so, allowing friendships to evolve. The unhealthy or needy individual reaches out to others only to fill the gnawing need, and tries to make friendships happen, to force positive interaction. Going back to Ken Keyes, Jr.'s, Living Love system, as explored in Chapter 5, needy people would be addicted to friends and the finding and making of friends, while healthy people would prefer friends, but not suffer when friends aren't immediately available. Acting out of need always produces bad judgment, negative energy exchanges, and dependent relationships.

BEING A FRIEND

The important thing isn't to get friends, but to ask yourself how you can be a friend. First to yourself, then to others. If you open yourself up honestly, the friendships will happen. If you frantically run around seeking friends, in desperate need of them, you'll either fail or end up with a lot of dependent and interdependent friendships.

THE OTHER EXTREME

It's useful here to note the other extreme, which is isolation. Some people are so afraid of being "needy" that they practically become hermits. These people see only two choices: unhealthy neediness or total independence and self-sufficiency. In their book *Shifting Gears*, Dr. George and Nena O'Neill talk about these narrow-minded people. "They mistakenly assume that the only alternate path is to become self-centered, rejecting intimacy and emotional closeness. Such people are so much in search of the self that they lose it. They transform their need for self-assertiveness into self-centeredness in a kind of superindividualism that ignores our needs for relatedness and interdependence with another. The philosophy of 'you do your thing, and I'll do mine and if we don't make it together, too bad' is the result. It is only through caring, both for ourselves and for others, that we can truly actualize ourselves, bringing our potentials fully into play. We must care enough about ourselves to find our own way of self-growth. And we must care enough about others to encourage them to find their own way."

TO HELP ME GROW

Creative relating, then, seems to be the kind of reaching out that supports your own growth and development. In *Ways of Growth*, the late, beloved psychologist, Sidney Jourard wrote, "You can help me grow, or you can obstruct my growth. If you have a *fixed* idea of who I am and what my traits are, and what my possibilities of change are, then anything that comes out of me beyond your concept, you will disconfirm. In fact, you may be terrified by any surprises, any changes in my behavior, because these changes may threaten your concept of me; my changes may, if disclosed to you, shatter your concept of me, and challenge you to grow. You may be afraid. In your fear, you may do everything in your power to get me to un-change, and reappear to you as the person you once knew.

"But if you suspend any preconceptions you may have of me and my being, and invite me simply to be and to disclose this being to you, you create an ambience, an area of 'low pressure' where I can let my being happen and be disclosed, to you and to me simultaneously—to me from the inside, and to you who receive the outside layer of my being.

"If your concept of my being is one that encompasses more possibilities in my behavior than I have myself acknowledged; if your concept of my being is more inclusive and indeed more accurate than my concept of my being, and if you let me know how you think of me; if you let me know from moment to moment how you experience me; if you say, 'Now I think you dislike me. Now I think you are being ingratiating. Now I think you can succeed at this, if you try'; if you tell me *truly* how you experience me, I can compare this with my experience of myself, and with my own self-concept. You may thus insert the thin edge of doubt into the crust of my self-concept, helping to bring about its collapse, so that I might re-form it. In fact, this is what a loving friend, or a good psychotherapist, does."

Dr. Jourard's concept of growth through friendship can give us a lot of food for thought. You might want to read over it several times and see how your friends appear from this perspective. It points to the two main prerequisites of a growing friendship and creative relating: self-disclosure and feedback.

If you can accept the simple truth of human relations and the human psyche, that good friendships help you grow, you can have a straightforward and healthy perception of the roles friends can and will play in your life, as well as your role as a good friend. In his book *Finding Yourself, Finding Others*, Clark Moustakas says, "A sense of relatedness to another person is an essential requirement of individual growth. The relationship must be one in which each person is regarded as an individual with resources for his own self-development. Self-growth sometimes involves an internal struggle between dependency needs and strivings for autonomy, but the individual eventually feels free to face himself if he is in a relationship where his human capacity is recognized and cherished and where he is accepted and loved. Then he is able to develop his own quantum in life, to become more and more individualized, self-determining, and spontaneous. We can help a person to be himself by our own willingness to steep ourselves temporarily in his world, in his private feelings and experiences. By our affirmation of the person as he is, we give him support and strength to take the next step in his own growth."

LOOKING BACK AT MAJOR GROWTH PERIODS

Make a list of the major growth surges you have taken in your life, the periods when you made decisive moves forward in your own development as an individual. This may have been a decision to take on a certain job or task, to move to a certain place, to learn some skill or profession, to get married, to get divorced. Look over all these major life decisions, the ones you feel were good and growing ones. What role did your friends play in these growth periods? Did they support you? Did they nourish you? Or did you feel alone? Also, look over your role in the growth periods of close friends, and whether or not you nourished and supported them.

UNDERSTANDING NECESSARY

To help you grow, your friends must understand you. In his book *On Caring*, philosopher Milton Mayeroff says, "To care for another person, I must be able to understand him and his world as if I were inside it. I must be able to see, as it were, with his eyes what his world is like to him and how he sees himself. Instead of merely looking at him in a detached way from outside, as if he were a specimen, I must be able to be *with* him in his world, 'going' into his world in order to sense from 'inside' what life is like for him, what he is striving to be, and what he requires to grow. *But only because I understand and respond to my own needs to grow can I understand his striving to grow; I can understand in another only what I can understand in myself.*"

In fact, one of the major destructive self-statements made repeatedly by people with unhealthy self-concepts is, "Nobody really understands me!" To make this statement, one would have to be devoid of intimate friendships. So one way to look at whether you have any good and nourishing friendships is to check out whether you feel you are understood *by at least one other person.*

WHO UNDERSTANDS ME?

What does someone who understands you really have to be aware of? Make a list of the things you think it would take to fully understand you. Such a list might look like this:

I am sensitive and need to be treated with tenderness.

Sometimes I have a strong need to be alone.

I like to be touched.

I am not always sure of myself, and like reassurance from friends.

I want honest appraisal of my behavior and actions.

When I'm sad, I want to be able to be with a friend without having to apologize or explain or hide my sadness.

Note, these are all personal understanding observations, things someone would know about you only if you told them. We often create our own traps by refusing to share the information that would enable someone else to understand us, and then deploring the fact that we are not understood. After having your list of personal observations, become aware of which of these you have shared with one or more friends. If there's something you have not shared with anyone, then chances are this is an area in which you are not understood by any other person.

People are often afraid of being understood, for fear that this would lead to rejection. A poor self-image is one that projects the statement "If you really knew me, you would not love me." It is true that someone who understands may not necessarily love you, but it is also true that no one can really care for you without understanding you, and anything less is merely some sort of pseudo-feeling. In his book *The Social Animal,* Professor Elliot Aronson of the University of Texas says, "Understanding does not always lead to attraction: I may understand you and decide that you are not *my kind* of person, but I would have difficulty concluding that you are not a person. Accordingly, I might choose not to be your friend or never to associate with you, but it would be very difficult for me to choose to hurt or to kill you without experiencing a great deal of guilt and emotional pain."

AN UNACKNOWLEDGED NEED

We often are not aware that a good friend can fill this need to be understood, and we may scramble around to get it from relatives, lovers, fellow workers, and assorted acquaintances. Psychologists have often noted that entertainers and other public figures are motivated by a need to be accepted and understood. In his book *The Four Loves*, C. S. Lewis pointed out that the modern world often ignores the value and virtue of friendship, while in ancient times friendship seemed "the happiest and most fully human of all loves." Lewis felt that few valued friendship because few really experienced it, and he wrote: "Friendship is—in a sense not at all derogatory to it—the least *natural* of loves; the least instinctive, organic, biological, gregarious and necessary. It has least commerce with our nerves; there is nothing throaty about it; nothing that quickens the pulse or turns you red and pale. It is essentially between individuals; the moment two men are friends they have in some degree drawn apart together from the herd. Without Eros none of us would have been begotten and without Affection none of us would have been reared; but we can live and breed without Friendship."

In today's world, friendship is primarily a spiritual and emotional need. It fulfills us in ways that may be difficult to measure. It nurtures us in aspects of our being that have little to do with physical survival. It is vital because we are more than mere survival machines; we are more than animals. Friendship is therefore a very human occurrence.

DIFFERENT LEVELS AT DIFFERENT STAGES OF LIFE

In an article entitled "Love, the Human Encounter," contained in the book *Love Today*, Dr. Everett Shostrom noted four levels of love at various stages of growth. *Affection* came at ages one to six, and is the type of love a parent has for a child. *Friendship* comes at ages six to twelve, and is a love involving peers with a common interest and respect for each other's equality. *Eros* is the romantic form of love, developing from thirteen to twenty-one. And *Empathy* is a charitable altruistic form of love which is expressed by a deep feeling for another person, and involves compassion, appreciation, and tolerance. Shostrom says that inappropriate training or serious problems at any of these four stages would mean that a person would develop distortions in the ability to love in an authentic manner as an adult.

It is the premise of this book, and of many humanistic psychologists, that a nourishing friendship is composed of *Affection*, *Friendship*, and *Empathy*. As an adult you have the capacity to reveal yourself more than you did when friendship first came into your life. And, if you had affection as a child, you have the capacity to deliver this affection to your friends now. Of course, some friendships may also include Eros, perhaps a friendship between a husband and a wife. We'll look at this in more depth in the next chapter, entitled Friends and Lovers.

But our purpose is not to analyze or catalogue; it is to experience, to feel. There are two facets of human communication that enrich and expand and enhance friendship. They permit the development of empathy, and usually result in affection and authenticity. They are self-disclosure and feedback.

SELF-DISCLOSURE

Before you are going to be willing to disclose yourself to another human being, you are going to have to trust yourself to that person's care, and you are going to have to trust that person not to take advantage of your disclosure. Therefore, self-disclosures occur most productively between people who have already developed a trusting relationship. However, one of the best laboratories for exploring this phenomenon is the group workshop, whether it be an encounter or sensitivity or therapy session. In this setting the group leader promotes a feeling of trust, and grants the group members permission to reveal themselves. It is contrived, but necessary, for most people are not used to this sort of opening up. In the group process you are invited to reveal yourself. Most people start out very tentatively, cautiously. But as the group provides feedback to the effect that your self-disclosure is acceptable, that it doesn't turn people off to you, then you will be willing to reveal more. An amazing euphoria can develop. There is hardly anything to compare with the joy of sharing some of your deepest fears and feelings, things you have held back for years out of fear that they would be unacceptable, and to have others accept them, and even feel closer to you for all your self-supposed weaknesses. For, in self-disclosure, you have revealed yourself to be human. And guess what? Those are all human beings out there, too! And the human part of them will respond to the human part of you. This is why, after a weekend group, many people report that they feel closer to some of the group members than they have to friends they've known all their lives. Self-disclosure, and the feedback it usually encourages, leads to intimacy.

In his book *Why Am I Afraid to Tell You Who I Am,* the Reverend John Powell says, "It is certain that a relationship will be only as good as its communication. If you and I can honestly tell each other who we are, that is, what we think, judge, feel, value, love, honor and esteem, hate, fear, desire, hope for, believe in and are committed to, then and then only can each of us grow. Then and then alone can each of us be what he really is, say what he really thinks, tell what he really feels, express what he really loves. This is the real meaning of authenticity as a person, that my exterior truly reflects my interior. It means I can be honest in the communication of my person to others. If I am willing to step out of the darkness of my prison, to expose the deepest part of me to another person, the result is almost always automatic and immediate: The other person feels empowered to reveal himself to me. Having heard of my secret and deep feelings, he is given the courage to communicate his own."

WHAT IS HOLDING YOU BACK?

Look over your list of friends and ask yourself the question: *What am I afraid to tell this person about myself?* Social scientist Tonia Sloman likes to play a game called Truth with her friends, saying, "You'd be amazed at the things people will tell you, if you only ask them." The game is simple. It can be played with one or more friends, but you probably would want to start out with one other person. You merely start asking each other questions, and the only rule is that you have to be absolutely truthful. One exchange might start out like this:

A: How do you feel about playing this game?

B: A little nervous. I'm trying to think up my own question, and also wondering what you are going to ask me. Are you nervous, too?

A: Yes, even though I suggested the game. I realize this will move us to a new level of intimacy, and that's a little scary. How do you feel about me right now?

B: I feel close to you, but I am wondering about your motivations in suggesting this game. In fact, I'd like to ask you, why did you suggest it?

A: Because I'd like to get closer to you, and know you better, and let you know me better. What does our friendship mean to you?

This gives you some idea. But, of course, you can move the questions into any area you choose, starting out lightly at first, then perhaps moving on to deeper feelings. It may seem a bit scary at first, but the game of Truth usually produces satisfying results.

I SHOULD

A Gestalt Awareness game you might play is based on the concept, outlined briefly in Chapter 5, that you operate best with no "shoulds" in your emotional makeup. But we all have some shoulds, things we believe we have to do. This game is played with two people. One of you goes first. For about five minutes, partner A catalogues all the things he or she believes he should do. And to each, partner B replies, "Bullshit!"

JACK AND TESS

Jack and Tess chose each other as partners at a weekend growth workshop in which this game was going to be played. They hadn't really gotten to know each other before playing this game together. Tess started out as partner A, and their initial dialogue went like this:

Tess: I should feed my cats more regularly.

Jack: Bullshit!

Tess: I should clean my apartment more often.

Jack: Bullshit!

Tess: I should feel guilty when I don't feed my cats or clean my place.

Jack: Bullshit!

Tess: I should always wait for a man to make the first move.

Jack: Bullshit!

Tess: I should write to my parents more often.

Jack: Bullshit!

Tess: I should try to improve myself.

Jack: Bullshit!

And so on. Tess went on for the full five minutes, listing all the things that she had been taught that she was supposed to do, or all the things she could feel guilty about if she didn't do them. When this interaction was completed, they reversed roles. Jack says he realized that he and Tess had a lot in common after the first few exchanges. He also had cats, and didn't keep his apartment too neat, and had a number of other similar shoulds. So, in addition to pointing out how many shoulds they each had, and that none of them were really necessary, they were, in effect, disclosing themselves to each other. They formed a good friendship. They both had healthy love relationships, but were attracted to each other as friends, and pursued that attraction.

Are your shoulds similar to those of your friends? You might try playing I Should with some of them.

In his book *Human Be-ing*, William Pietsch writes, "A real relationship only becomes possible when we are willing to reveal our emotions to another." Some examples of these emotional disclosures and the responses they might evoke:

> *"How do I feel? Well, frankly, I'm worried about tomorrow."*
> *"That bothers me too. What can we do about it?"*
>
> *"I'm troubled about what he might do."*
> *"I thought you were concerned. I'd like to help."*
>
> *"I feel badly about your leaving."*
> *"I'm going to miss you."*

Pietsch also says, "We may not be willing to risk the other person's seeing us as we are. If we set up a phony image of ourselves to relate to, the other person cannot know who we really 'are,' and we actually communicate 'I want your cooperation, but I don't trust you enough to let you know who I am.' "

FEEDBACK

Feedback and self-disclosure go hand in hand. Feedback may involve someone responding to your self-disclosure, or it may involve anything else you say or do. George and Nena O'Neill describe what they term "feedback friends" in *Shifting Gears*: "These are friends we respect and whose opinion we can rely on. These are the friends you probably have shared a continuity of experiences with. You can go to them when you are troubled, perplexed, worried, or have problems that you do not yet know how to solve. They are not mentors and do not necessarily give you advice; they give you honest feedback—they can explore a problem with you and are able to see you with clarity and objectivity."

In his book *Contact: The First Four Minutes*, Dr. Leonard Zunin gave an example: "At a recent workshop during a self-assessment session, a mature man of forty-eight, married and the father of three children, told us he was startled to find there was no one except his wife to whom he could confide his deepest feelings. 'She was in the hospital for a few weeks,' he said, 'with problems both emotional and physical. I could talk to my kids, but our interchange was limited to their awareness level. I wanted to spill my guts, to simply tell somebody how disturbing it was to have my wife away and sick, but there was nobody. My close 'friends' would have listened, but they were not clued in to me well enough; I wouldn't have felt safe in revealing myself. I finally got it all out on paper. Just sat and wrote what was in my head and heart, and I felt relieved; but there was no feedback. It's funny, because I was sure I had lots of friends I could turn to in an emergency.' "

We all need these intimate friendships, in which self-disclosure and feedback are an integral part of the interactive exchanges. In *Shifting Gears*, the O'Neills say, "In these intimate friendships we can open up facets of ourselves and gain new insights and perspectives about ourselves and others. We can stretch our minds with many friends—even old ones we know only in books—but there are few with whom we can stretch both our mental and emotional boundaries. Yet these are the ones that help us to grow in our dimensions of wholeness."

Sometimes we are not aware of our need for these intimate friends until we reach a crisis in our lives. As in the example cited by Leonard Zunin in *Contact*. But this ability to self-disclose and this need for feedback are not just for bad times. These qualities in a friendship can enrich us and help us be more than we are. Like any growing things, we need nourishment and careful attention to keep up the momentum.

Leo Buscaglia says, "For me, in a healthy friendship, there's got to be continual growth on the part of both individuals. I have to be doing my thing, and you have to be doing your thing, but we have to be open in sharing what we're doing, so that there isn't any mystery. Because the minute you don't understand what I'm doing, or I don't understand what you're doing, then in those shadows begins the process of our drifting apart. I want you to willingly want to tell me what you're doing, because you're enthused, excited. Another thing I would want in a friendship is what I call gentle honesty. I don't want brutality, and I don't want custard pies in my face, but I want you to gently be honest with me all the time. I want you to tell me if I smell, and I want you to tell me if I've offended you. I want you to tell me if I'm not helping you grow. Because it's only through honesty that I can understand what you're truly feeling. As sensitive as I am, I'm not psychic, and I don't know what you're feeling unless you tell me. When you tell me what you're feeling, I'll know, and I'll then have the choice to do something about it, or not to do something about it."

Can you be gently honest with any of your current friends? Can you accept their gentle honesty?

GENTLE HONESTY

One of the ways to be gently honest, perhaps the best way, is to simply give some loving, caring feedback along with any honest feedback that includes something you may see as a negative bit of information. For instance, "I really care for you, and appreciate you as a friend, and so I want to let you know that you have a habit which I allow to irritate me. If possible, I would appreciate it if you wouldn't crack your knuckles in my presence. I don't know for sure, but I think it may also annoy some other people."

How could you dislike someone who presented their honest feedback so gently? Think about how you would react to this kind of feedback.

The truth is that people respond more to us when we let them see our human side, some of the things which are not so perfect about us, and when we are willing to give them a view of their own humanness. In *The Social Animal*, Elliot Aronson says, "If two people are genuinely fond of each other, they will have a more satisfying and exciting relationship over a longer period of time if they are able to express whatever negative feelings they may have than if they are completely 'nice' to each other at all times."

Poet Ric Masten puts it more succinctly. "They are just other people out there, until I can be an asshole and they will still love me." Can you be an asshole and still have your friends love you?

Dr. Marjorie Toomis says, "One of the things that friends are good for is that they do give you different perspectives on the world, if you listen. But if you won't listen, you're not a very good friend anyway. A good friend gives you windows all over the place, on different parts of the world. I like friends who are doing different things, and then I can tune in to the different things and I don't necessarily have to do all those different things."

So you might look at your friends with a view toward whether or not they really give you some different perspectives on yourself. Or do you choose only people who will agree with you? Of course, sometimes you can get new insights into you own inner answers by asking your friends the questions you may not be willing to ask yourself. A true friend can give you new awareness of your own being. Ric Masten says, "You often go to a friend to hear what you have to tell yourself." He illustrates this with a poem:

i was talking
to myself again
in front
of the mirror
but
the glass man
only moved
his lips
with mine
and
said nothing
that'd help
so I
came to you
to hear
what it was
i had
to tell
myself
i chose you
above
everyone else

because
i knew
that you
would say
one can
only
help oneself
and that
is exactly
the kind of
smartass remark
i will not take
off a mirror

FEEDBACK FANTASY

The next time you are with a friend, imagine something about yourself that you would be unwilling to tell this person. It could even be something that is true about you, something you would never reveal to this person. Imagine yourself telling this friend, and imagine his or her facial expression and verbal reaction to the disclosure. There is a very good chance the response you imagine is not really the response you would get should you really reveal yourself.

SEYMOUR

Seymour was in an encounter group, composed of six men and six women. The psychologist gave the group an exercise in which they were supposed to reveal a secret, or something that embarrassed them. Seymour admitted that he was very embarrassed whenever he had an erection because he had a large penis and it stuck out in full view when it was erect. He said he had tried all kinds of binding underwear, but nothing worked, and he felt very anxious and uncomfortable whenever this occurred. The men responded with:

"Wow! That's something that's always gotten me uptight, too!"

"I'd be proud if mine stuck way out like that!"

"I know how you feel, it is *embarrassing."*

"If someone is looking there, then you're probably giving them a treat!"

"I can't understand why that upsets you, I feel good about myself whenever I have an erection."

The women responded with:

"That's a natural thing, it wouldn't bother me."

"I noticed you had an erection this morning, and it only made me curious to see your penis."

"As long as you were relaxed about it, it wouldn't make me nervous."

"I used to feel that way when I didn't wear a bra and my nipples got hard, like on a cold day. I was afraid the men would think I was getting aroused over them."

"Every part of your body is a beautiful thing, and a natural thing, and erections are just another part of your body responses, just like breathing, and laughing, and all the other things that happen."

"I think I would find you interesting, especially if I thought you were getting excited looking at me."

Needless to say, Seymour was surprised at these responses, at this feedback. He had expected ridicule, criticism. Instead, he got understanding. His uptightness over this issue diminished. For he was able to assume that those people in his everyday life would have similar responses.

SHARING THE FULL STORY

This brings us to another aspect of communication, one that many people ignore—the fact that whenever we verbally share some feeling, or conclusion, we are only sharing part of the total picture. Sometimes we don't have the time or opportunity to share more, but often we just don't think it's important to do so. For example, you call a friend up and say, "Hey, I'm feeling sort of lonely, can you come over?" Your friend responds with, "I'm really tied up now, or else I would, but I can't." That's not a mean reply. It's honest and out in the open, but it is far from the whole story. If the friendship really is an intimate one, with self-disclosure and feedback as an integral part of the interacting, then there are times when the process of decision should be shared. A fuller response might be, "I really hear what you are asking, and I would like to respond to your request, but I have some needs of my own right now, some things I have to work out, and I need to be alone to do that." Can you see the difference? Or, if you have to turn down a request from someone, realize that just giving them the final decision may seem like enough, but with some more information you may actually enrich the friendship through the act of explaining your refusal. For example: "I can't lend you my car right now. I lent it out last week to Smitty, and it came back with a dent. I know you will drive carefully, but I am nervous about it. I just wouldn't feel comfortable lending it out right now. I hope you can understand, because I really don't like disappointing you." This statement lets your friend see some of your vulnerability. Your nervousness over lending your car out. The friend can even empathize, as he or she has probably had similar feelings. It draws you closer together while still being an assertive statement.

Also, by sharing more of the story, we avoid narrow perspectives and misconceptions. You may often assume your friend knows what is happening with you from the sketchy picture you paint, but that assumption may be wrong. Wrong assumptions lead to wrong responses, as illustrated by this Ric Masten poem entitled "Who's Wavin' ":

i ain't wavin'
babe
i'm drownin'
goin' down
in a cold lonely sea
i ain't wavin'
babe
i'm drownin'
so babe
quit wavin' at me
i ain't laughin'
babe
i'm cryin'
oh why
can't ya see
i ain't foolin'
babe
ain't foolin'
so babe
quit foolin'
with me
this ain't singin'
babe
this here's screamin'

i'm screamin'
that i'm gonna
drown
and your smilin'
babe
and your wavin'
just like
you don't hear
a sound
i ain't wavin'
babe
i'm drownin'
goin' down
right here
in front of you
and your wavin'
babe
ya keep wavin'

hey
babe
are you drownin' too

oh

Which points to another problem in interpersonal communication. We often don't pay attention to where our friend is when we are engrossed in where we are. Being sensitive to each other is the best way to deal with this. If you have a problem, and you want to share it with your friend, check out first where your friend is emotionally. You might find out your friend also has a problem, and this mutuality of need can even bring you closer together. Otherwise you'll just be talking to a wall, and no real interaction will happen. Another Ric Masten poem illustrates how friends often just don't hear each other:

i have just
wandered back
into our conversation
and find
that you
are still
rattling on

about something
or other
i think i must
have been gone
at least
twenty minutes
and you
never missed me

now
this might say
something
about my
acting ability
or it might say
something about
your sensitivity

one thing
troubles me tho
when it
is my turn
to rattle on
for twenty minutes
which i
have been known to do
have you
been missing too

LISTENING

Do you listen to your friends, or are you just concerned about whether they listen to you? If you don't find a friend interesting enough to listen to, then this isn't really a friendship, it's just a warm body, and you may as well be talking to a robot.

Look over your list of friends and see if you can think of a time when you listened to each of them. At least as much as they've listened to you.

And listening may involve more than just your ears. It involves your inner perception. With time, you begin to understand what a friend means when he says, "Whew!" Leo Buscaglia says, "A real friendship affords total communication, and that's very refreshing. It allows me to talk to you, to understand the words you're using. So I can be more comfortable in your linguistic environment. When you use a word, I know what you mean by it, so I feel comfortable with you. And I know that when I use a word, it will communicate precisely what I'm saying, and you'll understand. So that the closer you get in a friendship, the more understandable are the symbols you use, so that you each feel more comfortable. I feel comfortable with you, talking about myself with you, and having you talk about yourself with me. It becomes such a nice comfortable thing to have a friend. I remember one of the things we always used to get a big kick out of as kids was the communication that my parents had with each other. They hardly needed to speak. They just looked across the room at each other, and one twinkled, and the other sparkled, and my mother would get up and get my father a beer. It was a crazy kind of a communication, but it was theirs, and they had developed it over the years, and it made a lot of nonsensical talking unnecessary. A friendship offers us other avenues of communication, so we don't have to get tied up in verbal knots."

NONVERBAL COMMUNICATION

It took a lot of years for Leo Buscaglia's parents to get their "twinkle" and "sparkle" together, but this doesn't mean you can't start having some nonverbal interaction with your friends right now. One exercise often used in sensitivity groups is to sit opposite each other with eyes closed, and explore each other's hands, then arms and shoulders and, finally, faces. You'll learn more about a friend's sensitivity in five minutes this way than by months of talking. Do it.

BEING REAL

The best thing about creative relating, using self-disclosure and feedback, is how good it feels to be real, to be authentically yourself! Leo Buscaglia notes, "One of the things I like in a friendship is to be accepted for me, so that I have to play the least amount of roles possible. In a friendship, I feel that the greater and deeper it is, the more genuine the two people can be. Therefore, it requires the least amount of energy to maintain. Because all the energy is concentrated on what is essential in the relationship, rather than all the fringe crap of building it."

And, in a chapter entitled Some Dimensions of Loving Experience, in

Love Today, Sidney Jourard wrote: "I love my friend, and he loves me. He loves a woman, and so do I. He loves his children, I love mine, and I love his. He loves my children, though neither he nor I know the other's so well as we know our own. But I love my friend. I want to know him. We make life richer, more meaningful, more fun for each other. My life is diminished without my friend being in it. I respect his projects, and he does mine. I help him when he wants it, and stand by when he does not. I wish him well in his projects. I know he reciprocates, because he has shown that he does. When he and I talk, there is no semblance between us. He discloses his experience to me in truth—he wants me to know him. And I do likewise. When he wishes to close off conversation he does so. I respect his privacy. He respects mine. I like the way he 'refracts' the world. When he discloses his experience of his world to me, my experience is enriched, because he sees and does things I cannot do directly. Imaginatively, I live more through his experience."

THE DIFFERENCES

Again, this subject of the differences between friends comes up. In the first chapter, psychiatrist Eileen Walkenstein declared that, for her, a healthy friendship was one that was unpredictable. Also in the first chapter, we quoted from Leo Buscaglia's *Love,* "If you know, accept and appreciate yourself and your uniqueness, you will permit others to do so."

There is no way you are going to be exactly like your friend in your tastes and opinions and feelings. Dr. Walkenstein says, "I can really only be intimate with you if you are not me, if you are there and I am here." Can you understand and *appreciate* the differences between you and your friends? If you like to ski, and your friend likes to play tennis, can you appreciate that difference, or are you always trying to convince your friend of how much more fun your sport is, and how he should give up his activity in favor of yours? *Acceptance* again, that most important word in human relationships. Can you accept that there are things you really care about that may mean less than nothing to your friend?

And each of us has a certain way of being, a unique way of operating in this world, a certain style. Psychiatrist Leonard Zunin says, "Do you respect each other's right to style? It has to do with tolerance. You don't have to love everyone's style, but if you look at your interaction with someone, what is their style of relating? And do you like that style or do you not like it? It's important to understand that they have a right to their own style, as do you. Do you respect each other's style?" Check this out with your list of friends. See if you can discern the differences in your styles of operating and relating. Honestly look at whether you respect the differences, and whether you feel your style is being respected and appreciated by your friends.

Do you really care for a friend, or do you care for the potential person you feel this friend would be if they listened to you and changed according to your demands? One of the ways in which friends manipulate each other is to hide initial dissatisfaction over another person's style or differences, making the self-statement, "I'll win him over and wait until I have influence over him, then I'll try to change what I don't like!" Have you ever felt this way about a friend? Can you see that it has nothing to do with acceptance and love and honest relating? The greatest insult you can offer anyone is to try to change them! And it's also the most futile effort we humans are capable of attempting. In his book *How I Found Freedom in an Unfree World*, Harry Browne says, "If you can accept the differences that exist between you and those you care for, you can make the most of what you have together. If you try to overcome the differences, you'll only make it harder to enjoy the things you *do* have together."

The problem seems to be that people often equate "different" with "separate." Just because someone is different from you doesn't mean they can't come together with you in a growing, creative relationship. Dr. Eileen Walkenstein sees us each having many, many facets. She says, "I think there isn't anyone who can meet you on every level. I'm multitudinous in terms of my facets, and so are you. If many of our facets meet, we have a lot of energy exchange in those many facets. If only one or two of our multitudinous facets meet, we have very little energy exchange, though we may still be what is known as thick and fast friends. I think a good criterion for a healthy friendship is to look at how much of myself I am able to share with a person, how many of my facets can be charged by that person's facets. Realizing again that there isn't anyone who can meet you on every level."

THINGS IN COMMON

Once you accept and appreciate the differences between you and your friends, enjoying each other's uniqueness rather than letting it entrap you in hopeless efforts aimed at changing the other person, you can focus your energy and attention on the things you have in common with your friends. Look over your list of friends. For each other person who is important to you, make two lists. One will be The Differences Between Us and the other will be The Things We Have in Common. If you can accept and appreciate the first list, you can go on to fully enjoy the second one.

It is true that the more things you have in common with a friend, the more relaxed and comfortable you will be with that person. In choosing friends, it is useful to be aware of this factor. It is all right to choose someone you have little or nothing in common with if you are choosing him or her to provide a Limited Friendship resource, perhaps as a tennis partner or someone to go shopping with. If, however, you are aiming at Intimate Friendship, then you may be creating a lot of troublesome obstacles by focusing on people with whom you have little in common. It is not impossible to create a loving, intimate relationship with someone who is completely different from you, especially if you are each moving into new life-styles that may have some similarities. But it does take more energy, and with the same amount of energy you might develop two or three deep friendships with people you share more common ground with. The choice is up to you, but it isn't really a choice unless you are aware of the relative difficulties and the alternative possibilities.

VALUES

Louis Mobley, founder of Mobley and Associates, helps groups of people find their common values, and the values in which they differ, so that both factors can be used in creatively relating. Mobley says, "It's worthwhile that you know that this man over here is different from you in terms of this, this, this, and that, because I'm convinced that creative activity happens, people who have a common purpose, and work together, find their creative opportunities when different values work together. Each can supplement the other. I think a lot of our commonalities, or our assumptions of commonalities, are formulated at very superficial levels, such as style of hair. Then we discover, after we've made commitments to friendships, that we don't relate at the value level with the people we've chosen. We need ways for people to find friends at the value level rather than at the superficial level." The way Louis Mobley does this is by using a tool he invented. Called

Valuing Simulation, or The Value Game, it involves a deck of cards on which various value statements are made. The players pick a few cards at random, then keep the value statements they want and try to trade the ones they don't like for ones they can agree with. Participants in the game then get together with other people who are holding similar value statement cards. Mobley says that people are often surprised to find whom they wind up with in groups. About half the cards represent traditional or establishment views, and half represent emergent or new views. Some of the value statements, with their opposite numbers:

Women should accept mothering as their natural role in life. Work outside the home is a choice for women, but is secondary to the maternal drive.

or:

Men can be as mothering as women, and women can work as productively as men. Both roles can and should be shared, as often as possible, in order to achieve greater equality between the sexes.

Work is as much a part of human nature as love.

or:

It is no longer necessary for everyone to work for a living.

Every person is capable of loving only one other person.

or:

People can love more than one person at a time.

Leaders determine the directions we take as a nation. We need more effective, sensitive and honest leaders.

or:

Leaders are symbolic figures today, who lead only as they are influenced by those around them.

These are only a few of the value statements. For more information on this game, and the various decks of cards available, write to Mobley and Associates, 5000 Sheppard Lane, Ellicott City, Maryland 21043.

Check yourself out first, using these four sets of statements. Find out which value statements you find most acceptable, least objectionable. Then look over your list of friends and see if you can guess how they would each respond. You might then choose to check out this perception with several of your friends. And you may end up being surprised. What really matters is not so much whether you agree in many of your values, but whether you even know what each other's values are. You can't accept the differences if you don't know them, and you can't enjoy the similarities if you aren't made aware of them.

It is also useful to see whether your values come from your own experience and evaluation of that experience or from the attitudes and admonitions of others. Dr. Abraham Maslow, in his study of "self-actualized" people, those who were most healthy and most fully used their talent and capacities, noted that they had values that were real and meaningful for them and not based on what others told them. Interestingly enough, the self-actualized person also tended to form very deep and intimate personal friendships with other people, though their list of friends usually was a very small one. In his book on Maslow's theories, *The Third Force*, Frank Goble said, "The self-actualizing people of the type Maslow studies are a tiny percentage of the total population, a fraction of one percent. They are very different from the average person, and few really understand them. Yet these superior people have a deep feeling of kinship with the whole human race. They are capable of sharing a type of friendship with people of suitable character, regardless of their race, creed, class, education, political beliefs, or color. This acceptance of others cuts right across political, economic, and national boundaries."

One of the things that might, however, dictate whether a healthy, strong individual will form a friendship with another person is whether the two persons have enough matching values to develop some common ground. This can indeed transcend differences in their backgrounds, and in their economic or social condition. Two people who believe it is more important to plant a new tree than to cut one down for lumber may have such a strong connection on this single value that they can form a deep friendship bond. And chances are they would find other values in common.

So look over your values and those of your friends. Make sure they are values you have honestly formed, without pressure or influence from the outside, and then seek out others with similar values for sharing experiences.

FINDING OTHERS

Dr. Leonard Zunin says, "There's always room in your life for another good friend. There are very few people that I've met in my entire life, less than a handful, who have all the good friends they want. I've met a number of people who have all of the acquaintances they want. I think people who really want friends, really need friends, would be much better off if they were able to define what they're looking for and then set out a plan, and actually pursue that plan. I tell patients who want a certain type of friend, 'Let's sit down and see what we can do to maximize the chances. I can't make guarantees. All I can say is that what you are doing now, if you keep doing it, is minimizing the probability. What can you do to increase that probability?' Also, I might ask whether the person toward whom you are reaching out has behavior that is in accordance with their own beliefs. Are they practicing what they preach? In other words, what do you believe in, and what do you do to back it up?"

Here again, it's important to note whether the values are true values. If they aren't, then you may have the destructive value-molding game, in which one person pretends to have certain values merely to entice the friendship of the other person. If, for example, you have a friend who says he shares your concern over the damage to the environment, and yet he refuses to fix his faulty exhaust system, which is causing part of the problem, you might begin to suspect he is merely paying lip service to that value.

Louis Mobley says, "People need to explore the whole range of values and then deliberately make choices. Otherwise you don't know whether it's a value or not. It may be something you're mouthing, but you really don't behave that way." The first step, then, in finding friends, is to know who you are and what you want.

WHAT DO YOU WANT IN A FRIEND?

To start with the basics, just focus inward and ask yourself whether you really want some new friends, or perhaps one new friend. What kind of person do you want this to be? What kind of values would you like him to have? What do you want from this friend?

Once you know what you want in a friend, you can probably figure out some good places to look for this person. If, for instance, it's important for you that your friend not overindulge in alcoholic beverages, you'd be pretty silly to look in bars. Yet you'd be surprised how many people are engaged in this kind of destructive and distorted friend-seeking, usually saying things like, "Well, where else are you going to meet people?"

EFFORT REQUIRED

It takes effort to meet people. You have to decide whether you want some new friendship energy, and then decide to go out and find it. If you wait for someone to come knocking on your door, or walking into your living room, you'll probably just end up making friends with door-to-door salesmen and burglars! There are millions of people out there, some of them looking for friends just like you.

First off, you have to admit you are looking for a friend. A lot of people assume that the desire for a new friend indicates they are not popular people, for if they were popular, friends would just come crawling out of the woodwork! This destructive assumption can prevent someone from reaching out in an otherwise appropriate moment. If you feel that admitting to another person that you want someone new in your life is an admission of some deep deficiency in your character, then you have serious relating problems.

So you want a friend and are willing to admit it—where does that leave you? Well, if you will simply make a list of your interests, the things you enjoy doing, the things you would like to learn about or learn how to do, and the major values you believe in, you will be off to a galloping start. If, for example, you are interested in the environment, there are any number of clubs and organizations in this area, including local chapters of the famed Sierra Club, and most of them plan outings, hikes, and campouts. There are also organizations devoted specifically to hiking or camping out, in both tents and recreational vehicles. If you like to read, you might check the library and other local organizations for groups that read the same book and then come together to talk about it. There are a number of these in almost every town and city, and it's an excellent way to meet people with similar interests. Or, if you would like to do something new and different, talk to someone in your local bookstore and suggest that everyone who buys a certain bestselling book come together at your place for a friendly discussion of that book at some not-too-distant date.

If you just let your mind roam freely, you'll come up with lots of your own suggestions via this personal brainstorming. Local colleges and universities are bound to have dozens of courses available to the general public in the evenings. If you like learning new handicrafts, you can take a course in one. Or a Chinese cooking class. Many of these schools also offer courses in the new therapies, in human relations, and in awareness and sensitivity, often featuring experiential exercises that allow the students to get to know one another in friendly ways. There may be TA or encounter groups, or sensitivity sessions held by growth centers, churches, or schools. Everyone likes to explore his own feelings, and this can really bring people together in close and satisfying interaction. There are also many organizations that have community projects going, or you may even think up a neighborhood project and enlist the aid of your community.

If you are doing something you enjoy, chances are you will enjoy the other people doing it, and vice versa. Here are twenty-four things that can bring people together:

Birdwatching. Sailing. Antique shows. Drawing classes. Cruises.

Theater groups. Film clubs. Scuba diving. Astrology lessons. Dog shows.

Collecting comic books. Building furniture. Making jewelry. Houseplants.

Bicycling. Flea markets. Health spas. Gourmet food clubs. Photography.

Auctions. Nudist camps. Karate lessons. Tennis lessons. Unusual pets.

The possibilities are limitless! Check your local newspaper for talks and seminars given by local organizations that might interest you. Look up organizations in your phone directory. Get on their mailing lists.

BEING OPEN TO FRIENDSHIP

Whether you have a strong need for new friends right now, or have a lot of good friendships, the most healthy way to facilitate continued nourishment seems to be to always allow yourself enough room for a potential new relationship. As you encounter people in your everyday life, you might ask yourself, "Can this person be a friend to me?" You may not be picking up what Dr. Edna Foa calls "friendship cues." Another factor that sometimes prevents us from reaching out is the unique way in which we each perceive the world and each other. In his book *Understanding Understanding*, Dr. Humphrey Osmond wrote, "The world as it appears to one person differs from the world as it appears to another. We are all occupying the same world 'out there,' but your subjective assessment of it 'in here' depends upon how we *perceive* the 'outside world'; and it is our perception of it that motivates our thoughts, feelings, and actions, hence our personalities or personal styles. Individuals perceive the same things differently and, so, *function* differently within the same setting. Have your ever wondered what someone sees in so-and-so, or why you're so fond of someone, or he of you? Have you ever wondered why some people seem unable to get along with each other? Confronted by the same circumstances in the 'outside world,' people respond differently—and characteristically—on the basis of their different subjectives, or 'inner worlds.' "

PETER AND RALPH

Peter and Ralph went bowling once a week. Peter noticed that for several weeks Ralph had seemed rather nervous and withdrawn. He assumed that Ralph was unhappy, and further assumed it was something he, Peter, was doing. He finally confronted Ralph and said, "What's wrong—have I done something to upset you? Aren't you enjoying our times together anymore? I used to really look forward to seeing you on our bowling night, but you've seemed so glum lately." Ralph then told Peter the problem was that he really wanted a good friend, like Peter, to spend more time than just one evening a week with. He had been afraid to approach Peter, assuming he would be rejected as a more intimate friend, and not wanting to invade Peter's privacy. Peter then confessed that he would really like to spend more time with Ralph, but he too had been afraid of asking for more than Ralph was willing to give. They decided to go away on a camping trip that very weekend, and spent much nourishing time together, even after Peter fell in love and got married.

Peter perceived Ralph's glum expression as being aimed at him, when actually it was a result of caring for him. Ralph felt Peter would not accept his friendship, and he too perceived Peter's emotional response incorrectly. This kind of isolation is all too common in our society today, with everyone afraid to ask for what he wants.

And sometimes you have to pay attention to more than just the simple exterior image the other person is projecting. In his excellent book on inner awareness, *The Natural Depth in Man,* Wilson Van Dusen says, "Perhaps the single most important basic skill that should be taught to all persons is the capacity really to see, hear, and understand others. Such a skill is useful in dealing with everyone—friends, relatives, or strangers. It enables one to understand a person more readily, bypassing much conversation and doubt. It enables one to respond more appropriately to others' needs. A friend may say all is going well with him, but you may see anxiety or depression in his face or gesture. A few gentle words reflecting what you see will deepen and make more real the whole basis of your relationship. What you might otherwise take as a deliberately obstinate attitude in another person may be backed by a consistent body rigidity. You can then see the attitude is not just directed against you, but it is part of the individual's whole life. The one seen and heard is generally better off when well understood. Your responses then fit where the other person is rather than where he's supposed to be."

In the case of Peter and Ralph, Peter was perceiving Ralph's glum expression as an indication of Ralph's possible dissatisfaction with the relationship. This also illustrates the need mentioned by Van Dusen to use a few gentle words to reflect what you see, before making judgments on it, before deciding you know exactly what is producing this response in the other person. If Ralph had kept on looking glum, and Peter had not approached him, they might have each become more isolated from the other, and eventually ended their once-a-week bowling ritual, never experiencing the nourishment their deeper friendship eventually provided.

THE MOMENT OF DECISION

Can you look over your list of friends and see for each the moment of decision, in which this relationship could have gone either way, either ending or moving toward the deeper relationship it became? This concept of decisions can be an important one. Dr. Harold Greenwald, a clinical psychologists, says all behavior is based on making decisions, some of which are unhealthy. He says, "People make decisions all the time, the major difficulty is that they don't want to be aware of them, because once you become aware of the decision, then you have to take responsibility for it. And most of us don't want to take responsibility. We prefer to think we're victims rather than the fact that we are where we are because we chose to be there. You may have the kinds of friends who give you payoffs for certain unfortunate decisions. For example, most friends will be very nice to us when we're sick, and they won't be nice to us when we're well. So, what we sometimes do is pick the kind of friends who will reward our most unfortunate kinds of behavior. People will say things like 'She always drags me down.' Not looking at the fact that they chose this friend, and not looking at what their goal was in choosing this particular kind of friend. If, for example, your original decision was to prove the world is no good, you'll pick friends to reinforce this. I've known people like that, and they'll tell me how all the friends they choose are no good, and they're now going to pick good friends. So they pick somebody, and pretty soon they goddamn well prove that this one is no good either. Some little fancied slight, insult, or so on, makes them reaffirm their original belief, their original decision. It's very difficult to decide to pick friends on another basis until you deal with what's going on behind the choices you make."

So, another way to look over your friends is to see if you can identify what life decisions were in operation when you chose them. Do your friends reinforce healthy decisions, such as to be loving, independent, and generous, or do they reinforce unhealthy ones, such as to be perfect, to have everyone love you, or never to be alone?

You can probably see how complex such life decisions can be. Can you also see that if there's so much hidden material behind every action you take in your life, there's just as much hidden material behind the actions of your friends and potential friends? Don't make simple judgments based on the obvious external manifestations of your friends' behavior. A lot more may be going on behind that sad expression or that smiling face.

PUTTING YOURSELF IN ANOTHER'S PLACE

One way to appreciate all that is going on inside another person, even though you will never fully perceive or understand that other person, is to put yourself in his place. Wilson Van Dusen tells how he used to do this in *The Natural Depth in Man*, describing how he would ride the San Francisco cable cars as a boy, and if an old lady got on he would study everything about her, and become her for a little while, reconstructing his world as this little old woman. Imagining her situation and her motivations. This is similar to Milton Mayerhoff's seeing someone as if with that person's eye.

Try this sometime with a friend. Just imagine you are this person.

Imagine how you would feel about what you are giving to this friend. If you are Dave and your friend is Howard, imagine you are Howard, and how you feel about Dave and what you are getting from Dave. Imagine why you have the expression you have on your face, why you do and say the things you are doing and saying. This exercise may give you a new understanding and appreciation of the other person.

It is all too easy to keep ourselves isolated from others. Part of our humanness has to do with our ability to go beyond façades, to make the effort to reach out.

In *Love,* Leo Buscaglia tells this story: "I recall an evening in a bar in San Francisco. I was with several good friends. The conversation was animated. We were all sharing reactions to a wondrous day's diversions. I saw a gentleman at a nearby table, sitting alone, staring at his half-filled cocktail glass. 'Why don't we ask him to join us? He seems so alone,' I said. 'I know what it means to be alone in a roomful of people.'

" 'Let him be,' was the consensus of the others. 'Perhaps he wants to be alone.'

" 'That's fine, but if I ask him, he'll have a choice.'

"I approached the gentleman and questioned whether he would like to join us or if he would prefer being alone. His eyes lit up with surprise. He accepted happily. He was a visitor from Germany. As he joined our table, he told us that he had traveled the entire length of the United States without speaking to anyone except hotel receptionists, tour guides, and waiters. Our invitation was a most welcome change. Of course, it must be admitted that some of the fault rested with the German gentleman, for part of the responsibility lies with each of us to reach out. If we take the risk, it is true that we may be rejected, but we must also remember that all men are also prospective friends and lovers."

Do you really believe this is true? Can you look at the people you meet and see in them the seeds of a prospective friendship? Do you automatically assume you know what would happen if you reached out to certain people, without ever making the effort?

We are beautifully complex creatures, and what a terrible mistake it is to think we know all there is to know about the desirability of another human being from just the limited exterior view they present to us. Look at yourself in the mirror. Could anyone really know the depth and full potential of you from just this body and the way it looks and the way it stands? Are you really giving other people a fair chance?

NEW FRIENDSHIPS WITH OLD FRIENDS

And perhaps you are not even giving your current friends a fair chance to be all they could be for you. In overlooking all of their potential, you are cheating yourself. By checking out at a deeper level than just what you see, by comparing more of your values and interests, by using new skills in self-disclosure and feedback, you may find some of your old friends can become exactly the new, creative relating partners you require.

Exploring new potential in old friends is sometimes harder than just finding new people, and you might make the choice based on how much energy you have and whether you feel it's worth expanding this current relationship with some new kinds of contact and communication.

POTENTIAL FRIENDS ARE EVERYWHERE

For a book on friends, there really isn't a whole lot of material on these pages devoted to finding new friends. The reason for this is simple: When you learn new relating skills, when you realize what you are really looking for in a friend, when you begin understanding others and realizing that they are much more than merely what they say or do, then the friendships will happen. All you have to do is decide what you want and then do something about that decision. You don't have to go on a desperate search for people. They are all around you. All you have to do is open your eyes and your mind and your heart. By knowing who you are and what you want, and reaching out warmly and honestly, you will attract the kind of people whom you will find attractive. It *is* as simple as that!

Finish the sentence: "One new thing I've learned about my friends is the fact that ———." And then go on to the next chapter.

CHAPTER 8

FRIENDS AND LOVERS

Sex and the sex drive has a lot to do with our attitudes toward friends, and the ways in which we have separated this part of our lives from all the other parts has led to some confusing distinctions between the terms "friend" and "lover." In the best of all possible worlds, there would be no difference between friends and lovers. They would all just be people, people to whom you related in different ways, depending on the unique qualities of your one-to-one interactions.

YOUR OWN DEFINITIONS

You are really the only one who can define what the terms friend and lover mean for you. And whether they can be interchangeable. In our culture we have so overemphasized the separation of the sexes and the pursuit of sexual fulfillment that we have distorted and perverted some basic areas of interpersonal interaction. For example, as children, very often there are strict rules for "boy play" and "girl play," with the two sexes never getting together except in awkward contact. Later, in adolescence, boys and girls relate to friends of the same sex as temporary substitutes until "love" comes along, or use such friends as sounding boards to discuss their romantic activities and aspirations. In young adulthood, friends of the same sex are easily dropped or ignored when a love relationship begins, and wedding bells often break up "that old gang of mine." What has happened is that the rewards of friendship with one's own sex have been largely unrealized and overlooked. At the same time there is a sharp distinction drawn between friends of the same sex and lovers or potential lovers of the opposite sex. At its worst, this perverse pattern leads to the dehumanization of both friends and lovers, so that they become objects. If you feel, for instance, that no lover can be your friend, or that you can't have a friend as a lover, then you have probably fallen victim to this destructive programming.

A lot of negative conditioning about friendship comes from this confusion. For instance, a young man may be interested in a young woman romantically, and she says to him, "But I just want to be your friend." Saying, in effect, that friendship is something less than lovership. In a chapter entitled Love Relationships in the Life Cycle, in *Love Today*, Dr. David Orlinsky says, "It is asked if persons of opposite sex can be 'just good friends.' Individual instances show that they can, but these are relatively infrequent, perhaps because of the degree to which erotic feelings are sublimated in friendship."

Thus, we seem to feel that sexual feelings are an unhealthy or an unnatural factor in friendships. We deny our sexuality when seeking friendship with members of the opposite sex. Hugh Prather put it so well in *Notes to Myself:* "I don't like the way I acted toward Alice. I was experiencing her as a very attractive girl, and yet the whole time I acted like an asexual nice-guy. When I feel like a man I want to act like one and not like a polite eunuch.

"You say you just want to be my friend. I know you mean you want to relate to my mind but not to my body. I can understand that, and will not ask you to relate to me in a way you don't want to. But likewise I refuse to castrate myself for you by pretending. If you want to have me as your friend you will have to accept my penis along with me."

SUE AND FRED

Sue and Fred have been friends for five years. They have traveled together, slept cuddled in each other's arms, massaged each other's nude bodies, and shared intimate confidences. But they have not sexually interacted. During most of their friendship, both have been in primary love relationships with other people, and have not had the need or desire to fill sexual roles for each other. They appreciate all the other facets of their relationship, and feel their sexual needs can be fulfilled in other ways with other people, while the friendship needs that are now being fulfilled would be very difficult to replace. The time they spend together, therefore, they choose to spend in other ways, to nourish parts of themselves that may not be nourished by other, sexual relationships. But they do not rule out the possibility that they may someday choose to change this and explore each other sexually. They admit they find each other attractive, and should either of them be sexually needy, the terms of their friendship may change to include this aspect of their lives. They are therefore saying that, though so far they haven't felt the need to nourish each other sexually, they are not setting up rigid restrictions that would lead to sublimation, denial, and frustration or resentment.

It's really a matter of choice. Fred and Sue are choosing not to have sex together. It is not a fear. They are not repressing their sexual feelings. They are not saying that having sex would be bad or ruin the friendship. They are just choosing not to experience that part of themselves with each other. They are making a free choice, for the moment. But if they felt uptight about their sexuality or held back feelings of attraction because they wanted to stick to what they felt a friendship "should" be, then they would be operating in a negative and unhealthy way.

Furthermore, these two friends of the opposite sex do choose to nourish each other physically with stroking, cuddling, and massaging. Psychologists agree that many sexual encounters are merely efforts to get the touching and cuddling that all humans require. Having some friends of the opposite sex who can provide this can take some of the burden and goal orientation away from one's sexual life. If Fred can go to Sue for some of his touch needs, he may not choose to engage in casual sexual encounters which can be dehumanizing and destructive.

The important thing is to be able to choose freely in any opposite-sex relationship.

JANIS AND TOM

Janis and Tom worked in the same office. Tom found Janis very attractive. Janis also found Tom attractive. She was in love with a man working on the oil pipeline in Alaska, a man who was going to be physically separated from her for six months. She felt she couldn't handle another sexual relationship, but she did want some warm human contact. She had hesitated approaching or responding too warmly to Tom for fear he would think she was leading him on and promising him something she couldn't deliver. She finally agreed to meet him for dinner. When Tom invited her back to his apartment for a drink, she really was wary, but she was also lonely. They had a couple of drinks. One thing led to another, and they started cuddling and kissing. Janis hadn't wanted to get into anything sexual, but her body was responding to Tom's caresses. Tom really hadn't planned to make sexual advances, but Janis was a lovely woman and obviously found him attractive. So they ended up in bed together. Just as they were about to have intercourse, Janis jumped up and ran out of the bedroom, crying hysterically. She finally was able to tell Tom that she really didn't want to have sex with him, even though she liked his warmth and his company. Tom told her that he was dating several very attractive women who provided him with all the sex he wanted. They agreed to keep spending time together, and to cuddle up together from time to time, without having sex. Tom began to talk about his experiences with other women, and Janis was able to give him some valuable insight from a woman's point of view. He provided her with some warm companionship and some of her touch needs.

If Tom had had a heavier investment in proving his masculinity, and had taken Janis' refusal to have sex with him as a put-down, the friendship never could have happened. Anytime a man or woman can only see members of the opposite sex as potential lovers, then a lot of possibilities are being ignored.

In his book *Friendship*, Myron Brenton writes: "When women and men see each other in stereotypical roles, as historically has been the case to now, only expectations based on 'You're a man' and 'You're a woman' are easily possible. Every encounter between a woman and a man then becomes heavy with unspoken demands: confirm that I'm desirable, acknowledge my virility, my orgasmic capacity, prove to me that I'm a sexual being—that's your role, that's your job. Such expectations make true cross-sex friendships difficult if not impossible to achieve."

One of the reasons cross-sex friendships may be becoming more possible is simply that sex is now more readily available to men and women, and the line between friendship and lovership may be beginning to fade. Coming to a friendship from a nonneedy, nonfrustrated space allows whatever is going to happen between a man and woman to happen naturally, mutually, spontaneously. In the example above of Janis and Tom, Janis was putting restrictions on the relationship, but she was not denying her attraction to Tom. She was willing to sublimate her own sexual needs, and Tom was having his fulfilled elsewhere. Chances are that their friendship could have been more fulfilling for both of them if there were no restrictions, but it was still a rather healthy relationship.

FRIENDSHIP VERSUS LOVERSHIP

In a conversation with the author, Bart Knapp, PhD, and Marta Vago, MSW, who are friends, lovers, and codirectors of Philadelphia's most highly respected therapy center, Laurel Institute, talked about the differences between the two relationship definitions. Marta Vago says, "It's a shame that there is such pressure from society to make relationships between members of the opposite sex into sexual ones, because there are many relationships that are mainly friend relationships and not lover relationships. And yet, with the pressure, a couple will make a heterosexual friendship into a sexual one. Some friendships can go under because the friendship is perhaps at its best when it's actually a true friendship, and it may deteriorate in value when it becomes a sexual one."

Bart Knapp says, "When a relationship is a sexual one, or is focusing on sexual differences, then it's focusing on *differences*. But with people as friends, where the sexuality is sort of outside it, then you're focusing on the common factor, the common factor of humanity. You're then focusing on *similarities* rather than on the differences, the aspect of sex. A friendship is based on a broader spectrum of factors. Sexually, the lovership focuses on a narrow spectrum, a more restricted range."

Marta Vago adds, "I would say a very strong friendship could include a sexual aspect as long as the basic friendship contract is one of friendship and not something else. But sex could be one of the ways in which the friendship could be expressed."

FRIENDS AS LOVERS

Perhaps only sexually satisfied men and women can have real cross-sex friendships, at least in terms of open sharing of feelings. Without desperate sexual neediness, cross-sex friends may find themselves enjoying each other sexually from time to time, as an expression of their caring for each other, as something that happens when they both have a sexual urge and happen to be in each other's company. If a man and woman who are friends find themselves between relationships, they may choose to satisfy each other's sexual needs rather than enter into casual sexual encounters with partners with whom they do not share the foundation of trust and caring they have established in the friendship. This can be a healthy manifestation of the friendship feelings as long as it is mutually agreed upon and done openly without manipulation.

EX-LOVERS AS FRIENDS

It seems to be an idealized image: the lovers moving from passion and romance to a warm and fulfilling friendship. In workshops entitled It's Over! Now What?, aimed at helping people cope with the end of love relationships, the author noted that almost every participant expressed a desire for a friendship with the former love-partner, or at least admitted that such a friendship would be desirable if it were possible.

BONNIE AND HERB

Bonnie and Herb lived together as lovers for three years. They mutually decided to end it and move on to other partners. They decided that they had grown as much as possible in this relationship. A few months after their separation, they met for one of their infrequent lunch dates, and shared the fact that they each missed some of the things they had enjoyed from each other during their love relationship, even though they were both in love with new partners. They decided to see each other more often, once a week at least. They even resumed some of their sexual activity, which had always been highly rewarding for them. They had no desire to resume the primary love relationship, but they did want to nourish and continue some of the good things that had developed over their three years together. There were also things they could say to each other that they didn't feel quite comfortable saying to their new love-partners. They had three years of trust behind them, and the awareness that nothing they said could damage the relationship they now had.

Rather than threaten their new love relationships, the friendship of Bonnie and Herb gave them each nourishment that they could take back into the primary relationships. They were able to check out many responses and awarenesses with each other. If Herb felt uneasy about something that was happening in his primary relationship, he might check out Bonnie's perceptions, and get the female point of view, thus being able to go back to his primary partner with some new perspectives for sharing. The friendship was not "platonic," it was not nonsexual, but the sexual activity they shared was just a once-in-a-while happening, a way in which they sometimes chose to share some of their warm feelings for each other. And the sharing and the trusting were the main factors in their relationship, and a feeling that they would be a part of each other's lives for a long, long time. Although they had both agreed at the end of their love relationship that they had grown together as much as possible, they now found that this new role of loving friends was fostering new growth for each of them.

This seems to be happening more and more, even with divorced couples, even after a lot of bitterness over the breakup. This is not to deny the difficulties, most of which have to do with our stereotyped images of what a lover should be and what a friend should be. The more we get away from what we believe and pay attention to what our actual experience is, the more possible this friendly transition will be.

Dr. Marjorie Toomim, a clinical psychologist, says, "One of the reasons people have so much difficulty staying friends after divorce is that they still really like each other. So they are ambivalent, and in our culture it's much easier to settle ambivalence by getting angry than it is to feel affection for someone that you can't have. It's sort of 'I feel I like you, but I also can't stand you' or 'I like you and you can't live with me.' Rather than be frustrated and like somebody that you can't have, or can't live with, or can't fulfill yourself with, it's easier to simply negate them and reject them, and get angry with them, and feed yourself reasons why you *should* be angry with them. It's an internal process."

The hardest thing in the world to do is to give up something you've been used to, something you've taken as your rightful due, something you've taken for granted. If you're really used to the passion and romantic love you have experienced in a marriage or any other love relationship, it's going to be very hard to give up that expectation and settle for what, in your mind, may be a lesser relationship. But, as so often is true in human behavior, the effort to surmount the difficulty pays handsome dividends. The richness of shared love, and trust built up over years of interacting, can provide a beautiful background for a nourishing friendship.

ROBERTA AND ROGER

Roberta and Roger were married thirteen years when their marriage broke up. There was a lot of mutual bitterness. They had an eight-year-old boy and an eleven-year-old girl, both of whom deeply suffered from the reflected pain of this bitterness. Roberta just did not want to be a wife anymore. She wanted to finish her education, she wanted to explore herself, and she couldn't see this happening inside the structure of her marriage. Roger wanted a wife, someone who would be there with a hot meal waiting when he came home from work. Roberta had been willing to fill that role for thirteen years, and had been happy in it. But she had changed. A year after their separation the divorce became final. Roberta got the house and custody of the children, but Roger was actively involved in his role as their father. The bitterness faded, and Roberta found herself asking Roger for financial advice, for help in planning which schools the children might attend, and numerous other domestic issues. They found themselves liking each other as people, even though the marriage and love relationship were over. They began going out to dinner with the children once a week, and even went away on a weekend ski trip together. When Roberta wanted to travel on her own to Europe for a month, Roger moved back into the house and stayed with the children. Their thirteen years of being together had built up a lot of connective facets. Though they both dated frequently, they found there were still things they felt most comfortable sharing with each other. Both describe their new relationship as a "freeing experience." Each honestly feels there is little or no chance they'll ever want to get back into a primary love relationship with each other, and they also feel that this is a friendship that will last their entire lives.

CHANGE WITHIN THE LOVE RELATIONSHIP

Another transition, with similar difficulties, is a move from romantic love to friendly companionship within an existing relationship commitment. Marta Vago gives an example of an everyday couple: "They start out as lovers, and they live together for a while, and over a period of time they become friends more than lovers. You may see a dropping off of sexual appetite, interest in sex, and there isn't the same intensity and investment in the sexual aspect of the relationship. This frightens many couples, and they think it means that they don't love each other. I think what has happened is that the pendulum has swung over more to the friendship end of the continuum, and because of that the lovership/sexuality is less important. It's not that the sexuality isn't there, but the relationship, in a sense, has become more full. And if we use the concept that friendship has one aspect of it, the sexual aspect, then we can see that once a couple really become friends, when there really is a good relationship, the sexuality is simply one aspect of the friendship, one facet of it. When they started out as lovers, the sexuality, the romantic part of the relationship, was much more important, and the friendship aspect was simply undeveloped, like an embryo in a fetal state."

Dr. Bart Knapp adds to this concept by saying, "The love and the sexuality is an adhesive for the relationship, and if it begins to shift into a friendship, the partners may see it as falling apart, because the adhesive is no longer binding. Yet there are other ways of binding the relationship."

In fact, the relationship that has sexuality becoming merely one facet of a fuller experience is a much richer and more fulfilling one. A number of psychologists feel that the myth of romantic love locks us into unrealistic expectations, and that the deeper empathy feelings of a loving friendship are far more nourishing. Poet Ric Masten says, "I think romantic love is a form of madness, the fiery passion that is. And I'm not sure there's any place for that in friendship. You wouldn't want to live day by day with someone you were crazy-nuts over."

BREAKING UP THAT OLD GANG OF MINE

Love relationships, and marriages, often have destructive effects on friendships that existed before the two individuals fell in love. Sometimes this is merely a time factor. In a primary relationship there is less time for outside friendships. But it is also true that jealousy and possessiveness often lie at the root of these discarded friendships. Saying "We don't need our friends, we have each other" may sound beautiful and romantic, but it may be a rationale for an unwillingness to risk the partner's displeasure by keeping up outside friendships. It's true that a powerful love experience can fill your life to the extent that you don't want anyone else in it, but this usually occurs only at the very beginning of a love relationship, when that time alone together is necessary to build a strong foundation of understanding and trust. If the trust and understanding really happen and then each partner reaches out for friends, the experience can be healthy and nourishing for the couple, and they will bring that health and nourishment back into the love relationship.

Look over your list of friends and see if you can determine how these friendships were affected by either the friend or you falling in love.

In *Open Marriage*, George and Nena O'Neill say, "The closed marriage contract demands that all friends must be acceptable to both partners. Each partner in the marriage is thus forced to give up any former friends his new mate doesn't like, or else sneak off to see them outside the house, meeting at the bowling alley or the hairdresser. Since no two people can possibly match all of one another's hook-up points, and since both premarital friendships and contact with other couples are subject to the veto of either partner, it is inevitable that the husband and wife in this situation will both become diminished persons."

Always relating to other people as a couple, and requiring that it always be on terms of couple-to-couple encounters, eliminates many friendship possibilities. In their book *Why Be Lonely,* authors Edward E. Ford and Robert L. Zorn say, "Close friendships are not developed in a crowd. Couples who go out with other couples often do not spend much time with each other during the evening. If they interact with many other couples, it tends to water down the relation-strengthening process and thus no building occurs. They do not have to work as hard at getting along with each other because there are so many others around. Close friendships are developed in one-to-one encounters. Doing things alone with another is very strengthening."

YOUR ONLY FRIEND

If your only friend, your only truly intimate friend, is your love-partner, then you have no other resource for the nurturing feedback that can enhance your relating skills and your awareness. There may be times when you just want to open up honestly and talk about what is happening in your primary love relationship. But if you have isolated yourself from all other friends, there is no one you can trust enough to talk to at this level. Not to mention the fact that if your primary love relationship should end, you may then not only lose a lover, but your best and perhaps only friend, a doubly traumatic experience, especially since the end of a love relationship is a time when we can really use a good friend. In a poem in the book *How to Survive the Loss of a Love,* poet Peter McWilliams illustrates this point:

all I need is
someone to
talk to
about
you
but

you
are the
only person
I can really
talk to. trapped.

And we may trap ourselves. It can be a way of putting the burden on the other person in a love relationship, saying, in effect, "I have given up all my friends, so you'd better stick with me or I'll be all alone in the world!"

Myron Brenton interviewed many people for his book *Friendship*, and says, "I encountered a few couples where both partners agreed that they sufficed unto each other and did not need friends. Much more often, where friendlessness prevailed, it was one of the partners who had no friends, relied completely on his mate, and in effect said, 'My spouse is everything to me, my best friend, my only friend, the one I always turn to.' And in almost every instance of this kind the partner on the receiving end of this overwhelming dependency would indeed feel overwhelmed. Would say to me, either directly or in a roundabout way, 'I wish he'd find a friend!' "

Just as your friends can reveal a lot to you about your emotional status, the ways in which friendships are interwoven into a marriage or other primary love relationship are indicative of the total pattern of relating. For instance, if one partner tries to make the other feel guilty because he or she has outside friendships, then there's a good chance that same partner will try guilt trips on other issues in the relationship.

AN OUTSIDE FRIEND

If you can see the importance of having an outside friendship, sit down with your love-partner and make an agreement that you will each have at least one friend who relates to you and you alone, not to the couple, not as a "joint" friend. If you do not now have any outside individual friendships, make a real effort to cultivate at least one apiece. As the friendship evolves, share with each other what you see as the value of having this outside friend.

If you honestly attempt this exercise in relating to a friend outside the primary relationship, you will most likely find that it will enrich your time together, allowing you to bring a fresh viewpoint back into the relationship.

If everything you do, and everyone you relate to, is always within the confines of the relationship, then they are indeed confines, a sort of prison. If you cannot feel comfortable having an old friend over to your home for a visit, just because he or she isn't also a friend to your love-partner, then you may be in a very restrictive and potentially damaging relationship. And if you do not accept your love-partner's friends, and are always putting them down, ridiculing them, trying to get your love-partner to get rid of them, then you are probably projecting your own insecurity. You might as well try to get your love-partner to give up all the foods you don't like, all the books you don't enjoy reading, all the music you don't like to hear.

TYRANNY OR DEMOCRACY

It all boils down to this: Is your love relationship a tyranny or a democracy? Is it something that enhances each partner's sense of self, or something that diminishes it? Looking at just how friends fit in can give the answers to these significant questions. Just ask yourself this simple question:

"Am I as free now to seek and relate to friends as I was before I formed this love relationship?"

HIS OR HERS?

Another major problem in having friends who relate only to the couple, and not separately to either or each individual, is that the friends may not know where to go when the relationship ends. As is only natural, they usually have stronger loyalties toward one partner than toward the other. If the friends are another couple, they may each have different loyalties, and may avoid contact altogether as a way of resolving that conflict. Each individual in a couple relationship is responsible for the friendship situation, and can avoid such conflict and potential confusion by investing some time and energy in developing and maintaining outside friendships.

STEPHANIE AND JOEY

Stephanie and Joey fell in love after meeting at a convention. Joey decided to move to Stephanie's city, and made friends with most of her close friends. He really enjoyed them as people, and saw no need to make additional friends on his own. After a few months, however, the romance withered, and Joey and Stephanie separated with some bitterness. Since they had been Stephanie's friends to start with, the friends all stayed with her and avoided Joey. He found himself all alone in a city in which he had no roots. It was a terribly depressing time for Joey. But he learned his lesson. He fell in love again just a few months later, but this time he cultivated many friendships of his own, as well as friends who could relate both to him and his new love-partner. A year later, when that love relationship ended amiably, he kept all of his friends, and some of the friends he and his love-partner had shared were able to maintain contact with both of them.

Friends *can* stick by both partners when a relationship ends. It's harder for them, and they'll want to do it only if they have honestly related to both people while they were still together. This can also support the kind of environment in which the former love-partners can build their own friendship. So, in a love relationship, the healthiest situation may be to have *my friends*, *your friends*, and *our friends*. Then there is friendship enough for everybody, and a lot of happy and nourishing interaction.

A NEW BEGINNING

For Joey, the bitter end of a love relationship and loss of those people he assumed to be his friends fostered new appreciation for friendship and new interpersonal strengths.

For those locked into rigid and stifling marriages, for instance, the end of the marriage can often open up powerful new awarenesses of the importance of friends and the realization that there were no valid friendships occurring during the marriage.

Research psychologist Susan Scholz says that women can learn a new appreciation for women friends after the end of a marriage: "In the traditional married state, most of the time women had friends that their husbands brought home. For the first time, the women I know who are divorced have been able to pick those people that they *wanted* to pick, based on their own needs and wants. This is certainly true for me and it's been super, because I don't think my ex-husband would have liked many of my friends."

The person Susan Scholz has picked to be her closest friend is college professor, Mary Ann Somervill. As mothers, PhDs, divorced women, professional women, and active members in the National Organization for Women, Susan and Mary Ann have much in common. But what really draws them together is their caring for each other as people. Their friendship transcends their roles, whether they are sharing baby-sitters or seats on the board of the local NOW chapter. May Ann Somervill says, "We can be ourselves and not have to be Dr. Somervill and Dr. Scholz." And she wrote this poem to describe her feelings about the friendship:

> We'll grow old together
> we decide
> as we contemplate
> our probable futures
> and who can understand
> the significance
> of our decision.
>
> A woman friend.
> Not a lover
> yet much loved.
>
> Many men will come and go
> passing through our lives
> drawing upon our time together
> but taking nothing from
> our feelings for each other.
>
> They come and go.
> We will remain
> and grow old
> together.

The emerging personhood of the American woman has helped blur the lines of distinction between friendship and lovership. This liberation movement has freed us all, by focusing on the humanness of each of us as people rather than on sexual stereotypes. In ancient times most deep friendships were between men in shared activities—hunting, making war or politics, or carousing. Women were supposed to be dutiful and inconspicuous. The dramatic change in this concept over the past few years has led to an appreciation of the cross-sex friendship. Now two people of the opposite sex can relate to each other, rather than just playing masculine and feminine roles. The woman-woman friendship has been an enriching fringe benefit of this liberating phenomenon.

In an article for the November–December, 1975, issue of *New Woman,* writer Diane de Dubovay noted that friendship between women in America is a relatively new trend: "Many women are beginning to realize that it's worth being friends with another woman—that a female friend can, in fact, be just as witty, stimulating, compassionate and worthy of admiration as a man, and that her friendship lacks the strain of physical and emotional bartering that often accompanies a relationship between a man and a woman."

And the nourishing qualities of the woman-woman friendship often overlap into the love relationships enjoyed by each woman.

YOU DECIDE

You, of course, have to decide what is best for you. You can decide whether you feel you want to have friendships with members of the opposite sex that include sexual interaction. And whether you agree that such friendships should focus on the friendship aspect of the relationship rather than on the sexual aspect. You also decide whether you want to have opposite-sex friendships that do not include sexual activity but do include touching and cuddling. And whether you want to pursue outside friendships while involved in a primary love relationship, agreeing that it's desirable to be a good friend to your love-partner, but not the only friend he or she has. And whether you feel it's possible to become a friend to your former love-partner when the romantic relationship has ended. And whether you agree that the liberation of the American woman has opened up new friendship possibilities.

But don't allow all the theories on the differences between friends and lovers confuse you. Decide for yourself what your definition of a friend is; what your definition of a lover is. When you meet someone, try to avoid the trap of immediately labeling the person as a friend or lover or acquaintance. Check your feelings out as the relationship itself progresses. What feels right, rather than what you think should be right, is usually what *is* right for you at that moment. Realize that there is value in having friends who are also lovers, and in having lovers who are also friends, and in having male friends, and in having female friends. At any given period in your life, you decide which will be most rewarding for you, in terms of what you need and want, and in terms of the amount of time and energy you have available. Of course, unless you experiment with some different kinds of friendships, you won't be able to make a real choice. Freedom of choice only occurs with an awareness of the alternatives.

Finish the sentence "One new thing I've learned about my friends is the fact that ———." Examine how you feel about this, and go on to the next chapter.

CHAPTER 9

ROOM TO GROW

If you subscribe to the concept that our friends can offer us a supportive interpersonal environment, an environment that encourages and nourishes our individual growth, then it follows that we have to allow room in our lives for the friends who will provide this environment.

If you accept the proposition that you are a moving, growing, changing organism, then you must also accept the proposition that you are doing so at your own individual pace. This means that the friends you have now may either not be growing at all or may be growing at a different pace than you. This does not make them better or worse than you, but your growth potential may be enhanced by having the freedom to interact with those people who are operating at your specific growth level at any given period in your life. If you fill your life to overflowing with old friends, and insist on holding on to them even though they may not be satisfying your current needs, you are limiting yourself. And you are missing the opportunity to interact with those people whose very reaction and response to you may be just what you need to support your personal growth.

As Myron Brenton says in *Friendship*, "We assume (or take for granted) that the kinds of relationship patterns we build up with friends, mutually gratifying as they are when we settle into them, will always stay that way. Of course, it is not something we should take for granted; that people grow away from each other is probably the top reason why friendships end."

Former psychologist and now famed spiritual leader Baba Ram Dass sees growth and increased spiritual awareness almost always changing friendship patterns: "You'll still be friends; you just won't share time and space anymore because you each will have gone on a different journey. No blame. As you keep awakening, you will find different people attract you. If you're involved in motorcycles, you want to be around motorcycle people. When you're busy going to God, you want to be around God people. If you're into both, you want to be around God people who ride motorcycles."

Though this last line from Ram Dass was delivered tongue-in-cheek, it points to a real issue. We may often needlessly end friendships when we demand that our friends do everything we do, are interested in everything we are interested in. Now, if your friend isn't interested in anything you are interested in, and isn't moving while you are, it may be time to separate. But getting rid of everybody who isn't a carbon copy of you will leave you all alone. Keeping just those friends who may happen to appear as carbon copies of you can leave you in even a worse condition: bored stagnation.

In his book *I Ain't Much, Baby, But I'm All I've Got,* Dr. Jess Lair says, "Once we have a clearer sense of who it is and what it is we really are, we drop away from a lot of people who are misery and trouble to us. It's not that there's something wrong with them, but those aren't the right people for us. As we drop away from those people, our life again can be different. I know after I had my heart attack, one of the things I looked at was some of the people I called my friends and thought were my friends. A lot of them weren't really; we were just kind of mutual enemies. And the minute that we each went our own separate ways, we were both happier because of it. I'm sure one of the ways you see this is in your friends of high school days, or particularly after you get away from them. Some of those people you look at and say, 'Oh, how could I have stood that person?' They were friends of convenience. We needed each other and clung together as to a life raft in the middle of the ocean. But there was no real friendship."

Perhaps one of Jess Lair's sentences will help you focus on another important aspect of allowing room to grow: *And the minute that we each went our own separate ways, we were both happier because of it.* So often people are afraid of severing connections with others for fear that the others will suffer. No one really suffers when the end comes to a relationship that was not a growing experience. It's part of what Jack Gibb fosters in his TORI communities: trusting that when you are being yourself, it will be accepted and acceptable. Dr. Gibb says, "I have in the past colluded with another person unconsciously. I like to talk a lot, and so I get a woman who will listen to me ad infinitum and adore me while I talk, and that's a good feeling, but it's a destructive relationship because there's no way that's going to last very long. Any relationship that's based on distrust or fear or collusion escalates the fear and distrust, and becomes a destructive relationship. But also, there are no destructive relationships that a person who begins to grow can be destroyed by."

A CLEAN SWEEP

Group leader Emily Coleman puts it in even stronger terms in her book, *Making Friends with the Opposite Sex:* "Make a clean sweep. Get rid of boring friends, whining friends, hostile friends, friends who talk your ear off and friends who sit quietly by, saying and doing nothing, letting you carry the whole burden of the conversation and the relationship. Trim down your list of friends to those who really inspirit you, and you'll find you have time and energy to seek new friends."

Emily Coleman sees this ability to end destructive or nongrowing friendships as an important skill in our culture: "With us having so many more people that we meet all the time, we have to develop the skill to get into a friendship quicker, to be able to make contact quicker, to be able to deepen it quicker, and we have to be able to cut it off when we move on, so that we don't leave loose ends."

LOOSE ENDS

Loose ends can be emotionally crippling. They usually come from just drifting apart from friends, not letting them know you are feeling the relationship is over or that you want it to be over. Sure, it's easier—it's not as scary just letting it slowly fade, but it also is dishonest and self-poisoning.

Dr. Leonard Zunin says, "I think how you've said good-bye to past friends is a very important thing. You say good-bye hundreds of times in life. You say good-bye to a favorite dress when it's too tattered to continue wearing. You say good-bye when you move from one city to another, when you change your job. You say good-bye to different stages of life. Some people can't say good-bye to being a teen-ager, some people can't say good-bye at a time of divorce. Some parents can't say good-bye when their children get ready to leave them. And some people can't say good-bye to friends, to friendships that have ended. The reason that I think it's so crucial to understand the elements of how we say good-bye is because that's not only a measure of our mental health and our stability, but it's also related to our ability to say hello. You're never fully there if you haven't said good-bye to something that has ended. Life is a series of partings and greetings."

Psychiatrist Eileen Walkenstein agrees. "As long as the person stays clutching onto a relationship that's really dead, they won't have their arms open and available for receiving any other kind of relationship. So there are times when you must cut loose of the corpses and the dead baggage."

Dr. George and Nena O'Neill comment on this in *Shifting Gears.* "The fact of moving into a new phase in your life will make it necessary to change some friends. You are going to be growing and it is going to be important to find other people who are growing and who will keep you growing. Just as we must be selective, focus on what is important to us and eliminate the options that confuse and distract us, so too we must exercise this ability with friends. This is not to diminish the importance and stability of old friends with whom you have shared past experiences and with whom you may share a whole commonality of interests. But you must move in the area of friendships, too. They become a vital part of our growth, lead us into new areas, stimulate us in thinking and provide new information."

In a column for *Ladies' Home Journal,* Dr. Theodore I. Rubin said, "It is an excellent idea to take stock of friends periodically, reviewing how you relate to them and how they relate to you. Friendships with people who consistently fill you with self-hate, destroy your self-esteem, and make you feel unhappy should be terminated."

IT'S HEALTHY TO LET GO

Thus the evidence seems overwhelming. Psychologists and psychiatrists seem to agree: moving out of destructive or nongrowing friendships is healthy, staying in stagnating relationships is not. Dr. Marjorie Toomim puts it this way: "Friends are expendable. As I have grown and developed, I've changed my friendships. I know that my clients are growing as their friendship patterns change. The people that they're interested in change. And they don't have anything to share in common with the people they knew two years ago. They're just not in the same place. They come in to start therapy, and the only kind of people they can possibly relate to are people that they don't see very often. People they would only go to a movie with, and then they'd go right home. Or people who are so involved in their work or their families that they really don't have time for my patients, except to do something like go shopping with them once in a while. And then, two years later, they're dealing with people with whom they can really communicate. And they like to spend long periods of time together. And they wouldn't bother to go see a movie with their friends; they wouldn't want to waste the time."

Can you see periods in your life where the letting go of friendships coincided with healthy growth in you?

Make a list of the friendships you've ended over the past few years, and after each name finish the sentence "Since I ended this friendship, I have ———." Fill in the blank with any positive movement or growth you have made, even if it feels unrelated to the friendship that ended. Then look at whether just the factor of free time, time that may have been spent in that friendship, didn't have something to do with that forward movement in your life. Or you may begin to see subtle connections.

CHARLOTTE AND KEVIN

Charlotte and Kevin were friends. They went to school together, where they studied art. Kevin was needy for people, and took up a lot of Charlotte's time. She didn't want to hurt his feelings, but eventually it began to become too much for her. She just sat Kevin down and quietly told him, "Look, you're a nice person, and I like you, but I don't like what's happening between us. I need time and space for myself and my painting. I don't want to argue about it, and I want you to respect my feelings, and understand it really has nothing to do with you, but I want to stop seeing you other than at school. I'd like to continue to be friendly there, but not outside." Kevin was hurt, and even cried. But Charlotte had made up her mind, and stuck to her decision. Kevin eventually made some new friends, now that he wasn't focused exclusively on Charlotte, friends that were willing to be there for him, and had more compatible needs. Charlotte got more into her painting. So much so that it showed a marked improvement, and she won a fellowship to study painting in Florence, Italy. There, she made new friends, and had a fantastic new life. A life she probably wouldn't have had if she hadn't ended her friendship with Kevin.

CELEBRATE THE TEMPORARY

We often cling to old familiar things, including friends. In his book *Celebrate the Temporary*, Dr. Clyde Reid says, "Sometimes people find a meaningful temporary friendship, then try to hang onto it. They quickly jot down names and addresses and promise to 'look you up' at a later time. They have not learned to celebrate a relationship for its temporariness and let it go. They are caught in the mindset which says that a relationship to have meaning must be ongoing. Disappointment is often the result when we try to re-create a contact that had meaning in a particular place and time. Letting go is a basic lesson of life, and is a necessity if we are to learn how to celebrate the temporary. We must let go of our bondage to possessions. We must let go of our family, our friends, even our life. So long as we cling to life as a permanent possession, it will not be as full as it can be."

To view all your friendships as temporary, as unfeeling as this may seem to you, will actually enhance the quality of those relationships, make them more human. For our lives are temporary things, and to cling, to hold on, is foolish as well as self-defeating. If you try to hold onto a friend beyond the time that this is a nourishing relationship, you do yourself and the friend untold harm. And by looking at all your friendships as permanent, you will be closed to new friendships, and you will often not put the energy needed into existing friendships. If you think this friend is going to be with you forever, you may put off telling him you care, always putting it off until tomorrow. There may be no tomorrow! And if you haven't yet discovered that, then already there is a fullness missing from your relationships. To treat each friendship as a precious gem that is here only for an instant is to enrich each moment you spend with that person, and to allow the parting to be just part of the ebb and flow of life, a natural event, not sad, just part of "what is."

OLD FRIENDS LOCKING YOU INTO OLD ROLES AND PATTERNS

Nongrowing friendships often lock you into rigid roles. If a new part of you is trying to emerge, it can often be prevented by your fear that it won't be acceptable to your current friends. If you were a truck driver, for instance, and were taking music lessons in your spare time, you might feel your truck driver friends would not accept this new role of yours, and so you would cover up a part of your personality when you were with them.

PHILIP

Philip was a shy, bespectacled nineteen-year-old. His one physical asset seemed to be his deep baritone voice. He took some training to be a radio announcer, and was offered a job in a small radio station several hundred miles from his hometown. Before leaving home, he got contact lenses, and decided to take advantage of the fact that no one knew him in the town he would be moving to. This meant he did not have to keep projecting the same shy image. He could experiment with new ways of being, new facets of himself. So, when he arrived in the small town, he pretended to himself that he was no longer shy, but was attractive and friendly. He reached out to people. He said to himself, "Even if I make a total fool of myself, I can always move away and never see any of these people again." With that as the worst thing that could happen, and by being willing to accept that possibility, Philip was able to break out of his former mold. When he visited his hometown, he found himself avoiding his old friends because they knew him as the old Philip, and would remind him of a part of himself he was changing. His new friends reinforced his new behavior, and soon it was no longer pretending; he really *was* more sure of himself and comfortable reaching out to people.

Teen-age marriages often lock the partners into their teen-age personalities, so, in effect, the couple never grows up. If one of them does, the marriage usually crumbles amid a lot of bitterness. Children who live with their parents into their twenties experience this same kind of role stagnation. They are surrounded with the interpersonal environment of their old role, and this makes it extremely difficult to grow or move into new roles.

Think of some of your old friends. Do they really understand who you are now, and encourage and support what you are doing now? Or do you have to hide part of who you really are from them?

In traditional marriages women are often locked into the old stereotyped role of housekeeper and mother. They sometimes have to leave the marriage in order to be the person they really are. Psychologist Susan Scholz says, "When we first formed our women's consciousness-raising group, we asked the question 'Why are we here?' The feeling was almost unanimous that we as women had not been able to form very strong friendships. We wanted to do that, and elicit the feeling of trust, to feel really trusting about other women. Because most of the friendships we had, had been through our husbands or through work. Or we got together on social occasions where we talked about idiot things, and we had never gotten into feelings that much."

ALIVENESS CHECK

One good way to check out your real feelings about your friends is to explore how alive you feel when you're around them. But first you have to get an idea of what aliveness feels like to you. You can do this by remembering a time when you felt as if you were bursting with life. It may have been watching a sunset, or making love, or doing a job well, or receiving some good news. To help you remember as totally as possible, get into a relaxed position, lying down with your eyes closed. Remember a specific instance of aliveness in your life, and really remember it with all your senses. What did it feel like? What did it look like? How did it smell? What sounds were associated with it? See if you can't generate in yourself right now the same feelings you had then. They have all been stored in your memory banks, and are there for recall if you just make the effort. When you really feel it, give this a rating of 10.

Now think about your friends. Have they ever made you feel this way? Have they ever, in any way, made you feel more alive? Can you focus on any such moment of aliveness, and give it a rating of 1 to 10?

Even more important, have you recently been feeling alive with your friends? Go over the list of people in your life and check out whether you feel they have any aliveness rating at all, in terms of how alive you feel in their company.

If *you* are not feeling alive in a relationship, you can be pretty certain that your friend isn't getting much out of it either.

FEELING GOOD ABOUT YOURSELF

Another good way to look at the nourishment you are getting from your friends is to check out how you feel about you in their presence. Psychologist Jack Gibb says, "What I want to do is create an environment for me in which I'll feel better about myself."

You've probably experienced this feeling. A sort of glowing sensation after parting from a friend, a feeling that you are a pretty terrific person to be with, an appreciation toward your friend for bringing out this feeling in you.

So, another potent question to ask yourself about a friend is: "When I am with this person, how do I feel about myself?" If you constantly feel insecure and insignificant in this friend's presence, then it probably isn't a nourishing friendship for you to be in.

The best kind of friend will stimulate feelings of aliveness and worthiness in you. These two criteria can really tell you all you need to know about which friendships to stay with and which ones to discard.

SAYING GOOD-BYE

What is the best way to tell a friend you want to end the friendship? It's important to put it in terms of feelings, and not say things like, "You are not a good friend for me." Instead: "I feel that this is not the friendship I need for where I am right now." Though someone may try to do so, you really can't argue with a feeling. If that's what you're feeling, that's what you're feeling, even if it's not rational, even if it's unfair, even if it hurts someone to hear it.

You can say it in gentle but firm tones, and you can look the other person in the eye when you're saying it, but it's very important to be definite, not hem and haw and sputter. You owe it to the other person to let him or her know exactly how you feel, and that you have made a decision. If you allow yourself to become embroiled in an argument, you've already lost.

How willing you are to end a destructive relationship may be a direct reflection of how good you feel about yourself, how emotionally healthy you are at that moment. When you don't feel good about yourself, you tend to want to hold on tightly to all your current possessions, including friends, trying to force them to conform to your needs, to affirm who you are. And, unfortunately, when you are feeling bad about yourself, you tend to surround yourself with people who reinforce that feeling, and you become very attached or addicted to those very people who are reinforcing this negative facet of you. To realize that this may be true is to move toward escaping from this interpersonal trap.

When you do feel good about yourself, you are aware that you cannot force a friend to stay with you if that friend really wants to go. In fact, you wouldn't *want* that friend to stay, because you too would realize that it is time for you to end the relationship. It might help to remember, then, that if your friend is hurt because you are ending the relationship, it has more to do with that friend's self-esteem than with anything you are doing. And staying on in the friendship isn't going to help that self-esteem!

IT'S ALREADY HAPPENED

There's an awareness you can have for yourself that can make life a lot easier and remove feelings of guilt when you have to terminate friendships:

When it is time to end a relationship, your decision to end it is not changing anything. It is merely confirming a fact: the fact that this relationship is no longer alive.

A veterinarian who tells a client that his horse has died, say of old age, is not to blame for the horse's death. It just happened; no one was to blame. The acknowledgment that the animal has ceased to exist has nothing to do with the death itself, it merely recognizes it. And when you announce to a friend, "I think our relationship is no longer nourishing," you are also recognizing a fact, broadcasting the news. Of course, the vet could pretend the horse was still alive, and the client might even go along with this pretense. But the horse would still be dead. You may also choose to pretend a friendship is still a friendship, and the other person may go along with this, but if it is dead it has ceased to exist, period.

OTHER ALTERNATIVES

There are many ways to handle destructive relationships. A flat good-bye may not be necessary. This is something you have to examine yourself, trusting to your feelings. You may want to change the relationship without ending it, perhaps by cutting down the amount of time you and this friend spend together. The destructive part may be the quantity of time spent together or something else that's a part of the relationship. This may possibly be eliminated, allowing some of the good parts of the friendship to survive.

BILL AND MARTIN

Bill and Martin had been friends for several years, and they divided their times together between playing tennis and drinking beer with the other men they knew. Martin decided he really wasn't getting any nourishment from either the beer or the time spent with those other men. He announced to Bill, "Bill, I am not going to our beer parties anymore. I hope you still want to be my friend, and I'd really like to continue our tennis games, but those sessions just don't do anything for me anymore, and I'm calling it quits." Bill was upset for a while; he still enjoyed the beer parties and having Martin's company during them. But he realized that the friendship was more important to him than guzzling beer in Martin's presence, so they were able to continue the friendship on the tennis courts.

THE END AS A BEGINNING

And finally, what really matters is how much your friends supported and allowed your own growth, not how long they stayed with you. One sure way to feel alive and good about yourself is to begin to take your life in your own hands, to begin to cut down any dead weight you've been carrying. And it's bound to have a positive effect on your remaining friendships. You'll feel freer with these people since you'll know you have them as friends by choice, not because you are incapable of saying good-bye to a friendship that is dead. And your friends will know they're there by choice, too! You'll have more time and energy to devote to the people who matter in your life, and to new people who may come into your life. You'll have given yourself room to grow, room for new beginnings, and you'll really appreciate yourself for providing such a nourishing gift.

Finish the sentence "One thing that I've learned about my friends is the fact that ———." Check out how you feel about this.

EPILOGUE

You now know more about your friends than you ever have before. You've gained much insight and awareness merely by focusing in new ways on these important and significant relationships. But insight and awareness alone don't count for much. Hopefully, you've also begun to apply some of the techniques, tailoring them to your own wants, needs, and life-style.

Even more important, hopefully you've come to realize that you are in charge. You are in charge of your own interpersonal environment. You've selected the friends in your life, and you've selected the ways in which you relate to them and the position you've given them in your life. To realize that you have chosen is to realize that you can choose to change. If you've chosen up to now to develop friendships with people you've encountered by chance, you may choose to change that by deliberately seeking out some new friends. Or, if satisfied with the friendships you have, you may choose to continue whatever patterns have been illuminated by this book. And even those will be enhanced by the deliberate decision to choose to continue behaving in that way.

You now have some suggested alternatives. You may choose to fantasize about your friends, or use Transactional Analysis to look at your friendships, or end destructive relationships, or experiment with self-disclosure, or form a chosen family, or you may choose to do exactly what you've been doing all along. But now it is a choice, because you can only really make choices when you have some things to choose from. This is a book of alternatives. You are responsible for the choices and for the results of those choices. And the best way to exercise that responsibility is to trust your own experience. As the Buddha once said: "Do not believe on the strength of traditions even if they have been held in honor for many generations and in many places; do not believe anything because many people speak of it; do not believe on the strength of sagas of old times; do not believe that which you have yourself imagined, thinking a god has inspired you. Believe nothing which depends only on the authority of your masters or of priests. After investigation, believe that which you yourself have tested and found reasonable, and which is for your good and that of others."

Also be aware that you have a choice each moment on how you will be spending that moment. You can use the moment to remember, to reflect or worry about something that has already happened. You can use the moment to plan for or worry about the future. You can use the moment to think about your friends. You can use the moment to experience a feeling about a friend. You can use the moment to be with a friend. Life can be a healthy balance of intellectual and emotional processing.

You can overanalyze and overuse the techniques in this book, and thus distort the purpose and direction. The main thing is to be. To be you, and to be you with your friends. All the exercises and methods and systems are merely tools to aid in that effort. Friendships are excellent human relations laboratories, but if they become laboratories instead of friendships, the point has been dramatically and catastrophically missed. The most important and potent and significant thing you can do with your friends is simply enjoy them. The happiest solution seems to be to strike a balance between the extremes of taking your friends for granted and studying them under a psychological microscope. And that too is something you are in charge of. You now have the tools, the friends and potential friends are out there, and you have to decide how to best bring them together. Whatever decision you make will be the right decision for you at that moment. And you can choose to change it in the next moment. It really is all up to you!

AUTHOR'S NOTE:

The main focus of this book has been on exploring your individual friendships. The Appendix goes a step beyond that and looks at the need for a sense of community. As a group leader for the past seven years, I have seen this emerge as one of the strongest of all the human motivations. You may find that a strong individual friendship can give you this sense of community, or that several separate friends can fulfill all these needs for you. I felt, however, that it was fitting that I include material which presented some other alternatives, and have adapted some of my most successful interpersonal exercises in a special fourteen-week program. The concept of a chosen family is not incompatible with the primary focus of this book, for that chosen family may either incorporate existent friendships or provide a source from which some individual friendships may develop. In any group, moreover, it is the one-to-one relationships between individual group members that determine the strength and direction of the group. So it is not a question of groupism versus individualism, but rather one of deciding whether you would like to get together a group of your friends or potential friends in this kind of a format. Also, as a group leader who has originated many techniques for building closeness and community, I have found that these are often easily adapted to one-to-one situations. You may, therefore, have no interest in a chosen family, but may still find many of the experiences in the fourteen-week program useful in building bridges of communication between you and individual friends.

Appendix

THE CHOSEN FAMILY

Early psychologists believed that human beings "needed" only the basic tools of survival, the purely physical needs of food, air, sex, and a place to live. But pioneering humanistic psychologist Dr. Abraham Maslow discovered that there are higher needs, ones that seem to separate man from the lower orders of life. The differences in Maslow's concept of needs and the theories of the earlier, more traditional research psychologists may stem from the fact that Maslow studied human beings, not animals in a laboratory. Apart from the purely physiological requirements, we have a need for safety and security, for love and belongingness, and for self-esteem and the esteem of others. When these are met, an even higher hierarchy of "growth needs" emerge, such as meaningfulness, justice, aliveness, beauty, and truth. But the need for love and belongingness, for being accepted by, and associated and friendly with others, is one of the four major sets of needs outlined by Maslow.

That need is not being fully met for most of us in our present culture. We often hear people refer to how nice things were in the good old days, but the truth is that the good old days weren't really any better, and may have been worse. People were mainly concerned with survival, and few had time to consider their higher needs. There was a stronger sense of family and community, but family and community had relatively little leisure time to fill. So, in addition to changing life-styles, we now have a lot more time to fill, a lot more time in which to feel isolated and lonely, a lot more time to think about our personal growth, and thus a greater need for the kind of support that growth can receive from a sense of belonging.

In *A Nation of Strangers*, Vance Packard noted, "We are rapidly losing several critical ingredients of a civilized, salutary society. We are seeing a sharp increase in people suffering alienation or just feeling adrift, which is having an impact on emotional and even physical health. We know there is a substantial increase of inhabitants suffering a loss of sense of community, identity, and continuity. These losses all contribute to a deteriorating sense of well-being, both for individuals and for society."

Can you sense this in your own life? Do you feel there is something missing, that a sense of community is not an integral part of your existence?

In *We, the Lonely People,* Ralph Keyes examined the highly mobile society that has evolved in the United States, and the transitory state of relationships. He says, "I can't argue against mobility and in favor of commitment for its own sake. I enjoy moving around, and like temporary relationships too much for that. What I am saying is that for the kind of community I've missed in the process, the intimate kind where people really come to know each other on many levels, I know that I'm going to have to stay put somewhere for a time. Having sat tight in San Diego for the eternity of three years, I've just slowly begun to realize some things about enduring friendship which were never clear to me before. Mostly what I've learned is that it's okay to make mistakes. People who expect me to stick around allow me to screw up more than I allow myself. Our friendship isn't dependent on my being nice and likable every minute we're together. And I've found also that my expecting people to be here next year, and remain friends with me, makes me more relaxed, more trusting, better able to share deep parts of me than I can with friends whom I see only occasionally."

The isolation and the need to belong can be seen and felt all through our society. Psychologists see it as a major factor in creating the problems that move people to seek help. Dr. Terry Levy, director of the Family Life Center at Biscayne College in Miami, says, "Isolation is a major problem. It has to do with the breakdown of the extended family, technology, the overcrowded but very alienated nature of the urban environment, isolation psychologically, socially, physically, and spiritually. People are feeling more and more isolated. I don't see the trend reversing itself at all. It's going to get worse."

HOPE AND OPPORTUNITY

Not a very cheerful prognosis from Dr. Levy, and many other social scientists, therapists, and human relations experts are equally as pessimistic. But this is not to say there is not a great deal of hope. True, our culture, our fears, the ways in which our cities are designed, even our high-rise architecture, is contributing to the problem. The old family structure has changed; most of the friendly old neighborhoods are gone. But there is something happening today that more than makes up for all that has been lost. For today, more than ever before in the history of mankind, we are concerned with the higher needs, the "growth needs" cited by Maslow. We are really interested in doing something about the isolation. And our increased mobility, free time, and access to new interpersonal skills give each of us more opportunity and more energy to develop a nourishing interpersonal environment.

Dr. Herbert Otto, chairman of The National Center for the Exploration of Human Potential in LaJolla, California, has coined the phrase "supportive interpersonal environment," which he describes as "the people around us who help us reach our full potential as total human beings." And the simple truth is that we now have more of an opportunity to select these people.

Family therapist Dr. Gerald Walker Smith says, "Because of the breakdown of the family, and all this, there's a much greater potential for real friendship now than there was a few decades ago. People aren't stuck with people they've got to be with because of some blood relationship, and that's nice. But the problem is that we aren't doing that. Instead, we're ending up being alone."

So we have the opportunity, but we're not taking it.

Herbert Otto says, "One of the most important things is to surround yourself with people who help you to validate the reasons for your existence or help you to explore the basic existential questions. You know: What are you here for? What's life all about? And to help you to clarify whether your behavior is consonant with your values. I see this as a part of the function of the supportive interpersonal environment. Of course it goes without saying that this environment offers you caring, love, enhancing of your self-esteem, giving you the strokes that you don't get elsewhere. And one of the main thrusts of the supportive interpersonal environment would be to stimulate your creativity. Surrounding yourself with people who turn you on, who stimulate you creatively. Theoretically this is all very beautiful, but when it comes down to the question of doing it, being with people who do this for you, or with whom you are experiencing this together, that's where I think we're fantastically short in our culture."

SUPPORTIVE INTERPERSONAL ENVIRONMENTS

There's no doubt, as Dr. Otto says, that we are short of these friendship environments in our society today. But they do exist, in many forms, in pockets of nourishment that offer hope for the future. Communes are one place in which this is happening, one place where building the supportive environment is usually the main focus. And the communes are not all composed of young people dropping out. Middle-class communal life-styles are evolving. People are exploring communal activities that may not involve a total sharing, but do provide a sense of belonging.

In New Jersey, a group of New York-based executives and their wives have developed a unique self-supportive communal baby-sitting system. There are six families involved, and each week one of the couples takes all the children into their home. The kids love it, romping together every weekend. The parents in charge can really pay attention to the children without feeling their privacy is invaded, since they are completely free five out of every six weekends. And it has enhanced the interpersonal contact between the twelve adults involved. They help one another plan activities for the weekends, and sometimes the couples not with the children plan trips and activities together.

In many communities groups of people are getting together on a regular basis to prepare a communal gourmet meal together, each person being responsible for one course. Some groups of friends have even gotten together for daily meals, thus cutting out a lot of duplicated effort and saving considerably on food costs, as well as providing valuable time together. Other groups of friends have organized food cooperatives, obtaining their food supplies cheaper and often fresher, dividing up the shopping chores, and having meetings to discuss nutrition and meal planning.

In New York, Dr. Jim Adams and Dr. Arline Rubin founded the Alternate Life Style Group in 1971. Group members get together to experience various interpersonal communication techniques and discuss communal activities. Some of the members are interested in living together communally, some in just sharing certain aspects of their lives with others. For instance, the group rented a summer house together, with some of the group members staying there all summer, others just visiting weekends.

In Miami, the staff members of Cornucopia, the Miami growth

center, all live together in a big old house, sharing chores domestically as well as their work activities.

In her book *Changing Your Life Style,* Dr. Frieda Porat tells of still another supportive interpersonal environment: "Six couples who lived in the same urban area—strangers to one another—met at a weeklong retreat with a leader well known for her encounter-group methods. The couples formed deep loyalties to one another and experienced great personal involvement during their marathon meetings. Despite differences in age and geographical placement of homes, they evolved in subsequent months a decision to move closer together by purchasing homes in a new housing development. This plan required a few members to change jobs, it forced children in two families to change schools, it disrupted all six families to some extent. Yet they felt a sense of community which they considered worth preserving. Although they bought separate houses, they continued deep personal contact in the voluntary association they called a 'commune of caring.' "

In Miami, David Robbins gave up his computer service company, sold his home, gathered up his family and some friends, and formed The Next Step, a spiritual growth community. They started out by renting a lodge in New Mexico for a summer, and then traveled cross-country in a caravan, seeking a place to put their roots. At this writing they still haven't settled, but were looking toward Colorado as a possibility.

A SENSE OF PURPOSE

It seems that the communes and other interpersonal environments that are most successful are those that have a sense of purpose—some goal or task they can work toward together, whether it encompasses their entire life-style or merely cooking one meal together each week. The purpose can simply be to build a sense of community together. Noted psychologist Jack Gibb developed the TORI Community experience, and TORI workshops are held around the country. TORI is an acronym for:

trusting—learning to grow in trust of myself and to share my person with others in ways that are fulfilling for each.

opening—making myself available to me and to the flow of life in the community around me.

realizing—discovering my self and what I want from each moment and from the process of living.

interdepending—discovering what it is to be deeply with others in the continuing creation of community.

THE TORI COMMUNITY

People are often surprised when they attend a TORI community-building weekend workshop. They expect a lot of structure, a lot of interpersonal games, a lot of direction. Instead, after a few warm-up exercises, the group is left alone. The only instructions people are given are to do whatever they want to do, to use the resource of the group and the facilitator as they wish. This can lead to frustration because "nothing is happening." But, in time, it goes beyond this, and everyone realizes that he or she has to be responsible for "making" it happen. A spirit of community emerges as people feel free to share their frustration or disappointment or fear. Jack Gibb believes it is important to create an environment where negative feelings are allowed, for they then seem to be transcended. It is not an encounter group or primal group where negative feelings are encouraged. They are merely allowed if they happen. In one such group, a young woman said she felt very angry with the group and with Dr. Gibb because she had not been approached by anybody even though she was desperately lonely. The group members begin to give her feedback to the effect that they were put off by her defensive posture, interpreting it as meaning she didn't want to make contact. They shared with her that they had been afraid to reach out to her for fear she would reject them. As she shared her feelings, a fascinating thing happened: The group drew closer together and began to then become a community. And the woman was accepted as she shared her fears, anger, and sadness. This reinforced openness on her part, for she saw that when she admitted her fear she was accepted, and people did reach out. Having to deal with her negative feelings brought everyone together and allowed others to reveal *their* negative feelings.

Jack Gibb says, "My diagnosis of the state of the culture now is that there are four needs. The simplest statement about my theory is that I'm aware there are tremendous fears and distrust that people have that they can't handle. The manifestations of that fear are a sense of lack of identity, and a sense of a lack of being, of not knowing who I am. So, the first need is for a sense of being, of knowing who I am, and trusting that. Then, a second disease of the culture is that closed, strategic, congested condition of people that's magnified in extreme security, secrecy, and so on, as manifested by Watergate. *Opening* is the second need. Then, people are struggling desperately to do what they 'ought' to do, and by nature that process is toxic. So the third need is to find out what they want to do. They discover what they want to do in the process of becoming free. The fourth disease is a sense of lack of community, of lack of togetherness, of lack of participation. Building community is the fourth need."

BUILDING COMMUNITY

Many churches are moving toward building community as a prime focal point, often supporting a number of intentional extended families. A number of organizations and individuals have initiated consciousness-raising groups for women, for men, for people.

Dr. Susan Scholz talks about the formation of her group, which includes about ten women who meet once a week to discuss various topics such as guilt, honesty, sex, and women's fantasies: "We all wanted to have a group of women we could really really trust and call our friends. I feel very strongly that I could call anybody in the group with a problem I had, and it would go no further than the group, and I'd get an honest appraisal of the situation without being put down. Once you're no longer a part of a family, you have to go elsewhere for some of those needs."

In *Love,* Leo Buscaglia tells this story about a visit he made to a little village on the great Tonle Sap lake: "Nature in Cambodia is very severe. Every year the monsoons come and wash everything into the rivers and streams and lakes. So you don't build great permanent mansions because nature has told you that they will only be washed away. You build little huts. Tourists look and say, 'Aren't they quaint but poor people! Living in such squalor.' It's not squalor. It's how you perceive it. They love their houses, which are comfortable and exactly right for their climate and culture. So I went to the lake. I found the people in the process of getting together and preparing for the monsoons. This meant that they were constructing big communal rafts. When the monsoons come and wash away their houses, several families get on a raft and live together about six months of the year. Wouldn't it be beautiful to live with your neighbors? Just think if we could make a raft together and live together for six months of the year! What would probably happen to us? All of a sudden we would again realize how important it is to have a neighbor—that I need you because today you may catch the fish that we will eat, or I like you because I can sit down and talk with you if I'm lonely and learn from you and understand another world. After the rains are over, the families once again live as independent units."

Leo says that most people react to this story by saying, "God, I wouldn't want to live with *my* neighbors for six months!" Would you? Do you even know them well enough to be able to make a real decision about it?

NEIGHBORS

You might imagine how you would make friends with your neighbors, as a potential chosen family. One therapist sent the following note to his neighbors in a luxury apartment complex:

"Hey! I've been living here three years, and I just realized I don't even know you. You are my neighbor, and I would like to know you, and I think you would like to know me, if you had the chance, if I had the chance. Let's make that chance. We still may choose to ignore each other, but at least then it will be from choice, and not because we never had the opportunity to get acquainted." He invited them all to his apartment for some cheese and wine. They sat around and told about who they were, and how they felt about meeting their neighbors, most of whom had never exchanged a word or a smile! They didn't all become intimate friends, but at least they began to know and trust one another, and several warm and nourishing relationships did develop. And no one put down the effort that man made! No one said he was trying to take advantage of them or use them. They all enjoyed the opportunity to get to know one another. Try it.

FRIENDS AS FAMILY

In effect, all of these systems and efforts are attempts to replace the traditional family, the extended family, with a selected or chosen family of friends. In *Friendship,* Myron Brenton says, "Whether we are young or older, in or out of communes, our friends are becoming more like extended family, in certain ways replacing or substituting for the aunts, uncles, cousins, grandparents, and other family members who comprised the larger extended family of old."

People are feeling this sense of kinship with their friends, and you will often hear people refer to their friends as "my second family." Actually, friends have more of a potential to fill the needs you have for nourishment than the old extended family ever had. The reason for this is obvious. We can choose our friends. As Volney Streamer put it, "We inherit our relatives and our features and may not escape them; but we can select our clothing and our friends, and let us be careful that both fit us."

In *Shifting Gears,* George and Nena O'Neill say, "If our families change in form through mobility, separation, divorce or other circumstances, we can build non-kin families of our choosing by selecting other persons we respect to share time and experience and feelings with us, our children and friends."

Some people now are experimenting with chosen grandparents, senior citizens from nursing homes or who live alone, who move in with them and their families, acting as resident baby-sitters and fulfilling many of the roles that used to be filled when older people were a part of every extended family. This fulfills a need for the older person, often isolated and stranded in our society, and a need for the highly mobile young family, giving them a sense of connection with the past and an important other viewpoint on life.

In *Making Friends with the Opposite Sex,* Emily Coleman says, "All people need others to play the roles of aunts, uncles, siblings, parents, grandparents, cousins and mates. When these family members don't exist or when they aren't available, or if their personalities don't jibe with ours, or when they can't play the roles we require, it is time to seek others with whom to relate as friendly family members. People need people. They need emotional support. They need families. But families can be 'intentional' families, handpicked. Families need not be limited to those related by blood or marriage. Since we all belong to the family of man, no person should automatically be 'off limits' to us. The person who sees himself as a worthwhile, responsible individual is capable of making his own meaningful choices, even when it comes to selecting his own 'family,' rather than merely making do with what he is given. He should be able to select as members of his family many people of whatever sex and age he wants for intimate relationships. No one but you should determine what kind of family will give you the emotional support you need. Only you can know what feels best to you."

THE SECOND-CHANCE FAMILY

One of the most innovative approaches to chosen families is the one developed by clinical psychologist Daniel Malamud, an adjunct professor at New York University's School of Continuing Education. It's a fourteen-week course entitled The Second-Chance Family: a New Medium for Self-Directed Growth. The class breaks up into groups of about eight members, and these groups become intentional families, meeting in class and on their own. Most of the groups stay together for at least six months after the course ends, and about half last for a year or more, with about a dozen groups now still meeting after two years or more. The course description seems to attract people who are truly interested in building a sense of family with others. It reads:

In a world that's increasingly crowded and impersonal, more of us need to belong to small groups in which we can share our dreams, discuss our dilemmas, act without façade, and support or challenge without intruding, forcing, or punishing. This workshop explores the creative possibilities of just such a new kind of family, based on personal ties of peers who relate to each other because of the common belief in personal growth. With the support of the family, each participant engages in novel self-confrontation games which aim to show that he has the power to discover hidden and undeveloped aspects of himself, that the self-directed cultivation of new and more satisfying ways of behavior is possible, and that he can evolve meaningful guidelines for his own life.

Talking about these second-chance families, Dr. Malamud says, "I see them as support groups. Apparently marriages and families, which used to be support groups, aren't the same anymore. So, in addition to a partner, it seems that there is a place for a group where you can be especially frank, perhaps in ways you can't even be frank with your intimate partner. Having a group is a special place where different kinds of intimacy are possible."

In deciding whether you want to build your own chosen family, either coming up with your own method of doing it or using the guidelines and group experiences outlined in this chapter, it does seem to be important that you have structure and commitment. Just "letting it happen" doesn't seem to work. Daniel Malamud states, "If there isn't a very conscious, explicit, and deliberate structure, with a clear goal that defines this group as one that is sharply and definitely different from the conventional social group, what you have is a bunch of chitchat, or the usual social interaction, which doesn't amount to very much. Even with a definite structure, it is extremely difficult for some time for members to get over the habitual type of social interaction. In other words, the temptation to socialize is very high, and it's something that I need to focus on again and again in my classes, preparing them for this to be seen as an experience that's *sharply* different from the social experience. Once a group really gets going, and the concept of openness and self-disclosure takes hold, the structure can be more relaxed and socializing can become entwined with the work. I myself am part of a peer group of therapist colleagues, and we've been meeting once a week for about five years, and by now we have a rather interesting balance of sociability and work. But certainly in the beginning I think it helps to have this be a very special place, something like a retreat where you leave all the usual stuff of your culture and go off in the woods somewhere. It has to be clear that this is a separate situation, and a separate place, with separate kinds of mores."

THE GOAL

In addition to structure and commitment, it's important to have a sense of direction and purpose, somewhere you want to head for, something you definitely want to get from your chosen family. Dr. Malamud's groups are called "second-chance" families because he sees them as giving you a second chance at having experiences you didn't have enough of in your first family, or a second chance at having some unfortunate experiences in your first family corrected. The goal can be simple and direct for your chosen family; it can be to bring together a group of people who can be friends and nourish one another, learning ways in which to communicate more fully and openly. Thus, the family of friends not only provides nourishment in and of itself, but it acts as a laboratory in which the participants can experiment with new behavior, most notably self-disclosure and feedback, and thus have new interpersonal skills develop which can also be used to enhance their lives outside the family group.

For his groups, Daniel Malamud sees this goal: "Learning who you are by allowing yourself to be yourself as much as you can be, in a group that cultivates ever-increasing tolerance, and later acceptance, and later welcoming, of all the trends in you, including trends that your culture taught you were 'bad.' And learning to accept your humanness as being part of the universal humanness, and getting to see that your ego is a system of beliefs which has prejudiced you against yourself, and which has tended to color your perception of yourself as being an exaggeratedly separate person who has to pursue certain goals which are considered 'good' and has to avoid other goals that are considered 'bad.' Helping you really become aware of how your belief system has led to your estrangement from yourself and other people and nature. The goal, for me, is very religious. One of appreciating my separateness and difference, but within the context of which I see that I am part of an infinite flow that is infinitely mysterious, and which, in a sense, takes care of me."

YOUR OWN GOALS

By now, you probably have a feeling about whether the idea of a chosen family of friends can fill your needs, can nourish and enrich you. Check that feeling out, go inside yourself and ask: "Do I feel I would enjoy having such a chosen family; would it make sense for me to make a commitment to work toward the establishment of this kind of unit, to devote perhaps one evening a week to this activity?"

You may decide that this idea doesn't fit you. Or you may realize you already have a chosen family of friends, which may or may not respond well to the upcoming exercises and experiences. Or you may decide this is an effort worth making, that you'll approach some people you know and see how they feel about it. However you decide, do it from a feeling level of awareness, and then the decision will have to be the right one for you right now.

Remember, it does take effort. It's all well and good to go with the flow of things, and to wish that a family of friends would just magically appear, but things usually don't happen that way. People usually have to be motivated, and it may be that the people you know have never even considered this as a possibility.

If you have decided to explore the chosen family concept either with an established group of friends or by bringing some new people together, the next step is obvious: to establish an awareness of what you want to accomplish in and with this group of people. This will have to be discussed with the others, but as the initial motivating force, you should first have a pretty good idea of at least one possible direction.

Dr. Malamud's fourteen-week time frame seems appropriate, for it gives the group enough time to establish comfort and trust, and to create momentum for future contact within the continuing family. Let us say a two-hour group session one night a week. You may tend to become overenthusiastic and want to spend much more time, but it is important to start out with moderate time demands that will not infringe on your other activities. As the group progresses, you may choose to plan some outings together, perhaps over weekends, but the core session continues at a regularly scheduled time on a set evening.

In order for the group to work cohesively, a definite commitment is needed from each family member. Someone who says he or she will try to make it when he or she can, will only drain the group energy. Barring emergencies or illness, everyone has to make every possible effort to be there for the group session. The initial contract is for fourteen weeks, and that is a firm commitment. You'll note that in the session for the fourteenth week, one of the projects is to decide whether the group shall continue.

Before beginning, make a consensus decision on whether new people will be allowed into the group after it starts. There is the danger that this will dilute the momentum, and you may choose not to permit it. The optimum numbers for group processing seem to be from six to ten people. Make your own decisions on this.

THE CIRCLE PROCESS

One of the best tools developed for group interaction is the circle process. It's simple and effective. You all sit in a circle, and whatever the sharing you are going to be doing, you do it one at a time, with no one responding or interrupting until it's his turn. You'll all be tempted to interject comments, but that temptation must be resisted. It's useful to pass around some object; you can have fun deciding what it can be, perhaps something symbolic, maybe even a copy of this book. Each person can only speak when he or she has the object in hand. Other times you may choose to open up the discussion, but when you are in the circle process, stay in it. One powerful advantage of this is that it equalizes the energy between highly verbal and relatively quiet members of the group. Also, people do not have to compete for attention, since everyone gets a turn. After the object has been passed around the entire circle, you may choose to permit someone to add something, as long as everyone else has the right to make an additional comment.

You can, of course, invent your own topics for discussion, even your own interaction games, but remember there is always the danger that the group can deteriorate into social chitchat if a firm structure isn't maintained, at least during the first few weeks.

One person can facilitate the group by reading out the agenda and starting each exercise or circle. Or, what may be an even better idea, each family member can have a turn at being in charge of the group.

Though it's important you have commitment and structure, and a purpose, it's equally important that you don't lose sight of the fact that the object is to form some nourishing relationships that feel good. If you get grim about it, no one is going to feel good or have any fun. Keep up the structure, but keep it up in a lighthearted way. Your family can be purposeful without being solemn and rigid.

In Dr. Malamud's classes, the group usually meets two hours each week in the classroom, and then an hour or two on their own in informal sessions. You may choose to stay together for a further hour or so and informally interact and discuss your feelings about the group and that particular evening's activities. Or you may find that two hours is plenty of time for all of you to experience the exercises fully and informally interact. As long as you stick to the initial structure, you'll probably find that informal interaction does not fall into the old chitchat patterns, but begins to achieve some deeper levels of contact. Check this out with one another and see if you can all feel the difference after several weekly sessions.

YOUR CHOSEN FAMILY: THE FIRST FOURTEEN WEEKS

WEEK ONE

Start right out with a circle process. Introduce yourselves, and exchange your feelings and expectations about this new chosen family project.

Next, share with one another those needs you feel this family can fulfill that are not now being met in your lives.

Choose a family name, something that fits your group and your hopes and aspirations for the family. You can either use the circle process or open it up for discussion and feedback. Some sample names: Loving Friends, The Butterfly Family, Free and Easy, The Family Circle, Our Gang, All in the Family, Us.

It's time to find out something about one another. Each person, in the circle process, makes three statements: Something I like about my body (I like my legs, I like my eyes, etc.); Something I like about my personality (I like my sense of humor, I like my warmth, etc.); and some talent or skill I have, something I do well and enjoy doing well (I like the way I knit, I like my cooking talent, I like my ability to dance well, etc.). Each person makes all three statements before passing the object on to the next member in the circle. When all have finished, go around again and state how you felt making these self-appreciative statements. Then, go around again, and each person shares how he felt hearing the other people's statements, as well as any feelings of closeness and empathy he may have felt toward any specific family members, and any surprises he may have had in hearing the other members' statements.

As a closing exercise, all family members sit in a tight circle. Place your hands in the center of the circle and begin to explore one anothers' hands with your eyes closed. Feel the different shapes and textures and temperatures. Then have all the hands cluster together for a minute or so, just feeling one anothers' energy.

For the second session, you are going to share some of your memories and feelings about your childhood. Members may want to bring some pictures of themselves as children, perhaps one or two per person, and, if possible, a toy or game they had as a child.

WEEK TWO

(Have some sheets of paper and pencils ready.)

Start the first circle process by sharing any thoughts or feelings you had during the week about the first session.

In the circle, each shares any picture or memento from childhood, tells about it, and completes the sentence "I was a ——— child." Fill in the blank with one or two words that most accurately described you.

Pass out the sheets of paper and pencils. Each member draws a picture of the home most remembered from childhood. Draw as accurate a diagram as possible of the favorite room in that home, the room each person spent the most time in as a child. Then share the pictures, and each person shares his feelings about that room, and tells about his activities in it. Go around in the circle again and share whether you feel you know more about one another by this sharing of childhood experiences.

Share one thing you each miss most from your childhood. An activity, a game, a special food, or some friend or relative. And whether you feel there is any way you can have the quality of that thing, or the thing itself, within the context of this adult family group.

From the past, we move to the future. Each member shares, taking as long as necessary up to five minutes, his or her dreams for the future. What he or she would like to accomplish; what kind of life-style he would like, what kind of relationships he hopes for. Also, what each of you is doing now to make any of these hopes and aspirations possible. End the session by closing your eyes and silently tuning into yourselves and your feelings.

WEEK THREE

You had no advance assignment for this week, nothing to look for or think about during the week other than last week's session itself. Each of you can share whether or not you would like to have some home-awareness assignment at the end of each session. From now on, one will be provided. You decide whether the group would enjoy doing it.

Let's see what we know about one another. In the circle process, each person can share what he or she knows about every other group member. You've spent time together, and learned facts and you've gotten some feelings about one another. In turn, each person now shares all he or she can, looking at each family member and talking directly to that person. For example: "I know you are interested in your children, and like to cook, and enjoy going to plays, and were a happy child, and are warm . . . " The member whose turn it is faces each other and talks to him or her, before the object is passed on for the next person's turn. Take your time with this exercise. After you've all gone around, open it up for discussion of whether each of you feels he or she was perceived accurately, and any feelings you have about making statements to others or having statements made about you.

Stand up and get in close together in a tight cluster, filling in every space, making some pleasant contact as you enjoy a group hug. Close your eyes and tune in to how it feels to be this close to these people. Then, in the circle process, share how you each felt doing this.

Next week we are going to discuss closeness and how close we feel toward the people in our lives. Exchange phone numbers, and agree that each of you will call one other member during the week and discuss your feelings of closeness to each other.

WEEK FOUR

Go into the circle process and discuss whether you called someone during the week, and how that felt. And any special moments of closeness you felt with another person during the past week.

Share your feelings about your own capacity for closeness and intimacy. Finish these two sentences: "The quality I have that really enhances my ability to be close to other people is ———." And: "Something that prevents me from being as close as I could be is ———." In the circle process, share your feelings on this issue of closeness.

One at a time, lie down in the middle of the circle on your stomachs. In complete silence, the family members gently begin rubbing the person in the center all over his or her back, from head to toe. Very gentle, featherlike strokes. Do this for two or three minutes, then gently rest the palms of your hands against the person's back, in a soft laying on of the hands, closing your eyes and sending thoughts of warmth and affection to this family member. No talking as you tenderly lift your hands, and the person slowly gets up to be replaced by the next family member. After you have all experienced the exercise, discuss your feelings in the circle process.

In the circle process, talk about a very special moment in your life when you felt especially close to another human being. Describe the setting and your feelings at the time.

Next week will be focused on decisions, so each of you agrees to make a definite decision of some sort in your life over the coming week. End the session with a group hug.

WEEK FIVE

(Have sheet of paper and pencil for each member ready for session.)

Discuss in the circle process your decisions during the past week, no matter how minor. Even deciding what to eat or what television show to watch can give you some awareness of your decision-making capacity. Share whether you felt you made decisive choices, and really made the choices you wanted to make or let outside influences affect those choices.

Each person in the family chooses a partner. If one person is left over, he or she will choose to join another pair to form a triad. Share with partners how you arrived at decision, which one of you made it, whether this reflects how you operate in your everyday life. Next, share with one another how you made the decision to participate in this family of friends, and how you feel about that decision.

Hand out a sheet of paper and pencil to each member. Taking ten or fifteen minutes, each person makes a list of ten major decisions he has made during his lifetime. When you are all finished, start the circle process, sharing the way you felt making out the list, whether you were surprised by anything on your list, and which you feel was the most brilliant and successful decision of all those you listed. Then share how you would be today, or what would be different in your life, if you had not made that decision.

In the circle process, see if you can each make a decision to do something that will give you pleasure and satisfaction during the coming week. Also, since next week will focus on aloneness, see if you can each make a decision to take some alone time in which to experience your self in complete solitude, even if for only an hour during the week.

WEEK SIX

(Have ready a sheet of paper and pencil for each family member.)

Share in the circle whether you were able to take an alone period for yourself during the past week, and how that felt.

Everyone closes his eyes and sits absolutely alone and quiet. Imagine that you are all alone this evening, that there is no one else present in the room. Stay with this for several minutes. Then see if you can become aware, still with eyes closed and in silence, that there are other people in the room with you. First sense them, then start slowly moving around on the floor and making cautious contact with the others. Finally, all come together in one huddle on the floor and silently enjoy the company and closeness. Go around in the circle and share your feelings about this experience.

In the circle, share the loneliest moment you can remember in your entire life. Really re-create the feeling and share that with the group. Then, in open discussion, talk about the differences between being alone and being lonely. How you each perceive these differences in your lives, and the advantages of alone time and the disadvantages of being lonely.

Hand out sheets of paper and pencils. Each member lists all the things he or she thinks would provide pleasure and nourishment and that could be done alone. Then, in the circle, share feelings about this, and whether you each feel you have nurtured that need we all have for alone time in our lives.

End the session with a warm group hug, but separate during the middle of it, each withdrawing into himself with eyes closed and then coming back together.

Next week is devoted to silliness, so see if you can do something silly during the coming week.

WEEK SEVEN

Share in the circle whether you did anything silly during the past week. Then go around again and share what the silliest thing you ever did was, and how it feels remembering it now.

Stand up and walk around one another. Then change your walk into a silly walk, bouncing, jumping, making silly sounds. Then encounter one another and either do or say something silly to each person you contact. Sit down, and go around the circle sharing how this all felt.

See if you can invent a silly game together and play it.

Go around in the circle and describe your feelings about silliness, whether you feel you are free to be silly or feel that this is something you should not be, something that isn't mature. Then, in open discussion, share how your parents reacted when you were silly as a child, and how you feel this influenced your current attitudes and feelings about silliness.

Sitting in the circle, one member starts by making a silly face and sound. The next member repeats that, and it goes around the circle. Then the next person comes up with another silly face and sound, and this goes all around the circle. When you have all led the circle in silly faces and sounds, share your feelings about the experience, and whether you felt uptight or embarrassed, couldn't wait for it to be over, or really enjoyed yourselves.

See if you can come up with a silly way to end the session. Next week is focused on sadness, so during the coming week try to be aware of any feelings of sadness you might have, even if only very brief ones.

WEEK EIGHT

In the circle, share any sad moments you had during the past week. Then go around again and share the saddest time you ever remember in your life and how it feels remembering it now.

Discuss openly whether you feel it's all right to experience sadness, or do any of you feel you should try to cover it up, hide your sad feelings? Can any of you remember being sad but pretending you weren't? Talk about some of the kinds of things that make you sad.

The author once wrote that "Being sad almost always involves a feeling that things have gotten out of control, that something has happened and there is absolutely nothing you can do about it." In circle, share your feelings about this statement and whether you have ever experienced moments like this.

In circle, see if you can each come up with a way to combat feelings of sadness, something you can do to start feeling better when all seems hopeless.

One at a time, in the circle, silently make a very sad face, really exaggerate it. Then go around and share how that felt.

Talk about the sadness you remember experiencing as a child, and how it might be different from any sadness you have recently experienced. Share whether you may be more or less willing to admit and share your sad feelings now than as a child, and whether you could feel comfortable calling any member of this family when you are feeling sad.

End with a warm group hug, and during it, each of you thinks of some happy thoughts. Next week is on pleasure, so try to remember all the good things that happen.

WEEK NINE

(Have sheet of paper and pencil ready for each member.)

In the circle, share any things that happened during the past week that gave you feelings of pleasure. Then go around again and share the most pleasurable experience you can remember, and how you feel remembering it now.

Stand close together in a cluster and close your eyes, making contact with as many other members as possible in your tight cluster. Start rubbing their backs, and arms, and heads, and try to give anyone you are making contact with as much pleasure as possible. Keep it up for a few minutes, then sit in the circle and share your feelings about the experience.

Go around in the circle, and finish the sentence "Some of the ways in which I limit my own pleasure are ———."

Go around in the circle and finish the sentence "Some of the ways in which I give myself the opportunity for pleasure are ———."

Hand out sheets and pencils. Each member makes a list of twenty things that would give real pleasure. These can be favorite meals, physical activity, certain accomplishments, various forms of entertainment, etc. Then, in circle, each shares his list and tells which of the items he would be most unwilling to give up, and everyone, shares how he feels listing these pleasures.

See if the group can come up with a comfortable way to give one another pleasure right here and now. Something that everyone agrees would feel good. Do it, Go around in circle and share feelings about doing it.

End with a warm hug. Next week we will focus on love, so see if you can experience some of that feeling during the coming week.

WEEK TEN

In the circle, talk about any love feelings you may have had during the past week. Then go around again and talk about the most loving moment you can remember, and how it feels to remember it now.

Stand up and walk around one another, then encounter as many of the other group members as you can, looking them in the eye and making some physical contact that expresses your capacity to love, some gentle touch that shows you are a loving person. Share your feelings about this in the circle process, and whether you feel you are a loving person.

In pairs, discuss with one another where you are right now in terms of love relationships and where you would like to be a year from now. Come back into the larger group and, in circle, share what you feel you could personally do to be a more loving person and to have more love in your life.

One person at a time stands in the middle of the group, and all the other members stroke and give that person loving attention for one minute, in silence. After everyone has had a chance in the center, go around in the circle and share feelings about the experience.

Chances are, during the past ten weeks, you have had some warm feelings toward some of the group members. Let each person share these feelings with those people who evoked them. Then share in the circle how you each felt about doing this.

End the session with a warm and loving hug. Next week is devoted to your sexuality, so you might think about this facet of your life during the coming week.

WEEK ELEVEN

In the circle, share any feelings or thoughts about your sexuality that you had during the past week, anything you feel comfortable sharing about your actual sexual activity, and your feelings related to that activity. Then go around in the circle again and share what for you was the peak sexual experience of your life.

In open discussion, share how you first heard the "facts of life" as a child, and if your parents told you, what their general attitude was (approving, cautious, warm, disapproving, etc.), and whether you feel they had a healthy sexual facet as part of their individual personalities and their interaction together. Then, as much as you feel comfortable doing, share your first sexual experiences, how you felt, and whether you feel this has had any influence on your current sex life.

In the circle, share whether you subscribe at all to the old stereotype that men should be the aggressors and women passive during sexual activity. Then, if your family is a sexually mixed group, have the men sit on the floor and the women stand up and walk around eyeing the men as if they were objects being considered for purchase. The women should touch the men if there's something they want to check out, and can kid among themselves, while the men remain silent. Finally, each woman selects a man, or men, if the numbers are uneven. And the pairs or triads sit down and discuss their feelings about this exercise.

In the circle, each person completes the sentence "Something I think I could do to enhance the quality of my sexual experiencing is ———." Then go around again and complete the sentence "As a lover, I would describe myself as ———." Go around a third time and share your feelings about both these statements. End with a warm family hug. Next week is on fantasy, so see if you can imagine something you would really like to have happen to you in the near future.

WEEK TWELVE

In the circle, share your feelings about imagining something you would really like to have happen to you in the near future. Then go around again and share the favorite fantasy of your life, whether it is recent or from childhood, and your feelings about remembering this fantasy now.

Turn the lights low, and everyone find a comfortable prone position. Eyes closed, take a few deep breaths to relax, and then imagine yourself in your favorite place. Imagine that you have one wish that will be granted to you in this place; whatever you desire will come to you. Spend four or five minutes on this fantasy trip. Then, in the circle, share as much of your fantasies as you want to, and how you felt having them. Don't worry if they weren't too vivid or if you couldn't get into them, as this may be an area you need practice in.

Stand up, and each of you imagine you are an animal or an object. Walk around as if you were that animal or object, even encountering other members in that role. No talking, but you can make sounds if you wish. After a few minutes of this, continue to walk around, but transform yourself to your normal role. Sit down and go around the circle, sharing feelings about this fantasy.

Lie down in a star pattern, with your heads toward the center, feet spread outward, on your backs with eyes closed. Your heads can be touching, and they should be close enough so you can talk in moderate tones and be heard by everyone. You are going to have a group fantasy. One person starts by setting the scene. It can be the jungle, or outer space, or anywhere real or imagined. The fantasy involves an adventure your chosen family is going to have, so include all the members at one point or another. It might start out with "We're climbing a snow-covered mountain peak, and Jim starts screaming and yells out, 'I don't believe it! It's a ———.' " And then the next person continues the story, filling in the blank. You keep going around, building up the adventure and involving more of the members in it. Have as much fun with it as possible, and you'll probably feel when it's right to end the fantasy. Then sit up and share how this group fantasy felt.

In the circle, share how you imagined the family group would turn out when it first started, whether it has turned out that way, and whether you feel good that it has or hasn't met your fantasy expectations.

Imagine you have just entered the Olympics as a team for the Group Hugging Competition. Do your stuff for the judges.

Next week we'll be talking about "things," so plan to bring one of your favorite objects, something that has real meaning for you.

WEEK THIRTEEN

(Have a sheet of paper and pencil for each member.)

In the circle, share the object you brought, showing it to the group and telling how you feel about it and why it's important to you. If you forgot an object, or couldn't bring it for some reason, share what you would have liked to bring, and your feelings about that. Then go around again and share what you consider to be the favorite object you have had in your entire life, and your feelings at remembering this.

In open discussion, talk about the many things and objects that have played important roles in your life, that have sentimental value. Include your favorite childhood object and tell what happened to that.

Hand out sheets of paper and pencils. Each person make a list of My Favorite Things, and list on his sheet ten objects that play a role in his current life. Then, in the circle, share your feelings about making this list.

Stand up, and each of you pretend you are one of your favorite objects, standing absolutely still for a minute or two, really getting into the feeling that you are no longer human. Then begin to come back to your human form, and go around and gently touch one another to confirm your return to humanness. Sit down and go around the circle, sharing your feelings about this experience.

In the circle, share feelings about some things you would like to have, but haven't had a chance to have yet. And complete the sentence "The thing I would most like to have in the future is ———." It has to be an object, something material.

In the circle, each person imagines that he or she has unlimited resources and is going to give a present to each of the other family members. Then, in turn, each member tells the other what he or she would give him or her. It should be an object that hasn't been mentioned yet, but one you think would be really enjoyed. It could be a feast, or a yacht, or a trip around the world, or anything you feel would give them real pleasure. After everyone has dispensed his present, share your feelings about doing this.

End the session with a group hug. The next session will be on endings and beginnings. During the week, think about this aspect of your life, and especially how you feel about the way the family has begun, and the fact that the structured sessions are going to end.

WEEK FOURTEEN

In the circle, share your feelings about the beginnings of this family and the fact that this is the last formally structured session.

In open discussion, talk about how you each see beginnings and endings, and the roles these play in your life. Do you feel you begin things well, laying good foundations? Do you ever end things badly, feeling hurt and bitter and experiencing a great sense of loss?

In the circle process, talk about how you feel the group should go about continuing, what you would like to see happen now, and whether you can come up with some suggestions for ways of keeping up the good feelings.

After the circle, open it up for general discussion. To start with, decide if you want to allow more people in, to keep meeting at the same time, and to continue the structured part of the sessions. There are a number of books with interpersonal exercises, including several mentioned in the text and in the Bibliography of this book. Perhaps one of you will want to take on the task of obtaining some of these books, and possibly designing another fourteen-week program. See if you can accomplish one definite task: to come up with a plan for next week's session.

Sit in the circle. Each member nonverbally goes over to another with some physical expression of how he or she feels about the other. Each member makes nonverbal contact with every other person in the group. When you have finished, you have the option of sharing your feelings about it or just enjoying in silence whatever happened. End with a final family hug.

INTERNAL FEELINGS EXTERNALIZED

You may have noticed an interesting thing happening as your family meetings progressed. The more you got to know one another, and about one anothers' thoughts and feelings at all sorts of different levels, the closer you felt toward your family members. This is not an unusual phenomenon in group processing. It is real, and has to do with opening yourself up to others in a trusting atmosphere. The way you were each feeling inside was projected out to the group, and this created a synergistic reaction, bringing back the good energy of the group to each individual.

If, for whatever reason, you did not choose to get together and try a family format, you'll probably find that a lot of the exercises are useful in one-to-one encounters between friends. You may even choose to try out this aspect first, before moving on to a group experience.

ATTACHMENT

You can become too attached to your chosen family, so that you are not willing to reach outside of it for new experiences and new people. This is a natural inclination; certainly understandable if you feel a deeper level of comradeship and warmth in your family than you have ever felt outside it. But, at best, the family is a cocoon from which to emerge as a healthy butterfly, returning for nourishment from time to time.

Leo Buscaglia says, "I think it's important that people use their chosen family not as a refuge, not as a place to hide, but as a place in which they can safely grow. Creating a safe place is nice, as a place to grow, but that's only a beginning. You have to go beyond that. Too often these are refuges that keep people down rather than allow them to continue to grow. If there is a function of the chosen family, it's to be a place where people can be nurtured and loved. They can always come back and get their wounds mended, but, as far as a healthy family is concerned, it's not a place to hide, it's a place to grow in and leave."

Dr. Susan Scholz agrees, saying, "I think everybody needs a refuge. And it's okay, as long as you're functional out in that other world, and as long as you don't expect the same kinds of responses from other people that you get from your extended family, and as long as you're not uptight when you don't get the same responses from people in the outside world. Essentially, it's a discrimination problem. If you can discriminate when to be warm, tender, loving and giving, like you are in your extended family, and when not to be because it won't be accepted, that's fine. I see not having the refuge, and being out in that other world, as dangerous."

RETREAT AND REFUGE

Daniel Malamud mentioned that the chosen family could act as a retreat, a separate place. Leo Buscaglia and Susan Scholz call it a refuge. You can decide for yourself whether your chosen family fills this role for you, and whether you want it to. One thing to look out for is the possibility that your group can become a rigid, closed entity. If you'll remember, in the chapter Systematic Perceptions, TA therapists Dr. Bart Knapp and Marta Vago talked about groups based on *We're OK, you're not OK*—the kind of cliques that produce an extremely defensive attitude and a "we" against "they" mentality. This kind of group can stunt rather than promote growth, and it's something you might discuss with your family. One way you might encourage contact with the outside world is, after you have established yourselves as a cohesive unit, to help others form their own chosen families based on your experiences. If this develops, once in a while all the chosen families can get together for a big "family reunion" type of celebration.

To some extent this is a totally new life-style, and as such it is very flexible. It needs structure and commitment to function, but you and your friends can decide on that structure and commitment, and tailor it to fit your needs and wants. Happy choosing!

ANNOTATED BIBLIOGRAPHY

AUTHOR'S NOTE

Much of the research for this book was in the form of discussions and interviews with psychologists, psychiatrists, social scientists, social workers, and group leaders. However, I found a great deal of highly useful information in the books listed herein. I've quoted from most of them in the body of the book, and am happy to recommend them. I've made some personal comments on each book, and at times have included a quote to provide a sample of the contents. When a book was available both in hardcover and paperback, I chose to list the hardcover publisher only, but followed this with the initials PB to indicate that the book is available in paperback. Also, some of these books may have become available in paperback since this book went to press, so I suggest you check with your local bookstore.

Awareness, by John O. Stevens (Real People Press, Box F, Moab, Utah 84532, 1971) PB. There are many useful exercises here to build awareness and communication. Particularly useful for connecting with friends in new ways is the chapter entitled Pairs.

Be the Person You Were Meant to be, by Dr. Jerry Greenwald (New York: Simon and Schuster, 1973) PB. This book impressed me so much I immediately called Dr. Greenwald and interviewed him. It neatly divides human behavior into toxic and nourishing categories, and has many examples with which you can compare your own behavior patterns. The chapter on Nourishing and Toxic Relating can provide many cues to your friendship patterns. In it Dr. Greenwald says, "We can learn only from our own experience how to discriminate between relationships which are nourishing, healthy, and gratifying and those which are frustrating and will tend to make us ill. Our awareness of how we experience our interaction with others provides us with the raw data from which to recognize and reach out for nourishing relationships and, equally important, to minimize those which are ungratifying and toxic."

Beyond Success and Failure, by Willard and Marguerite Beecher (New York: Julian Press, 1966) PB. One of the best and most overlooked of all the really helpful self-help books, this can teach you a lot about dependency and self-reliance. In their chapter Food for Thought, the Beechers talk about friendship, and write: "Our real friends are those for whom we have a warm willingness to participate on a live-and-let-live basis. The number of our friendships is limited only by our ability to be a friend; not to those who give us the shirt off their back."

Beyond the Couch, by Eileen Walkenstein, MD (New York: Crown Publishers, 1972). A provocative and robust work, you'll be entertained and fascinated by this psychiatrist's attack on the medical and mental health establishment, and gain much insight from her concepts of positive and negative energy charges and her plea for us to simply be human with each other.

Born to Win, by Muriel James and Dorothy Jongeward (Reading, Massachusetts: Addison-Wesley, 1971) PB. Many TA therapists seem to agree this is the best book giving a general overview of Transactional Analysis. The Gestalt awareness experiments are very useful in building self-concepts and understanding what happens when you relate to your friends.

Celebrate the Temporary, by Clyde Reid (New York: Harper & Row, 1972) PB. A potent little volume with a unique philosophical approach focused on appreciating the now and realizing that each moment is only here for a temporary stay. Clyde Reid says, "I have visited old friends and spent an evening talking about past events and mutual acquaintances. When I have come away, I have often felt a sense of frustration at having lived only in the past. Something dies when relationships get stuck in this reviewing of past history with no new input of fresh experiencing."

The Challenge of Being Single, by Marie Edwards and Eleanor Hoover (Los Angeles: J. P. Tarcher, 1974) PB. Perhaps the best book written about being single in today's world. Check out the chapter Reaching Out for New Friends for such tidbits as this: "Good companions allow us to be ourselves at the same time that we enjoy their company. They don't overwhelm us with either their presence or their needs. They are fun to be with, and they make doing something we enjoy more enjoyable. And they are there because they like us and care about us."

Changing Your Life Style, by Dr. Frieda Porat with Karen Myers (Secaucus, New Jersey: Lyle Stuart, 1973). Some of the best material ever written on the subject can be found in the section on communes, including some fascinating examples of chosen families.

Come into the Mountains, Dear Friend, by Susan Polis Schutz (Blue Mountain Arts, PO Box 4549, Boulder, Colorado 80303). A beautifully designed book of poetry, with a lot of it focused on friendship. The illustrations by Stephen Schutz add to the specialness of this thin paperback, and make it a real bargain at $2.95.

Coming to My Senses, by John Robben (New York: Thomas Y. Crowell, 1973). A hard-to-find gem of a book with very personal observations by a man who has obviously become very self-aware and has done a lot of growing. For example: "Many of my friends are seeing psychiatrists, and many others probably should be. No one I know is in touch with himself, and those who are finally trying to be are going through terribly painful times. They don't know anymore what the truth is because so much of what they do is bound up in commitments they made long ago, which they now either can't get out of, or don't know how to get out of, or wonder if they even want to get out of."

Contact: the First Four Minutes, by Leonard Zunin, MD, with Natalie Zunin (Los Angeles: Nash Publishing Corporation, 1972) PB. A book filled with useful material, based on the premise that in the first four minutes of any interaction lie the foundations for every subsequent happening. Some very useful exercises here, plus tips on contacting people in person, by letter, by telephone, verbally and nonverbally. Dr. Zunin writes: "A friendship may start in four minutes, but it has to be cultivated like a plant. You water it with attention, fertilize it with mutual interchange, prune it with awareness; and its roots go deep. Real friendship flowers when you need it most; you have given it the best you have, and it's ready—when you are—to reciprocate, absorb, please or console."

Decision Therapy, by Dr. Harold Greenwald (New York: Peter H. Wyden, 1973). This is a book developing Dr. Greenwald's concepts that everything that happens to you has to do with decisions you make in your life. A lot of case histories for his psychotherapy practice illustrate this premise. He writes: "As I use the term, a decision is a choice between alternatives of behavior; a choice of the way one organizes information, or the way one chooses to look at the world. I use the analogy of a map. We all have our own map of the world." A very important book indeed!

Emotional Common Sense, by Rolland S. Parker, PhD (New York: Harper & Row, 1973). A useful book on avoiding self-destructiveness, with some excellent suggestions on coping with depression and enhancing sexual relationships, as well as chapters on self-understanding and social understanding. Dr. Parker writes: "The need for contact with other members of our species is built into our nervous systems. Perhaps it is the stimulus for our very feeling of being alive and human."

Fantasy Encounter Games, by Dr. Herbert Otto (Los Angeles: Nash, 1972) PB. A host of fun-filled and enlightening games to play with your imagination and those of your friends. Dr. Otto writes: "Adult play is important. We need to play more to recreate ourselves, to regenerate, to allow ourselves more pleasure and to recharge our energies so that we can actualize more of our potential."

Finding Yourself, Finding Others, by Clark E. Moustakas (Englewood Cliffs, New Jersey: Prentice-Hall. A Spectrum paperback, 1974). Comments by Moustakas and other noted writers, poets, and therapists on feeling alive within yourself and with others. The passages are thought-provoking and flow beautifully one into the other. Moustakas writes: "For most people partial communication and relationship are preferred to the risks of honesty and openness of self-expression and self-disclosure."

The Four Loves, by C. S. Lewis (New York: Harcourt, Brace & World, 1960). An important book for anyone interested in understanding what love is all about. The four loves are: Affection, Friendship, Eros, and Charity. Some of the ideas may seem antiquated, but they all stimulate awareness. Lewis writes: "Friendship arises out of mere Companionship when two or more of the companions discover that they have in common some insight or interest or even taste which the others do not share and which, till that moment, each believed to be his own unique treasure (or burden)."

Friendship, by Myron Brenton (New York: Stein and Day, 1974) PB. A broad sociological overview of friendship in conversational language, which can give you much valuable information about the history, importance, and structure of friendship.

Gestalt Therapy Verbatim, by Frederick S. Perls, MD, PhD, (Real

People Press, Box F, Moab, Utah 84532, 1969) PB. Fascinating discourses on Gestalt therapy from its creator, along with transcriptions of actual therapy sessions with the master. The book contains a lot of thought-provoking and useful material, and one sentence that can stimulate weeks of discussion: "Our manipulation of ourselves is usually dignified by the word 'conscience.' "

Handbook to Higher Consciousness, by Ken Keyes, Jr. (Living Love Center, 1730 La Loma Ave., Berkeley, California 94709). The book that outlines and presents instructional material on Ken's Living Love system. Includes the twelve pathways to higher consciousness, which are excellent tools for looking at yourself and how you relate to friends and others. Also goes in depth into the concept of addictions versus preferences, and Ken's ideas on how to stop suffering. This is an underground bestseller, and deserves to be.

The Heart of Friendship, by Muriel James and Louis M. Savary (New York: Harper & Row, 1976). A sentimental testimonial to the value of friendship, with lots of anecdotes about famous friends and quotes from philosophers. This is mostly a book *about* friendship, and as such is interesting and useful, though I would have liked to have seen some of the kinds of exercises that made *Born To Win* by Ms. James and Dorothy Jongeward so potent a tool for self-discovery.

How I Found Freedom in an Unfree World, by Harry Browne (New York: Macmillan, 1973) PB. A fine self-help book designed to show you that you are really in charge of your own life and can be as free as you choose to be. Browne says, "Freedom *is* possible, and you can have it—if that's what you really want."

How to Meditate, by Lawrence LeShan (Boston: Little, Brown, 1974) PB. The best book ever written on meditation. Includes some hard-hitting comments on some of the overly commercial meditation techniques being peddled today, and some fine meditation exercises, including many which can be shared with friends.

How to Survive the Loss of a Love, by Melba Colgrove, PhD, Harold H. Bloomfield, MD, and Peter McWilliams (Leo Press, 5806 Elizabeth Court, Allen Park, Michigan, 48101). This is an expansion of an earlier McWilliams poetry book, this time adding the comments of a psychologist and psychiatrist to his survival poems. One of many useful tidbits of advice: "When making new acquaintances ask questions that require more than a 'yes' or 'no' answer."

Human Be-ing, by William V. Pietsch (New York: Lawrence Hill, 1974) PB. A book about dissolving the walls between you and others, between you and yourself. A lot of entertaining and informative examples and illustrations. Pietsch says: "A complete break in a relationship is usually not necessary, however. Standing up for one's self may simply mean a break in the 'old' type of relationship, and accepting a 'new' relationship with the same person ('a re-negotiation of the contract')."

I Ain't Much, Baby—But I'm All I've Got," by Jess Lair, PhD (Garden City, New York: Doubleday, 1972) PB. A down-to-earth personal sharing from a remarkable philosopher/teacher, originally privately issued for his students. This book built up a nationwide audience by word-of-mouth, and has become one of the great self-help bestsellers.

Interpersonal Perception, by R. D. Laing, H. Phillipson, and A. R. Lee (New York: Springer, 1966) PB. Sometimes a bit technical, nevertheless this is a valuable book aimed at exploring and explaining the experiences, perceptions, and actions which occur when two people get together in dyadic interaction. Particularly useful is the Interpersonal Perception Method questionnaire.

Love, by Leo Buscaglia (Thorofare, New Jersey: Charles B. Slack, 1972). The next best thing to hearing and seeing Leo in person, this is a book that overflows with wise and witty and fascinating material. Leo says, "Man is by nature a social being. He finds that he feels more comfortable in his aloneness to the degree to which he can volitionally be involved with others." This is a hard book to find in your local bookstore, but well worth the effort to specially order it.

Love Today: a New Exploration, edited by Herbert Otto (New York: Association Press, 1972) PB. A series of essays and articles on love, which are filled with facts and feelings.

Making Friends with the Opposite Sex, by Emily Coleman (Los Angeles: Nash, 1972). A very difficult book to find, since the publisher never printed enough copies to fill the demand. It's worth finding, though, and it covers much more than man-woman relationships. Emily is one of the best group leaders around, and the kind of person who makes you feel good about being you. Some of this comes across in the book, though it could have been edited with more care.

Man, the Manipulator, by Everett L. Shostrom (Nashville, Tennessee: Abingdon Press, 1967) PB. I must confess my reluctance to recommend this book is based purely on the fact that Dr. Shostrom is the one psychologist who refused to be interviewed for *Friends.* But this doesn't take away from his many accomplishments and the fact that this is the best book written on the subject of manipulation. Also, there was no way I could write about manipulative relationships without quoting from it, and giving Dr. Shostrom credit for some pioneering work in this area.

My Needs, Your Needs, Our Needs, by Jerry Gillies (Garden City, New York: Doubleday, 1974) PB. Needless to say, this is one of my favorite books. The major complaint I've received since its publication is that I limited myself by focusing on man-woman love relationships. Many people have written to tell me that they've used some of the exercises for friendship interaction, parent-child and teacher-student communication, and self-awareness.

A Nation of Strangers, by Vance Packard (New York: David McKay, 1972) PB. A book about rootlessness in American society, offering examples of some new approaches to combat alientation in our culture. A fascinating book, and the kind that makes you want to go out and hug a friend after reading it.

The Natural Depth in Man, by Wilson Van Dusen (New York: Harper & Row, 1972) PB. I can't understand why more people don't know about this most remarkable book on inner experience. You can't read it without coming to some new awarenesses for and about yourself.

Notes to Myself, by Hugh Prather (Real People Press, Box F, Moab, Utah 84532, 1970) PB. A beautiful sharing journal with many passages that will touch you deeply, others that will amuse you. For example: "The way to be most helpful to others is for me to do the thing that right now would be most helpful to me."

On Caring, by Milton Mayeroff (New York: Harper & Row, 1971) PB. A philosophical masterpiece on what caring for others and being cared for is all about. Milton Mayeroff writes: "When the other is with me, I feel I am not alone, I feel understood, not in some detached way but because I feel he knows what it is like to be me."

100 Ways to Enhance Self-Concept in the Classroom, by Jack Canfield and Harold C. Wells (Englewood Cliffs, New Jersey: Prentice-Hall, 1976). Aimed at children, the one hundred experiences in this book can help anyone grow in self-esteem. The authors have taken and adapted techniques from all the really innovative people in humanistic psychology and education, including Jerry Gillies, and this work promises to be around for a long time as a classic.

Open Marriage, by Nena O'Neill and Dr. George O'Neill (New York: M. Evans, 1972) PB. One of the most important books ever written on interpersonal relations, and many of their ideas for marriage can be applied to friendships. Particularly useful is the chapter on Open Companionship and its section on the Friendship Genealogy, in which the O'Neills say, "You will very likely find that the incidence of friendships decreases sharply with marriage, that upon acquiring a mate you began to shut the door upon new acquaintances, and thus upon the new experiences that other people lead us to. Stop and reflect a moment on the amount of pleasure, stimulation and growth you have denied yourself by closing the door on such friendships, by presenting the couple-front to all comers. It can be a sobering thought."

Peoplemaking, by Virginia Satir (Palo Alto, California: Science and Behavior Books, 1972) PB. A book primarily written for parents, but with a wealth of information and positive awareness for anyone. I particularly like her suggestion that you treat your relatives as people, for I think we often overlook the potential friends among our relatives. Virginia Satir writes: "The cure for this gap is for each to get acquainted with the other as persons, who change from time to time, applying the same means to get to know one another as do any two people seeking to get acquainted." This book also contains some of the best conceptualization of self-esteem ever written, in the chapter Self-Worth, including Virginia Satir's famed Declaration of Self-Esteem.

Portraits of Loneliness and Love, by Clark E. Moustakas (Englewood Cliffs, New Jersey: Prentice-Hall, 1974) PB. In comments from Clark Moustakas and others, this book beautifully illustrates the differences between loneliness and solitude, and how loneliness is really a part of the loving process.

Psychological Dimensions of Social Interaction; Readings and Perspectives, edited by Darwyn E. Linder (Reading, Massachusetts: Addison-Wesley, 1973) PB. Often reads like the textbook it is, but some of the papers and articles provide much useful material for exploring interpersonal interaction.

Shifting Gears, by Nena O'Neill & George O'Neill (New York: M. Evans and Company, 1974) PB. A book about how to take charge of your life in a swiftly changing society, including all aspects of life, with a lot of thoughtful exploration of the importance of friendships and other interpersonal contacts.

The Social Animal, by Elliot Aronson (New York: Viking, 1972) PB. A valuable look at human behavior from the point of view of social psychology. The chapter on communication in sensitivity groups is one of the clearest and most intelligent reports on this controversial subject. I also like "Aronson's Law," which states that "People who do crazy things are not necessarily crazy."

The Third Force, by Frank Goble (New York: Grossman, 1970) PB. A look at the psychology of Abraham Maslow, with very thorough chapters on self-actualization and Maslow's theory of basic needs. An important book for anyone interested in learning about the basic view of humanistic psychology.

The Transparent Self, by Sidney M. Jourard (New York: Van Nostrand Reinhold, 1971) PB. One of the most important books in humanistic psychology, focused on self-disclosure and authenticity. Dr. Jourard writes: "There is probably no experience more terrifying than disclosing oneself to 'significant others' whose probable reactions are assumed, but not known."

Understanding Understanding, by Humphry Osmond with John A. Osmundsen and Jerome Agel. (New York: Harper & Row, 1974) PB. Some rather complex ideas here, but worth plowing through for some useful concepts on human behavior, especially as regards understanding ourselves and others.

Ways of Growth, edited by Herbert Otto and John Mann (New York: Grossman, 1968) PB. A great compendium of articles by leading figures in humanistic psychology and the human potential movement. The opening chapter, Growing Awareness and the Awareness of Growth, by Sidney Jourard, is considered by many to be the best explanation/exploration of personal growth ever written. And the eighteen other chapters all contain useful and fascinating material.

We, the Lonely People: Searching for Community, by Ralph Keyes (New York: Harper & Row, 1973). Keyes is one of the finest of the contemporary nonfiction writers, and here presents a powerful look at how we are losing our sense of community, and some real possibilities for holding onto it and expanding it in the future.

Who's Wavin'?, by Ric Masten (Sunflower Books, Palo Colorado Canyon, Coast Rt. #1, Monterey, California 93940) PB. Some of Ric's poems appearing in *Friends* hadn't yet been published when he gave them to me, though they may be by the time you are reading this. This booklet contains the title poem, which I used in chapter 7, and "When

Sybil Comes," which I used in chapter 6. Since Ric publishes his little paperback books himself, you might want to write to him at Sunflower Books for information and a price list. He also has several records of poetry readings and his witty and penetrating folk songs.

Why Am I Afraid to Tell You Who I Am?, by the Reverend John Powell, SJ (Argus Communications, 7440 Natchez Ave., Niles, Illinois 60648, 1969) PB. John Powell has built up quite a following with this and several of his other commentaries on growth and humanness. These are beautifully designed paperbacks, with a lot of thoughtful views on life and love. One statement I like: "To reveal myself openly and honestly takes the rawest kind of courage."

Why Be Lonely?, by Edward E. Ford and Robert L. Zorn (Argus Communications, 7440 Natchez Ave., Niles, Illinois 60648, 1975) PB. Based on the Reality Therapy approach, this book does much to explain loneliness and offer some solutions. One really potent line from the book: "People are out there, but you have to reach out." If everyone would really accept this simple statement, there wouldn't be very much loneliness left in this culture.

ADDITIONAL RESOURCES

TORI (see Chapter 10)

For more information on Jack Gibb's TORI concepts, TORI workshops, and any TORI communities which may be located near you, write:
TORI Associates
Box 694
La Jolla, California 92038

Association for Humanistic Psychology

AHP is an organization of some five thousand people dedicated to fostering human growth and dignity. It is not a professional organization, though many psychologists and psychiatrists belong. It's a great place to meet growth-stimulating friends, especially at the regional and national conferences, filled with many workshops and beautiful people. Write:
The Association for Humanistic Psychology
325 Ninth Street
San Francisco, California 94103

Living Love (see Chapter 5)

For information on Ken Keyes, Jr.'s, Living Love workshops, books, and tapes and records, write:
Living Love Center
1730 La Loma Avenue
Berkeley, California 94709

Jerry Gillies

To be kept informed of any Jerry Gillies workshops or lectures in your area, or just to say hello and offer any comments you may have on this book, write:

Jerry Gillies
PO Box 431803
South Miami, Florida 33143